D0016013

THE
AUTHORITARIAN
MOMENT

THE
AUTHORITARIAN
MOMENT

How the Left Weaponized America's
Institutions Against Dissent

BEN SHAPIRO

BROADSIDE
BOOKS

HarperCollins books may be purchased for educational, business, or sales promotional use. For information, please email the Special Markets Department at SPsales@harpercollins.com.

Broadside Books™ and the Broadside logo are trademarks of HarperCollins Publishers.

FIRST EDITION

Library of Congress Cataloging-in-Publication Data has been applied for.

ISBN 978-0-06-300182-4

21 22 23 24 25   LSC   10 9 8 7 6 5 4 3 2 1

To my children, who deserve to grow up in a country that values
the freedoms promised by the Declaration of Independence
and guaranteed by our Constitution

CONTENTS

THE
AUTHORITARIAN
MOMENT

INTRODUCTION

According to the institutional powers that be, America is under authoritarian threat.

That authoritarian threat to America, according to the Democratic Party, establishment media, social media tech bros, Hollywood glitterati, corporate bosses, and university professors, is clear—and it comes directly from the political Right.

And that authoritarian threat, according to those who control vast swaths of American life, manifested itself most prominently on January 6, 2021.

On that day, hundreds if not thousands of rioters broke away from a far larger group of pro-Trump peaceful protesters and stormed the United States Capitol, many seeking to do violent harm to members of Congress and the vice president of the United States. Their goal: to overturn the legally constituted results of the 2020 election.

The images from January 6 were indeed dramatic—and the rioters of January 6 did indeed engage in acts of criminal evil. Pictures of barbarians dressed in buffalo horns and idiots carrying Trump flags and military gear–clad fools carrying zip cuffs made the front pages globally. Sitting congresspeople and the vice president of the United States were rushed to safety, shielding themselves from the droogs beyond.

All Americans of goodwill—on all political sides—decried the January 6 riots. Vice President Pence personally oversaw the counting of the electoral votes; Senate Majority Leader Mitch McConnell (R-KY) condemned the rioters as vile cretins, then moved forward to the certification of the election.

But according to the Left, the January 6 riots weren't merely an act of universally condemned criminality. They were the culmination of right-wing authoritarianism. Jonathan Chait of *New York* magazine wrote, "We entrusted a sociopathic instinctive authoritarian with the most powerful office in the world. What did we think would happen?"[1] Paul Krugman of *The New York Times* suggested, "one of our major political parties has become willing to tolerate and, indeed, feed right-wing political paranoia. . . . The GOP has reached the culmination of its long journey away from democracy, and it's hard to see how it can ever be redeemed."[2] Greg Sargent of *The Washington Post* explained, "Trump's GOP has an ugly authoritarian core."[3] Lisa McGirr wrote in *The New York Times*, "Republicans will certainly seek to pivot from the riot, but the nativism, extreme polarization, truth-bashing, white nationalism and anti-democratic policies that we tend to identify with President Trump are likely to remain a hallmark of the Republican playbook into the future."[4]

"If you voted for Trump," said Don Lemon of CNN, "you voted for the person who the Klan supported. You voted for the person who Nazis support. You voted for the person the alt-right supports. That's the crowd that you are in. You voted for the person who incited a crowd to go into the Capitol and potentially take the lives of lawmakers."[5]

Score settling would be necessary. Charles Blow of *The New York*

Times asked, "What do we do now as a society and as a body politic? Do we simply turn the page and hope for a better day, let bygones be bygones? Or do we seek some form of justice, to hold people accountable for taking this country to the brink?"[6] Joy Reid of MSNBC called for "de-Baathification," à la the post–Iraq War purge of Saddam Hussein's military.[7]

Indeed, the American Left argued, the greatest threat to America's future came from right-wing authoritarianism—which, naturally, the Left conflated with white supremacy and conservative philosophy. To fail in the quest of ridding America of this threat would spell the end of the republic.

Authoritarianism had to be stopped.

But what if the most dangerous authoritarian threat to America wasn't the several hundred evil conspiracists, fools, and criminals who breached the Capitol?

What if the most dangerous authoritarian threat to the country wasn't a properly despised group of agitators making asses of themselves by charging into the Hall of Democracy, variously dressed in military gear, animal skins, and buffalo horns?

What if the primary threat to American liberty lies elsewhere?

What if, in fact, the most pressing authoritarian threat to the country lies precisely with the institutional powers that be: in the well-respected centers of journalism, in the gleaming towers of academia, in the glossy offices of the Hollywood glitterati, in the cubicles of Silicon Valley and the boardrooms of our corporate behemoths? What if the danger of authoritarianism, in reality, lies with those who are most powerful—with a ruling class that despises the values of half the country, and with the institutions they wield? What if the creeping authoritarianism of those who wield power has been slowly growing, unchecked, for years?

What if authoritarianism has many strains—and the most virulent strain isn't the paranoia and fear that sometimes manifests on the Right, but the self-assured unearned moral virtue of the Left?

THE AUTHORITARIAN INSTINCT

Something there is in man that loves a dictator.

In the book of Samuel, the people of Israel, threatened from without by warring tribes and within by dissention, seek to end the age of judges: they want a king. They have been warned repeatedly about the disastrous consequences of such a choice. God tells Samuel that the people have "rejected Me"; Samuel excoriates the people, telling them that a king "will take your sons" and "take your daughters" and "take your fields and your vineyards" and "take the tenth of your flocks"—that, in the end, "you shall be his servants, and you shall cry out in that day because of the king you chose, and the Lord will not answer you in that day."

And the people answer: "No, there shall be a king over us; that we also may be like all the nations, and that our king may judge us, and go out before us, and fight our battles."[8]

Human nature does not change.

This is the unfortunate truth of human history: because man is a threat to man, human beings seek safety and satisfaction in authority; because man is a threat to man, human beings seek the possibility of a *remolding* of man, a remolding to be achieved through the exercise of power. Human beings, all too often, trust not in the moral authority of a God above, looking down benevolently on humanity, providing ethical guidelines for building fulfilling lives and rich communities. Instead, they look to the earthly authority of a king, a leader, an institution. It took just a few weeks from the splitting of the Red Sea for the Jews to embrace the Golden Calf.

Human beings are ripe for authoritarianism.

For most of human history, authoritarianism manifested in centralized governmental systems: monarchies, oligarchies, aristocra-
cies. The widespread democracy of the post–World War II period
is extraordinary, and extraordinarily fragile: human beings may be
granted freedom, but freedom has a short shelf life.

Democracy is threatened chiefly by ochlocracy: the rule of the
mob. Mob rule transforms freedom into authoritarianism in two ways:
through reactionary brutality, in which citizens seek protection from
the winds of change, without and within—a form of brutality largely
associated with the political Right; and utopian brutality, in which citizens seek to escape present challenges through the transformation of
mankind itself—a form of brutality largely associated with the political Left. Often, the two forms of brutality feed on each other, creating a downward spiral into tyranny. This is precisely what happened
in Weimar Germany, where the utopian brutality of German communists came into conflict with the reactionary brutality of German
Nazis. The winning side implemented the most vicious tyranny in the
history of mankind; the losing side was an offshoot of one of the most
vicious tyrannies in the history of mankind. Neither side sought the
preservation of a democratic, rights-based system.

The Founding Fathers of the United States saw in mob rule the
greatest danger to their nascent system—and they put in place governmental checks and balances in order to protect individual rights
from the frenzied whims of the riotous mass. The Constitution was
designed to check ambition against ambition, passion against passion.
James Madison famously abhorred "faction"—by which he meant "a
number of citizens, whether amounting to a majority or a minority of
the whole, who are united and actuated by some common impulse of
passion, or of interest, adverse to the rights of other citizens, or to the
permanent and aggregate interests of the community." He posited two

possible ways of preventing faction: one, "by destroying the liberty which is essential to its existence; the other, by giving to every citizen the same opinions, the same passions, and the same interests." Both ways would end in authoritarianism.[9] The solution, he suggested, lay in checks and balances, in creating such a diffusion of interests that combination would become nearly impossible.

For a while, it worked.

It worked for two reasons.

First, the checks and balances built by the founders were wondrous in their durability. The hopes of would-be authoritarians were routinely stymied by the balances of federalism, of separation of powers. Those checks and balances remain durable today: the constitutional system's series of speed bumps certainly blunt momentum. Despite the best attempts of members of both parties to completely override the constitutional order, excesses are often mitigated, at least in small part.

Second, and more important, the American people broadly rejected the impulses of the mob—they rejected both the utopianism of left-wing authoritarianism and the reactionary nature of right-wing authoritarianism. Core American freedoms—freedoms of speech and of the press, freedoms of religion and association—were widely perceived to be beyond debate. If oppression deeply marred American history—and, of course, it did—it did so against a backdrop of American liberty, more and more broadly applied to more and more Americans. The Founding Fathers were united in their support for a culture of freedom—particularly freedom of thought and speech.[10]

THE AUTHORITARIAN MINDSET

But beneath the surface, the authoritarian mindset always looms.

In 1950, Frankfurt School theorist Theodor Adorno, along with

University of California, Berkeley, researchers Else Frenkel-Brunswik, Daniel Levinson, and Nevitt Sanford, authored a book titled *The Authoritarian Personality*. The book, an attempt to explore the origins of anti-Semitism, posited that people could be classified via the use of a so-called F-scale—F meaning "pre-fascist personality." Adorno et al. posited that such personalities were churned out by the American system. The authors suggested, "The modification of the potentially fascist structure cannot be achieved by psychological means alone. The task is comparable to that of eliminating neurosis, or delinquency, or nationalism from the world. These are the products of the total organization of society and are to be changed only as that society is changed."[11]

Because Adorno was a leftist and a Freudian, the analysis was deeply flawed; the very possibility of a left-wing authoritarianism was ignored by Adorno. Still, right-wing authoritarianism is quite real. Following in Adorno's footsteps, Harvard social scientist Robert Altemeyer utilized a "Right Wing Authoritarianism" (RWA) scale, attempting to detect three character traits:

"Authoritarian submission," or willingness to submit to established and legitimate authorities;

"Authoritarian aggression," or aggressiveness approved by the authorities against a particular "outgroup";

"Conventionalism," defined by adherence to approved social conventions.[12] Altemeyer found that right-wing authoritarianism was unnervingly common.

Surprisingly, Altemeyer found that left-wingers were not at all susceptible to authoritarianism. Altemeyer concluded that left-wing authoritarianism was "like the Loch Ness Monster: an occasional shadow, but no monster."[13] Perhaps that had something to do with the fact that the "Left Wing Authoritarianism," or LWA, scale-loaded the questions.[14] In fact, when University of Montana social psychologist

Lucian Conway simply rewrote Altemeyer's exact questions, replacing only the right-wing premises with left-wing premises, he found that "the highest score for authoritarianism was for *liberals* on LWA." Conway explained, "Our data suggest that average Americans on the political left are just as likely to be dogmatic authoritarians as those on the political right. And those left-wing authoritarians can be just as prejudiced, dogmatic, and extremist as right-wing authoritarians."[15]

The *content* of the dogma is merely different: as sociologist Thomas Costello of Emory University et al. writes, left-wing authoritarianism is characterized by three traits that look quite similar to those of right-wing authoritarianism:

"Revolutionary aggression," designed to "forcefully overthrow the established hierarchy and punish those in power";

"Top-down censorship," directed at wielding "group authority . . . as a means of regulating characteristically right-wing beliefs and behaviors";

"Anti-conventionalism," reflecting a "moral absolutism concerning progressive values and concomitant dismissal of conservatives as inherently immoral, an intolerant desire for coercively imposing left-wing beliefs and values on others, and a need for social and ideological homogeneity in one's environment."[16]

In reality, there are authoritarians on all sides. Even Adorno came to take this view: during the student protests of the 1960s, Adorno, who taught at the Free University of Berlin, was confronted by student radicals. He wrote a plaintive letter to fellow Frankfurt School theorist Herbert Marcuse complaining about the left-wing authoritarianism he saw in the student protesters who occupied his room and refused to leave: "We had to call the police, who then arrested all those they found in the room . . . they treated the students far more leniently than the students treated me." Adorno wrote that the students had "display[ed] something of that thoughtless violence that once belonged to fascism." Marcuse, a strident left-wing authoritarian himself—he infamously proposed that "repressive tolerance" required that dissenting right-wing views be censored[17]—then chided Adorno, stating that "our cause . . . is better taken up by the rebellious students than by the police," and argued that violence by the Left was merely "fresh air."[18]

Authoritarians rarely recognize their own authoritarianism. To them, authoritarianism looks like simple virtue.

THE AUTHORITARIAN QUESTION

So, if there are authoritarians on the Right and on the Left—and if the two feed on one another, driving America ever deeper into a moral morass—where does the true risk lie?

To answer that question requires us to evaluate two more questions. First, which form of authoritarianism is more common in the halls of power?

Second, which form of authoritarianism is more likely to be checked?

Let's revisit January 6 and its aftermath with these questions in mind.

There is little doubt that the rioters of January 6 were right-wing authoritarians. They invaded the Capitol building in order to stop the workings of democracy, overthrow the constitutional process, and harm those seeking to do their legal duty. They participated in authoritarian submission—they believed they were doing the work of President Donald Trump against a corrupt and effete establishment. They participated in authoritarian aggression—they believed they were empowered to do harm in order to defend Trump and take on the legislative branch. And they were engaged in conventionalism—they felt they were defending established values (the flag, the vote, democracy itself) against a revolution from within.

On January 6, these right-wing authoritarians invaded the Capitol. And, contrary to popular opinion, the system held.

As it turns out, authoritarianism on the right was checked, in large measure, by *members of the right*. It was Vice President Mike Pence who sent a letter to President Trump explaining that he would do his duty "to see to it that we open the certificates of the Electors of the several states, we hear objections raised by Senators and Representatives, and we count the votes of the Electoral College for President and Vice President in a manner consistent with our Constitution, laws, and history. So Help Me God."[19] It was Senate Majority Leader Mitch McConnell (R-KY) who congratulated Joe Biden on his victory immediately after the Electoral College vote. It was Republicans in the Senate who abandoned their electoral challenges immediately upon the reconvening of the electoral counting, after the Capitol building was cleared out. It was Republican governors and secretaries of state who certified their state votes.

The institutions held.

Many in the media termed January 6 a "coup," but it was never a coup in any proper sense: a coup requires institutional support. Certainly the rioters had no institutional support. In fact, Trump himself never explicitly called for the Capitol riot, stated in his speech that morning that he wanted the protests to be "peaceful," tweeted that he wanted everyone to go home in the midst of the riot (the vast majority of his supporters at the rally already had), and eventually—far too late, of course—put out a statement in which he acknowledged his defeat and told his supporters to remain peaceful. Trump might have authoritarian tendencies, but he did not wield authoritarian power. And beyond Trump himself, not a single major institution in American society supported the Capitol riots. Few even supported the president's efforts to challenge the election beyond the Electoral College vote.

As a matter of fact, whatever personal authoritarian tendencies

Trump may have had were checked *throughout his administration*. Trump had certainly engaged in authoritarian rhetoric—he utilized violent language, he suggested weaponization of the legal system, he called for breaches of the Constitution. And *nothing happened*. His much-maligned attorneys general refused to violate the law. He didn't fire special investigator Robert Mueller. His anger at the press translated mostly into increased ratings for his enemies; CNN's Jim Acosta, who spent every waking minute proclaiming that he was endangered by Trump's overheated talk, became a household name thanks to his grandstanding. At no point did Acosta fear arrest or even deplatform-ing. The shock of January 6 was that the guardrails collapsed for a brief moment in time after holding for years on end. And then the guard-rails were re-erected, including by some of Trump's erstwhile allies.

Now let's turn to the other side of the aisle.

In the aftermath of January 6, America's institutional powers swung into action on behalf of authoritarian measures.

Establishment media broadly promoted the idea of deplatforming mainstream conservatives and conservative outlets. CNN reported that the Capitol riot had "reignited a debate over America's long-held defense of extremist speech." Naturally, the media quoted "experts" like Wendy Seltzer, affiliate at Harvard's Berkman Klein Center for Internet & Society, to the effect that free speech primarily benefited those who are white.[20] Nikole Hannah-Jones, the serial social media prevaricator and Pulitzer Prize–winning purveyor of historical fiction about the inherent evils of America, quickly asked for a "reckoning" in the media.[21] Max Boot suggested in the pages of *The Washington Post* that Fox News be removed from Comcast, or that the Federal Communications Commission be empowered to censor cable net-works, stating, "Biden needs to reinvigorate the FCC. Or else the ter-rorism we saw on Jan. 6 may be only the beginning, rather than the end, of the plot against America."[22]

This wasn't just talk. Nearly every social media company in America promptly removed President Trump's accounts, even while acknowledging that they could not justify that removal on the basis of their stated policies. Major corporations announced they would cut funding to any Republican who had challenged electoral votes, despite never having done so to Democrats.[23] Senator Josh Hawley (R-MO), who had supported challenging electors (without serious legal basis, it should be noted), had his publication contract pulled by Simon & Schuster.[24] Harvard Kennedy School of Government dropped Representative Elise Stefanik (R-NY) from its senior advisory committee for making "public assertions about vote fraud in November's presidential election that have no basis in evidence."[25] Godaddy.com kicked AR15.com, the biggest gun forum in the world, offline.[26]

The most dramatic and immediate reaction to the Capitol riot was the institutional move against Parler. Parler had been launched in August 2018 as an alternative to Twitter; conservatives had been complaining about Twitter's opacity and discrimination against conservatives relative to leftists. Parler was the supposed free market solution. Then, in the aftermath of the riot, Apple's app store removed Parler, as did the Google Play store. The excuse: supposedly, Parler users had coordinated with regard to the January 6 protests, and Parler had allowed inflammatory and threatening material to remain up. The final blow came when Amazon Web Services—a company that merely provides cloud-based web infrastructure for companies—canceled Parler altogether, taking it offline. AWS, Parler CEO John Matze wrote, "will be banning Parler until we give up free speech, institute broad and invasive policies like Twitter and Facebook and we become a surveillance platform by pursuing guilt of those who use Parler before innocence."[27]

As it turned out, Facebook and Twitter had been used by Capitol protesters to coordinate as well. Neither company lost its cloud infrastructure. But leftist members of the media didn't react to that hypocrisy by calling for Parler's restoration—they reacted to it by calling for *further censorship against Facebook and Twitter.* Joe Scarborough of MSNBC—who throughout the 2016 race spent inordinate time pumping up Trump—ranted, "Those riots would not have happened but for Twitter, but for Facebook. . . . Facebook's algorithms were set up to cause this sort of radicalism to explode. . . . Facebook and Twitter set up their business models in a way that would lead to the insurrection."[28] Other tech journalists mirrored that sentiment—a sentiment they had been pumping for years, hoping to shut down social media companies that distribute alternative sources of media.

Meanwhile, governmental actors talked of revenge—and of using the Capitol riots to achieve long-sought political goals. Representative Alexandria Ocasio-Cortez (D-NY) stated that Congress should put together a "media literacy" commission in order to "figure out how we rein in our media environment."[29] Representative Cori Bush (D-MO) called for every single member of Congress who "incited this domestic terror attack" to be removed from Congress.[30] Senator Ron Wyden (D-OR) averred at NBCNews.com that the only way to prevent another Capitol riot was the addition of Washington, D.C., as a state, a renewed Voting Rights Act (likely unconstitutional), and universal mail-in voting.[31] As Joe Biden entered office on January 20, Representative James Clyburn (D-SC), who had compared Donald Trump to Hitler and Republicans to Nazis,[32] said that Biden should simply act unilaterally via executive action to implement his agenda if Congress balked: "If they're going to throw up roadblocks, go on without them. Use your executive authority if they refuse to cooperate . . . you can do big things and you can do great things. You can do things that are lasting."[33] It is worth noting that there is no clause of the Constitution whereby the president can simply implement his favored policies without congressional approval.

To sum up: on January 6, a group of radical extremist Trump supporters—right-wing authoritarians—stormed the US Capitol, where they were quickly put down. The institutions survived; the insurrectionists were roundly derided, disowned, and prosecuted.

Immediately thereafter, left-wing authoritarians took full advantage of the situation to press forward revolutionary aggression, top-down censorship, and anti-conventionalism targeting not just the rioters, but conservatives and individual rights more broadly. This perspective was mirrored across nearly every powerful institution in American society.

So, let us repeat the question.

If there is a serious threat to free speech, does it come chiefly from right-wing authoritarians? Or does it come from the left-wing authoritarians in media, big tech, and government?

If there is a threat to democratic institutions, does it come chiefly from right-wing authoritarians? Or does it come from the left-wing authoritarians in government, who broadly disdain the Constitution and believe in the implementation of their worldview from the top down?

If there is a threat to our most basic liberties, whom should we most fear: the dumbasses in clown suits invading the Capitol on January 6? Donald Trump, a man who talked like an authoritarian but did not actually govern as one? Or the monolithic leftists who dominate the top echelons of nearly every powerful institution in American society, and who frequently use their power to silence their opposition?

LIFE UNDER LEFT-WING SOCIAL AUTHORITARIANISM

Deep down, Americans know the answer to this question.

More than six in ten Americans say they fear saying what they think, including a majority of liberals, 64 percent of moderates, and

fully 77 percent of conservatives. Only self-described "strong liberals" feel confident in saying what they believe these days.[34] To be a
left-wing authoritarian is to feel the certainty of anti-conventionalism,
the passion for top-down censorship, the thrill of revolutionary aggression.

Tomorrow belongs to them.

For the rest of us, a society run by left-wing authoritarians is extraordinarily burdensome. It is to be surrounded by institutional
hatred. If you are conservative—or merely non-leftist—in America,
the hatred is palpable.

They hate you in academia. They hate you in the media. They hate
you on the sports field, in the movies, on Facebook and Twitter. Your
boss hates you. Your colleagues hate you—or at least have been told
they should.

They hate you because you think the wrong way.

Perhaps the problem is that you attend church regularly. Perhaps
it's that you want to run your business and be left alone. Perhaps it's
that you want to raise your children with traditional social values. It
could be that you believe that men and women exist, or that the police are generally not racist, or that children deserve a mother and a
father, or that hard work pays off, or that the American flag stands for
freedom rather than oppression, or that unborn children should not be
killed, or that people should be judged based on the content of their
character rather than the color of their skin.

Maybe the problem is that you won't post a black square on your
Facebook page to symbolize your support for the Black Lives Matter
movement. Maybe the problem is that you won't kneel for the national
anthem or cheer for those who kneel. Maybe it's that you haven't put
your preferred pronouns in your Twitter profile, or hashtagged with
the latest pride symbol for the latest cause, or used the proper emoji in
your text messages.

Or maybe it's just that you have friends, or family members, or even acquaintances who have violated any of the thicket of cultural regulations placed upon us by our supposed moral betters. Guilt by association is just as damning as guilt through action or inaction.

The reasons they hate you are legion. They change day to day. There's no rhyme or reason or consistency to them. One day, you might be a ballyhooed champion of justice for standing up for gay rights or feminist ideals; the next day, you might be told that you have been banished to the cornfield for your refusal to acknowledge that a man calling himself a woman is not in fact a woman (Martina Navratilova or J. K. Rowling). One day, you might find yourself a hero of the intelligentsia for your cynicism about religion; the next, you might find yourself a villain for the great sin of suggesting that cancel culture breeds radicalization (Sam Harris or Steven Pinker). One day, you might be a well-respected opinion maker, considered de rigueur reading for your complex take on economics and sociology; the next, you might be considered a privileged white male worthy of excommunication (David Shor or Matthew Yglesias).

This is not a question of Democrat or Republican. Not one figure named above would identify as a Republican, let alone a conservative. There is only one thing in the end that unites the disparate figures deemed worthy of the gulag in our ongoing culture war: refusal. Like Herman Melville's Bartleby, it is simple refusal that demands compulsion. The standards matter less than the simple message: you will comply, and you will like it.

The consequences for those who do not are quite real. As a prominent conservative, I always warn those who aren't prepared for social, cultural, and familial blowback not to associate with me publicly. There are consequences for treating conservatives as human. That's why every birthday, I'm amused but unsurprised to receive a bevy of kind wishes from liberals via text message—and none publicly in places like Twitter, where the mere recognition that a conservative was born of woman is enough to earn unending scorn.

Such situations are far from hypothetical. In June 2018, prominent Hollywood actor and producer Mark Duplass approached me about getting together—he was producing a film dealing with gun rights, and wanted to speak with someone on the Right to get a more accurate point of view. I thought that was shockingly decent of him, given Hollywood's permanent and thoroughgoing determination to caricature conservative positions; I told him so, and suggested he come by the office for a discussion.

We ended up spending about an hour and a half together. As he left, I gave him the usual warning: don't mention that we've met publicly, unless you're prepared for the fallout.

He didn't listen. In July, a couple of weeks later, he tweeted this shocking message: "Fellow liberals: If you are interested at all in 'crossing the aisle' you should consider following @benshapiro. I don't agree with him on much but he's a genuine person who once helped me for no other reason than to be nice. He doesn't bend the truth. His intentions are good."

The world fell in on poor Mark. After trending on Twitter publicly, and surely receiving a boatload of nasty notes privately, Mark quickly deleted his tweet, and then replaced it with a Maoist struggle session of hot-button social justice warrior thoughtvomit:

So that tweet was a disaster on many levels. I want to be clear that I in no way endorse hatred, racism, homophobia, xenophobia or any such form of intolerance. My goal has always been to spread unity, understanding and kindness. But I am going to make mistakes along the way. Sometimes I move too quickly when I get excited, or fail to do enough research, or I don't communicate myself clearly. I'm really sorry. I now understand that I need to be more diligent and careful. I'm working on that. But, I do believe deeply in bi-partisan understanding and I will continue to do my best to promote peace and decency in this world right now. That said, I hear you. And I want to say thank you to those who reached out with constructive criticism. I have genuinely learned so much and wish everyone all the best.[35]

Well, almost everyone.

Honestly, I felt rather sorry for him. Duplass has to work in this town. And Hollywood is a one-party ideological dictatorship. That said, I did warn him. And cowardice is indeed a form of sin.

Naturally, Duplass's craven apology to the world for having ac-knowledged that a conservative is indeed human brought cheers from the usual suspects (Vox's Zack Beauchamp headlined, "Duplass was right to take back his praise").[36] Order had been restored; the binary moral universe ruled by the woke priestly caste had been maintained.

And it *will* be maintained.

Because Duplass isn't alone. This sort of stuff happens *all the time*. Just about a year after the Duplass incident, I attended a rather tony political summit—perhaps the only real ritzy cocktail party I've ever gone to. One of the other attendees happened to be one of the more prominent left-wing podcasters in the country. After a few pleasant-ries, I suggested that perhaps we ought to do an election-year cross-over podcast. "The numbers," I said, "would be extraordinary. And I know my audience would love it. We're always having on guests who disagree."

"I'm sure your audience would be cool with it," the podcaster an-swered. "But mine would murder me."

He wasn't wrong. Which is why when I meet prominent people, from conservative sports stars to libertarian tech magnates, from right-wing Hollywood creators to goodhearted liberals in the media world, I do so quietly. I'm not in the business of taking billions of dollars off the market capitalization of major corporations or getting studio heads fired simply by confirming with whom I lunch. Those who violate ideological quarantine risk being treated as lepers in this environment.

Now, I'm lucky. I speak my views for a living. But tens and tens of millions of people aren't so lucky. For them, the consequences of speaking non-leftist views publicly in our absolutist time are grave. The authoritarian Left seeks to quell dissent. And they use every means at their disposal to do so.

Every day, I receive dozens of letters and calls from people asking how to navigate the minefield of American life. It's easily the most common question I receive.

"My boss is forcing me into diversity training, in which I'm told that all white Americans are inherently racist. Should I speak up about it? I'm afraid I'll be fired."

"My professor says that anyone who refuses to use preferred pronouns is a bigot. What should I write on my final? I'm afraid he'll grade me down."

"My sister knows I voted for Republicans. Now she says she doesn't want to talk to me. What do I do?"

The consequences of woke cultural authoritarianism are real, and they are devastating. They range from job loss to social ostracism. Americans live in fear of the moment when a personal enemy dredges up a Bad Old Tweet™ or members of the media "resurface" an impolitic comment in a text message. And the eyes and ears are everywhere. One simple tip from someone on Facebook to a pseudo-journalist activist can result in a worldwide scandal. Your boss cares what you say. So do your friends. Cross the social justice warriors, and you will be canceled. It's not a matter of if. Only when.

The only safety from the mob is to become a part of the mob.

Silence used to be possibility. Now silence is taken as resistance. Everyone must stand and applaud for Stalin—and he who sits down first is sent to the gulag.

So repeat. And believe.

Perhaps the most galling aspect of our culturally authoritarian moment is the blithe assurance whereby Americans are informed that they are exaggerating. There is no such thing as cancel culture, our woke rulers assure us, while busily hunting down our most embarrassing political faux pas. There's nothing wrong, they say, with calling your boss to try to get you fired—after all, that's the free market just working! Why are you whining about social media censorship, or about social ostracism? People have a right to tear you to shreds, to end your career, to malign your character! It's all free speech!

In a certain sense, they're not wrong: your boss does have a right to fire you; your friends and family do have a right to cut you off. None of that amounts to a violation of the First Amendment.

It simply amounts to the end of the republic.

Free speech and free exchange of ideas die when the attitude of philosophical tolerance withers. Government authoritarianism isn't the only way to kill American freedom. Cultural authoritarianism works, too. It has always worked. Writing in 1831, the greatest observer of America and democracy, Alexis de Tocqueville, summed up the threat of democratic despotism in terms that sound shockingly, eerily prescient:

> Under the absolute government of one alone, despotism struck the body crudely, so as to reach the soul; and the soul, escaping from those blows, rose gloriously above it; but in democratic republics, tyranny does not proceed in this way; it leaves the body and goes straight for the soul. The master no longer says to it: You shall think as I do or you shall die; he says: You are free not to think as

I do; your life, your goods, everything remains to you; but from this day on, you are a stranger among us. You shall keep your privileges in the city, but they will become useless to you; for if you crave the vote of your fellow citizens, they will not grant it to you, and if you demand only their esteem, they will still pretend to refuse it to you. You shall remain among men, but you shall lose your rights of humanity. When you approach those like you, they shall flee you as being impure; and those who believe in your innocence, even they shall abandon you, for one would flee them in their turn. Go in peace, I leave you your life, but I leave it to you worse than death.[37]

This is the America we currently occupy. As Axios reporter Jim VandeHei writes, "Blue America is ascendant in almost every area: It won control of all three branches of government; dominates traditional media; owns, controls and lives on the dominant social platforms; and has the employee-level power at big tech companies to force corporate decisions . . . our nation is rethinking politics, free speech, the definition of truth and the price of lies. This moment—and our decisions—will be studied by our kid's grandkids."[38]

There is no respite: your employer requires your fealty to woke principles; corporations require that you mirror their political priorities; the media treat you as a crude barbarian. There are no distractions: Hollywood mocks your morals and damns you for adherence to them; the sports world requires that you mimic the popular perversities of the moment before being allowed to escape; social media controls the flow of information you can see, while preventing you from speaking your mind. And each day you wonder if today will be the day the mob comes for you.

This book is about how our authoritarian moment came to be. It is about the takeover of our most powerful institutions by a core of radicals, and about the miasmatic hatred and dire consequences Americans face for standing up for heretofore uncontroversial principles.

But it is also about something more.

It is about how to fight back in the *right way*.

Because buried in authoritarianism is always one deep flaw: its insecurity. If authoritarians had broad and deep support, they wouldn't require compulsion. The dirty secret of our woke authoritarians is that *they are the minority*.

You are the majority.

It's not that everybody hates you. It's that millions of Americans are afraid to say that they *agree with you*.

We have been silenced.

And now is the time for the silence to be broken by one simple, powerful word, a word that has meant freedom since the beginning of time:

No.

CHAPTER 1

HOW TO SILENCE A MAJORITY

On November 8, 2016, a bombastic reality television star became president of the United States. Donald Trump became president despite months of media hysteria and extraordinary attacks on his campaign and his character; he became president despite the confident predictions of the pollsters and pundits that he had virtually no chance.

Most of all, the pollsters and pundits got Trump's level of support wrong because they got Trump supporters wrong. Trump's supporters, they believed, were a diamond-hard core of bigots, annoying but generally unthreatening—a set of "deplorables," in Hillary Clinton's phraseology.

Then Trump won.

This presented the political elitists with two possible choices: they could engage in some well-earned introspection, considering the possibility that they had missed something vital in American political life and reexamining their premises about the nature of the American public; or they could castigate tens of millions of Americans as moral and intellectual deficients.

They chose the latter.

After some initial media coverage, in which Brooklyn-based, Gucci-loafer-wearing would-be-journalistic–Jane Goodalls covered Trump supporters as mysterious, grunting gorillas-in-the-mist; in which graduates of the New York University School of Journalism, fresh-faced and bright-eyed after classes with Lauren Duca on how to bitch about Tucker Carlson in *Teen Vogue*, traveled to fabled primitive red state America—a chaotic and brutal place filled with chain restaurants and Walmarts and churches, and characterized by a serious lack of culturally sensitive vegan restaurants and artisanal coffee shops and Planned Parenthood facilities; in which said ace reporters talked to Poor Old Billy, a down-on-his-luck former factory worker merely aching for some Democratic subsidy programs . . . the journalistic establishment came to a conclusion: Trump voters were, as they had originally thought, and as Hillary Clinton had once said, deplorable. They were, as Barack Obama had once characterized them, bitter clingers, desperately clutching to God and guns and racism, wearing their hard hats to decaying factories, then turning them in for white hoods at night to terrorize the neighborhood minorities. Trump voters were poor white Americans in dying Rust Belt towns, hoping to stop demographic shifts by voting Trump. (It somehow escaped attention that some 2.8 million New Yorkers voted for Trump, or 4.5 million Californians. There are lots of Republicans who don't sit around in diners wearing trucker hats.)

This was a convenient narrative. It certainly relieved journal-ists of the obligation to leave their comfort zones, both literally and figuratively—no need to spend a night in rural Ohio rather than the comforts of the Upper West Side, or to bother discussing uncom-fortable issues with the rubes. It also allowed journalists to abandon the practice of journalism more broadly. Now, instead of focusing on Trump's policies, they could simply focus on his tweets, the id-driven manifestations of their original thesis: every tweet could be read as a confirmation of their hypothesis about red-state Americans. Now, instead of examining all sides of various political controversies, they could simply assume the sinfulness of their opponents, and demand surrender. Journalism became a search-and-destroy mission, directed not merely at Trump but at Trump's supporters.

This wasn't much of a change, as it turned out. Republicans of all stripes had always been the problem, not just Trump. Before Trump was a glint in the media's eye, the media had targeted a small-town plumber who had the temerity to ask Barack Obama a question about his tax policy; they dug up his tax record, his home address, his plumbing license. Mitt Romney, the most milquetoast human being of the modern era, had been castigated by the media as a racist and a bigot. John McCain, who would later be hailed as an anti-Trump hero, was hit with similar slander.

The media itself had shifted on Trump personally over the years. For years, he'd been treated as easy clickbait, a genial figure of comedy and an outsized figure of wealth and pomposity, an icon of garish frivolity and entertaining charlatanry . . . up until the point he declared himself a Republican candidate for the presidency. Even then, Trump received late night phone calls from Jeff Zucker and advice from Joe Scarborough. Then he won the Republican nomination. Overnight he became the fonthead of evil—because overnight he became the symbol of his supporters, not the other way around. After all, it wasn't as though the media would have treated Ted Cruz or Marco Rubio as anything but pariahs had either won the nomination. As Trump would later argue, they hated him mostly because they hated his supporters.

This created an extraordinary amount of loyalty to Trump among Republicans—Republicans felt that Trump had merely taken bullets otherwise aimed at them. And they weren't totally wrong. The political slings and arrows *were* aimed at them. Trump just made an easier, more convenient, and more justifiable target. The media wasn't the only institution committed to the narrative that all conservatives—or at least the ones who hadn't flipped and joined the Lincoln Project, earning Strange New Respect™—were vicious racists, know-nothing xenophobes, bigoted idiots. Nearly *every major American institution* was committed to the same idea.

Conservatives felt the left-wing authoritarianism. They understood it on a gut level. And they hated it.

They felt the top-down censorship from social media, which deemed their speech "hate speech" and their worldview "harassment." They felt the anti-conventionalism from Hollywood, which painted conservatives as the great threat to a more beautiful, tolerant, and diverse country, and from their bosses, who declared their fealty to tolerant, liberal ideals while not-so-subtly threatening to fire dissenters, and from their friends and family, who told them in no uncertain terms that they were not welcome at the table. They saw the revolutionary aggression of a radical Left directed against fundamental American ideas—and patted on the back by all of America's most powerful institutions.

Conservatives were to be treated as outsiders. Anyone who voted for Trump was to be banned from polite society, to be treated as a gangrenous limb. Better to lop them off from the body politic than allow their poison to fester. In fact, it wasn't enough merely to silence conservatives who didn't actively oppose Trump. Silence, as the nonsensical woke slogan went, was violence. Conservatives had to be *outed*. Even those who might not feel themselves sympathetic to Trump had to be outed if they so much as engaged in *conversation* with Trump voters, or even those open to engaging in conversation with Trump voters. Such discussions, the logic went, would serve to humanize the inhuman, to tolerate the intolerable. Excision of the occasional Trump supporter was utterly insufficient—*exorcism* of the very concepts that could lead to the presence of Trump support had to be undertaken. Confessions had to be forced. Purity tests had to be administered. Struggle sessions had to be initiated.

Symbols of loyalty would be demanded: properly self-righteous hashtags on Twitter; anti-Trump bumper stickers on cars; semantically overloaded, tautology-laden lawn signs plunked into well-manicured grass. Statements of dissociation would have to be undertaken: dissociation from newly identified code terms like "meritocracy" and "Western civilization" and "color-blindness." Dissenters would be lumped in with Trump supporters. The Overton Window—the window of acceptable discourse—would be smashed shut, then boarded over.

And, our cultural leftist authoritarians thought, it had worked.

In 2018, Democrats won an overwhelming electoral victory, swamping Republicans across the country and seizing control of the House of Representatives, flipping 41 seats blue. Support for Democrats washed through the suburban areas of the United States, flipping 308 state legislative races in favor of Democrats. That was without Trump on the ballot.

With Trump on the ballot—the symbol of evil himself, bigotry and racism and vulgarity and brutality made Orange Flesh—surely Democrats would usher in a never-ending Golden Era of dominance, and cement Republicans into minority status for a generation.

And sure enough, one week before the election of 2020, Joe Biden was apparently ahead in the polls by nearly double digits. Democrats had a generic ballot advantage in Congress of nearly seven points.

Triumph was at hand.

Except it wasn't.

It turns out that if the major cultural institutions in a society declare all-out war on a large percentage of the population, those people don't convert—they go underground. And that's precisely what they did. They fibbed to pollsters, or didn't pick up the phone at all. They didn't tell their friends and family how they were voting. They didn't post on Facebook or Twitter. They didn't tell their bosses their real thoughts about Joe Biden or Kamala Harris or Alexandria Ocasio-Cortez.

Then they entered the polling places, and they voted.

And they voted against those who had declared them the cultural enemy.

Donald Trump may have lost the election, but Republicans across the land didn't. Republicans outperformed the polls across the board. Many pollsters had projected that Trump would lose by double digits nationwide; instead, Trump personally won more votes than any other Republican in American history, and more votes than any candidate in American history outside of his opponent, Joe Biden. Some pollsters had suggested that Republicans would easily lose the Senate and drop a dozen seats in the House. Instead, Republicans nearly maintained the Senate (losing control only because of Trump's asinine intervention in two winnable Georgia Senate races), gained seats in the House, maintained their stranglehold on state legislatures in a redistricting year, and nearly retained the White House, too.

The elevation of a geriatric nonentity like Joe Biden was no endorsement of the Democratic agenda. It was far more likely a rejection of Trump's personality—which came as little surprise after years of erratic tweeting, bizarre personal behavior, and extraordinarily savage media coverage. Trump underperformed Republicans in nearly every state with a competitive Senate race; Republicans swept into power in New Hampshire, where Trump lost by nearly eight points. Trump bled in the suburbs; had he lost the suburbs by the same margins he did in 2016, he would have been reelected. So Americans may have rejected Donald Trump personally. But the silent majority—a majority the media, the pollsters, and the experts completely missed—broadly rejected the Democratic agenda, in truly shocking fashion.

Americans didn't vote in defiance of the polls because they were racists. They didn't vote in favor of Trump because they were bigots. They didn't vote for Susan Collins in Maine and Thom Tillis in North Carolina and Steve Daines in Montana because they were benighted rednecks committed to a vanishing demographic majority. Latinos didn't vote in outsized numbers for Trump because they were suddenly "white," even though Pulitzer Prize–winning prevaricator and much-ballyhooed mountebank Nikole Hannah-Jones of *The New York Times* declared them so. Black males didn't vote in surprising numbers for Trump because they had abandoned their race, as Joe Biden himself implied. Suburban white women didn't vote Republican because they had decided they were in love with Donald Trump's casual grossness with women.

These Americans voted the way they did because they are Americans, and because they demand to be heard. Because they refuse to surrender to the alliance of the authoritarian Left and their liberal enablers. Because they never agreed with the media or their bosses or their idiot nephews in college carrying around copies of unread Ta-Nehisi Coates books to get laid. Because they won't be bullied into putting up meaningless symbols on their social media pages, or into declaring that all police are racists, or into cheering on the idea that America ought to be denigrated.

They went quiet. They didn't go away.

And then they weren't quiet anymore.

That's why the pollsters got it wrong. It wasn't because pollsters are purely incompetent. It's because pollsters can't pry answers out of those who have been intimidated into silence. As Eric Kaufman, professor of politics at the University of London, observed, pollsters didn't actually get it wrong with white non-college-educated voters—those who are likely to feel the least peer pressure from the self-empowered newfangled cultural fascisti. They got it wrong with *precisely the people most likely to feel pressured*: white college graduates. As Kaufman concludes, "If America cannot reform its regime of speech discipline, it has no hope of overcoming its yawning cultural divide."[1]

In order to overcome that yawning cultural divide, however, we must first acknowledge the obvious: our divide *is* cultural. It is not economic. It is not racial. It is cultural.

THE CULTURE WAR

Our philosophical betters—the elitist opinion makers who claim to understand the deeper meaning in our politics—generally present two explanations for division in America: race and class. Both are utterly insufficient.

The Marxist theory of class-driven division has long provided a shoddy explanation for real-world phenomena. During World War I, Marxist theorists were firmly convinced that international warfare would certainly result in a revolution by the working class, only to find that workers of the world were actually Brits, Frenchmen, Germans, and Russians. Today, Thomas Piketty explains Trump by appealing to rising income inequality[2]—but can't understand just why Trump voters continue to reject the overt redistributionism of the Democratic Party. By Marxist theory, Trump voters should have become Bernie voters over time. They aren't.

The racial theory of American politics is similarly non-explanatory. That theory supposed that Trump's outsized white support in 2016 was evidence of a white majoritarian backlash to an ascendant minority coalition. But that theory was firmly debunked in 2018, when white suburban voters handed a majority to Democrats in Congress, and in 2020, when Trump increased his vote share among minorities but *lost vote share* among white voters, and white men particularly. If racial animus were the driving force behind Trumpism, or Republicanism more broadly, that wouldn't have manifest itself in a 55 percent Cuban vote for Trump in Florida, or in Trump closing the gap in majority-Latino Rio Grande Valley districts like Starr and Hidalgo counties from 60 and 40 points in 2016 to 5 and 17 in 2020.

Trump didn't overperform estimates among Latino and black voters because he was a racist. He overperformed because the elitists in our institutions *declare things racist even when they aren't*. Joe Biden suggested that Trump engaged in full-time dog whistling, despite Trump's repeated denunciations of white supremacy and his unprecedented outreach to minority communities, including a criminal justice reform program largely opposed by many in the grassroots conservative community. But as it turns out, elitist white Americans and woke "anti-racism" advocates who largely overpopulate the media, corporate America, social media halls of power, and Hollywood don't have a read on broader minority viewpoints. When these elitists declare that standing with the police is a "dog whistle," voters of all stripes tune out.[3]

In fact, that sort of labeling—the attempt to turn all political opposition into evidence of personal malevolence, the mainstreaming of anti-conventionalism, combined with top-down censorship and incentivization of revolutionary aggression—is the reason for the backlash against down-ballot Democrats.

Our culture wars aren't about anything so mundane as marriage, policing, or even abortion. Our culture wars are about a simple question: Can we agree that freedom of speech is more important than freedom from offense? Can we hire, work with, and break bread with people who may differ on the nature of the good life, but agree on the individual freedoms that come along with being an American?

If the answer is no, you're probably a leftist. If the answer is yes, you're part of the silent majority.

And perhaps you're only silent because you don't know that you're *in the majority*.

Why don't you know that?

Because for three generations, there's been an ongoing, successful attempt to wrest institutional control from the apolitical, and to weaponize those institutions on behalf of the authoritarian Left. Most Americans tend to think individually, both philosophically and strategically: they spend their time attempting to convince friends and family of their viewpoints, rather than infiltrating institutions and using the power of those institutions for mass marketing. Leftists have no such qualms. Most Americans, trusting in the free market and free speech, insist that people be left free to make choices they don't like, and oppose the exercise of institutional power; leftists militarize powerful forces in a variety of fields to achieve their political ends.

The authoritarian Left has successfully pursued a three-step strategy to effectuate their takeover of the major institutions in our society. The first step: winning the emotional argument. The second step: renormalizing the institutions. The third step: locking all the doors.

CONVINCING AMERICANS TO SHUT UP

The Left has spent decades gradually suppressing most Americans— and encouraging conservatives to suppress themselves. The process began with an appeal to politeness; that appeal became a demand for silence; then the demand for silence became an order to comply, repeat, and believe.

This was a heavy lift, and it didn't happen overnight. The Left began with a simple recognition that both conservative and liberal philosophies have soft underbellies. For conservatives, the soft underbelly is a militant insistence on *cordiality*. Conservatives were, until Donald Trump, deeply concerned with personal *values* in their politicians— but they were insistent on them in daily life. One of those virtues was peacefulness, affability, treating thy neighbor as thyself. As philosopher Russell Kirk suggested, conservatives believe in peace and stability, in human imperfectability and in community.[4] If we believe in peace and stability, that requires tolerance; if we believe human beings are imperfectible, we shouldn't be too quick to judge; if we believe in the value of community, we must be willing to forgive small slights. These are nuanced ideas, but all too often conservatives boil them down to *being proper*. And by being proper, conservatives all too often mean being *inoffensive*.

But being inoffensive is a bastardization of the call to decency. Conservatism doesn't merely believe in anodyne cordiality—a cordiality that looks the other way at cruelty, or requires silence in the face of sin. Conservatism promotes certain values that come into conflict with leftist values. Conservatism relies on moral judgment, too. Conservatism believes that friendship relies on willingness to steer those we love away from sin: as the Bible states, "You shall not hate your brother in your heart. You shall surely rebuke your fellow, but you shall not bear a sin on his account."[5]

Nonetheless, leftism identified in conservatives a fundamental willingness to go along to get along—to see cordiality as virtue itself. And it wasn't difficult for leftists to transmute some conservatives' desire to be cordial into a political principle: anything considered offensive ought to be barred. This principle—we can call it the Cordiality Principle—manifested in ways directly contrary to the conservative ability to speak freely. Conservatism believes in standards of right and wrong, of good and bad. Distinguishing between good and bad requires the exercise of judgment. The Left suggested that judgment was itself wrong, uncivilized, vulgar. Judgment was, of course, *judgmental*. And this was bad. To be judgmental was to offend someone, and thus to violate the Cordiality Principle.

"Equality" and "inclusion" and "diversity" and "multiculturalism" became the bywords of the day. As conservative philosopher Roger Scruton writes, "In place of the old beliefs of a civilization based on godliness, judgment and historical loyalty, young people are given the new beliefs of a society based on equality and inclusion, and are told that the judgment of other lifestyles is a crime. . . . The 'nonjudgmental' attitude towards other cultures goes hand-in-hand with a fierce denunciation of the culture that might have been one's own."[6]

This Cordiality Principle gained serious traction in arenas ranging from arguments over religion to pornography to abortion to same-sex marriage. Many conservatives became uncomfortable standing up for their own principles in polite company, or in moral terms—better not to be perceived as *Not Very Nice*.

The soft underbelly of liberalism to the Cordiality Principle was obvious. For liberals, compassion isn't merely a principle: it is an ersatz religion. Where conservatives define virtue in accordance with religious precepts or natural law, liberals define virtue *as empathy*. Liberals see themselves as compassionate, at root; they see themselves through the lens of kindness. And it simply isn't "nice" to quarrel with others, no matter how demanding. Niceness lies at the core of everything; better to bite one's tongue than to start a fight, which might be seen as intolerant.

The Cordiality Principle was just the beginning. The second step came when leftists began to contend that judgmentalism wasn't merely a violation of the Cordiality Principle, it was an actual harm. The argument shifted from "Just Be Nice" to "Silence Is Required."

Now, traditionally, offense has not been considered a serious harm.

J. S. Mill famously posited the so-called harm principle—the notion that activity that actually harms someone ought to be condemned, or even legally barred. But Mill himself rejected the conflation of harm and offense—just because someone found something offensive, Mill argued, didn't mean that it ought to be regulated or socially banned.

The distinction between harm and offense, however, can be murky. Philosopher Joel Feinberg points out that few of us believe that people should publicly have sex with one another; that's a crime against our sense of cordiality. Offensiveness, he says, can in fact be a harm. To that end, Feinberg posited a balancing test: on one hand, society would balance the "seriousness of an offense"; on the other hand, society would balance "reasonableness of the offending conduct." If offensive conduct did not seriously offend anyone, for example, and was personally important to the offender, the conduct would be allowed. If, however, the offense is "profound," the balance could shift, and shift precipitously.[7]

The authoritarian Left has artificially shifted Feinberg's balance. Every offense to particularly "vulnerable groups"—meaning groups defined as vulnerable by the Left in a kaleidoscopically changing hierarchy of victimhood—represents the possibility of profound offense. Those who engage in such offense must be silenced.

Thus, the Left has posited that even minor offense amounts to profound damage—hence the language of "microaggressions," which posit by their very nature that verbiage is an act of violence. Microaggressions range from the utterly anodyne ("Where are you from?" is apparently a brutal act, since it presupposes that the subject of the question is of foreign extraction) to the extraordinarily counterproductive (references to "meritocracy" are deeply wounding, since they presuppose that free systems reward hard work, thus condemning the unsuccessful by implication).

Microaggressions require no intent—intent is not an element of the crime, since we may not be aware, thanks to our "implicit bias," of our own bigotry. They do not even require actual evidence of harm. Subjective perception of offense is quite enough. The culture of microaggression is about magnifying claims of harm in order to gain leverage. That leverage can grow to astonishing proportions: woke staffers got a reporter for *The New York Times* fired for using the n-word to explain why and when using the n-word was wrong. *Times* executive editor Dean Baquet even repeated the authoritarian Left's favorite mantra: "We do not tolerate racist language regardless of intent." *Regardless of intent.*[8] If you can be racist without intent, silence becomes the only protection for most Americans. After all, as Berkeley leftists chanted when I spoke there in 2017, "Speech is violence."

But now the Left has gone even further. Now, *silence* is violence. This idiotic, self-contradictory slogan has been picked up by a myriad of politicians and thoughtleaders. The idea is that if you remain silent in the face of an evil—an evil defined by the Left, naturally—then you are complicit in that evil. It's no longer enough to oppose racism, for example; you must carry around a copy of Robin DiAngelo's *White Fragility*, announce your white privilege for the world to hear, and prepare for your inevitable atonement. If you don't, you will be deemed an enemy.

Now, don't mistake the slogan "silence is violence" as a call for open speech. Far from it! "Silence is violence" means that you *must* remain silent, but only after "doing the work"—learning why your point of view is utterly irrelevant, ceding all ground to woke leftists, and becoming a crusader on behalf of their point of view. If you refuse, you will be targeted. Abject apologies will be demanded. The only way to escape the social media brute squads is to become a member, baying in unison.

THE RENORMALIZATION OF AMERICAN INSTITUTIONS

All of this might remain a fringe phenomenon relegated to the wilds of Twitter and college campuses, but for a simple fact: the culture of authoritarian leftism has now hijacked nearly all of Americans' major institutions and cultural touchstones.

Universities, once bastions of free thought, are now philosophical one-party systems dedicated to the promulgation of authoritarian leftism. Corporations, petrified of legal liability—or at least hoping to avoid accusations of insensitivity or bigotry—have caved to this culture. They have enforced a culture of silence in which tens of millions of employees fear speaking their minds for fear of retaliation. Social media have banned people who refuse to abide by social justice dictates, and social mobs, egged on by eager activists in the media, mobilize daily to target the un-woke. Culturally apolitical spaces ranging from sports to entertainment have been mobilized on behalf of the Left, weaponized in pursuit of the cultural revolution.

How did this happen? How did colleges, supposedly protectors of open inquiry and free speech, turn into the bleeding edge of censorship and ideological compulsion? How did the media, supposedly committed to the business of facts and First Amendment freedoms, fall prey to the iron grip of the woke? How did corporations, oriented toward apolitical profit making, turn away from the vast majority of their audience and toward pleasing a vocal but small minority?

The answer lies in a process that author Nassim Nicholas Taleb labels "renormalization." This process allows a motivated minority to cow a larger, largely uninterested majority into going along to get along. Taleb gives a simple example: a family of four, including one daughter who eats only organic. Mom now has a choice: she can cook two meals, one for the non-organic family members and one for her daughter; or she can cook one meal with only organic ingredients. She decided to cook only one meal. This is *renormalization* of the family unit, which has converted from majority non-organic to universally organic. Now, says Taleb, have the family attend a barbecue attended by three other families. The host has to make the same choice mom did—and the host chooses to cook organic for everyone. This process of *renormalization*—the new normal—continues until broader and broader numbers have been moved by one intransigent person.

The process applies in politics as in life. "You think that because some extreme right- or left-wing party has, say, the support of ten percent of the population," Taleb writes, "their candidate will get ten percent of the votes. No: these baseline voters should be classified as 'inflexible' and will always vote for their faction. But some of the flexible voters *can* also vote for that extreme faction. . . . These people are the ones to watch out for, as they may swell the number of votes for the extreme party."[9]

It's not enough, though, to have a lone stubborn person. You need a tipping point—a certain number of people within a whole in order to create a renormalization cascade. While each minor demand made of the broad majority might seem reasonable, or at least low-cost, over a long enough period of time, people fight back. It's one thing to hold one block party with organic ingredients. It's another to demand, day after day, that everybody in the neighborhood turn in their hamburgers for organic tofu. At a certain point, a long train of minor demands amounts to a major imposition. Even the American Founding Fathers were willing to tolerate a "long train of usurpations and abuses" for a while. Only after it dawned on them that those demands pursued "invariably the same Object, evinc[ing] a design to reduce them under absolute Despotism," did they declare independence.

The process of renormalization can only go so far unless a tipping point is reached. That tipping point, however, does not require a majority. Not even close. If *all* the intransigent actors get together, a core can be formed, which triggers the tipping point. Physicist Serge Galam has posited that in some cases, only about 20 percent of a population is needed to support an extreme view in order to cause radical renormalization. One way of creating such an intransigent minority coalition: the activation of what Galam has called "frozen prejudices," at the risk of appearing intolerant or immoderate to a broad majority, while still maintaining a solid core base.[10] In other words, start with a motivated core group; don't worry about who you alienate; appeal to the prejudices of vulnerable groups, who are then forced to choose between the core group and its most ardent enemies. Make the choice binary.

This is, in a nutshell, the strategy for the authoritarian Left. By putting together an intersectional coalition of supposedly dispossessed groups motivated by a common enemy—the system itself—they can move mountains. They can build a coalition of people who look the other way at revolutionary aggression, who endorse top-down censorship, who believe deeply in anti-conventionalism. And when the ascendant authoritarian leftist coalition uses its momentum against those who populate the highest levels of institutional power, offering job preservation or temporary absolution in return for surrender, institutions generally surrender. And then those institutions cram down these authoritarian leftist values. That's how you get Coca-Cola, a company with over 80,000 employees, training its workforce to be "less white" in fully racist fashion, noting that to be "less white" means to be "less arrogant, less certain, less defensive, less ignorant, and more humble"—and claiming that this discriminatory content was designed to enhance "inclusion."[11]

SHUTTING THE OVERTON WINDOW

Within institutions, the authoritarian Left's incremental demands have been taken up, one by one: from diversity training to affirmative action hiring, from charitable donations to internal purges. But for the generalized impact of institutional takeover to be felt requires one final step: the renormalization of our societal politics in favor of censorship.

Those who work within hijacked institutions remain a small fraction of the general population—but they can renormalize the society more broadly if they can convert liberals into leftists. American politics is, broadly speaking, divided into three significant groups: conservatives, leftists, and liberals. Liberals may share redistributionist goals with leftists, but can be distinguished from leftists with a simple test: asking whether those who disagree ought to be silenced. The American Civil Liberties Union, for example, used to be liberal—it stood up for the right of Nazis to march through Skokie, Illinois. Now, however, the ACLU is fully leftist—in 2018, the ACLU promulgated an internal memo explaining, "Our defense of speech may have a greater or lesser harmful impact on the equality and justice work to which we are also committed . . . we should make every effort to consider the consequences of our actions. . . ."[12]

The bulk of mainstream Democrats—and the vast majority of Americans—don't stand in favor of top-down censorship. But increasingly, the Democratic Party leadership has shifted from liberal to leftist. This means threatening action against social media companies for allowing dissemination of nonliberal material, or seeking regulation targeting corporations who do not mirror the liberal agenda.

Renormalization takes place by inches. Instead of simply calling for outright bans on broad swaths of speech, leftists have insisted that the Overton Window—the window of acceptable discourse, in which rational discussion can take place—ought to be gradually closed to anyone to the right of Hillary Clinton. This means savaging conservatives as racists and penalizing liberals who deign to converse with conservatives.

This means that liberals are left with a choice of their own: they can either choose to form a coalition with leftists, with whom they agree on most policy goals, but with whom they disagree on fundamental freedom principles; or they can form a coalition with conservatives, with whom they disagree on policy goals, but with whom they agree on fundamental freedom principles.

That choice is, so far, up in the air.

On the one hand, there are liberals who still stand for free speech—or at least appear to do so. In June 2020, 153 liberals ranging from J. K. Rowling to Noam Chomsky signed a letter decrying the rise of "the intolerant climate that has set in on all sides." These prominent thinkers explained, "The free exchange of information and ideas, the lifeblood of a liberal society, is daily becoming more constricted. . . . .The way to defeat bad ideas is by exposure, argument, and persuasion, not by trying to silence or wish them away."[13] This was a heartening development. But not one Trump supporter appeared on the letter. Which meant that the question remained an open one: did these liberals mainly seek to avoid the radical Left's censorious purges themselves, or did they truly hope to open up the Overton Window beyond themselves?

Whether liberals side with conservatives in defense of free speech and individualism or they side with leftists in pursuit of utopia remains an unanswered question. The jury is still out. But time is running out for liberals to decide. Matthew Yglesias, one of the signatories on the *Harper's Weekly* letter and a cofounder at Vox, was berated by members of his own staff for deigning to join up with the likes of Rowling, who has been unjustly accused of transphobia. Unsurprisingly,

Yglesias stepped down from his position at his own website just a few months later, citing that incident: "It's a damaging trend in the media in particular," Yglesias told Conor Friedersdorf of *The Atlantic*, "because it is an industry that's about ideas, and if you treat disagreement as a source of harm or personal safety, then it's very challenging to do good work."[14]

The threat to core American values is only increasing.

CONCLUSION: WILL AN AGE OF HEALING EMERGE?

On the night the media announced their projection that Joe Biden would be president-elect of the United States, Biden sought to put the culture war genie back in the bottle. This was, in and of itself, rather ironic, given Biden's role in stoking the culture wars, from destroying the Supreme Court hopes of Robert Bork to suggesting that Mitt Romney wanted to put black Americans back in chains. Still, Biden expressed that the way forward for the country lay in unity rather than recrimination. "Now," Biden intoned, "let's give each other a chance. It's time to put away the harsh rhetoric. To lower the temperature. To see each other again. To listen to each other again. To make progress, we must stop treating our opponents as our enemy. We are not enemies. We are Americans."[15]

This was undoubtedly a nice sentiment. But conservatives remained suspicious; time and again in politics, unity has been used as a club to wield against those who disagree. There are two types of unity: unity through recognition of the fundamental humanity of the other and unity through purification. Given their long experience of watching the Left's political quest to cleanse the country of conservatism and conservatives, conservatives remained wary.

They were right to be wary.

The same day Biden gave his "unity" speech, former first lady Michelle Obama—a supposedly unifying figure in her own right, according to her media sycophants, despite her long record of divisive statements—claimed that Trump's 70 million voters were motivated by love for the "status quo," which meant "supporting lies, hate, chaos, and division."[16]

Biden, naturally, said nothing.

Meanwhile, Democrats and media members called for political de-Baathification of Trump supporters. Former Clinton labor secretary Robert Reich called for a "Truth and Reconciliation Commission" to root out Trump supporters. Democratic National Committee press secretary Hari Sevugan tweeted that "employers considering [hiring Trump staff] should know there are consequences for hiring anyone who helped Trump attack American values," and pushed the Trump Accountability Project—a list of Trump employees and donors to be held accountable for Trump's presidency. Representative Alexandria Ocasio-Cortez (D-NY) suggested "archiving these Trump sycophants for when they try to downplay or deny their complicity in the future."[17] Members of the Lincoln Project, a group of former Republicans-cum-Democrats who raked in tens of millions of dollars in donations to attack Trump and Republicans during the 2020 cycle, called on members of the law firm Jones Day to be inundated with complaints for the great crime of representing the Trump campaign in court.[18]

Meanwhile, Democrats with the temerity to call out the woke, militant wing of their own party were subjected to claims of racism and bigotry. Even elected Democrats, it turned out, were deplorables. When moderate Democrats complained that they had nearly lost their seats thanks to the radicalism of fellow caucus members pushing "defund the police" and socialism, Representative Rashida Tlaib (D-MI) called them bigots seeking to silence minorities.[19] Progressive groups including the Justice Democrats, the Sunrise Movement, and Data for Progress issued a memo declaring that fellow Democrats who wished not to mirror the priorities of the woke were participating in "the Republican Party's divide-and-conquer racism."[20]

The battle to silence the silent majority remains ongoing. It is likely to accelerate, not to decelerate, as time goes on.

To understand how to combat it, we must first understand the history and program of our new cultural fascisti; next, we must understand how deeply our core institutions have been weaponized; and finally, we must understand our own weaknesses, and seek to correct them.

CHAPTER 2

HOW THE AUTHORITARIAN LEFT RENORMALIZED AMERICA

In 2012, President Barack Obama won reelection. He did so despite winning 3.5 million fewer votes than he did in 2008, and 33 fewer electoral votes; he did so despite winning the same percentage of the white-vote-losing Democrat John Kerry did in 2004; dropping support from 2008 among Americans across all age groups and education groups; and losing voters who made above $50,000 per year.

Obama had barely gotten his head above water in the approval ratings by the time of the election, the economy had stagnated (in the two quarters just prior to the election, the gross domestic product had grown just 1.3 percent and 2.0 percent)[1], and Obama had performed in mediocre fashion in the presidential debates. Nonetheless, he became the first president since Ronald Reagan to win two elections with a majority of the popular vote.

So, what did Obama do to work this magic? He put together a different sort of coalition. Obama won because he held together a heavily minority-based, low-income coalition: 93 percent of black voters,

71 percent of Hispanic voters, 73 percent of Asian voters, 55 percent of female voters, 76 percent of LGBT voters, 63 percent of those making below $30,000 per year, and 57 percent of those making between $30,000 and $50,000 per year.[2] Obama became the first president since FDR in 1944 to drop electoral and popular vote support and win reelection anyway.

The story of Obama's 2012 victory is the story of the transformation of American politics. In 2008, Obama had been a different sort of candidate running a quite familiar campaign: a campaign of unification. Ronald Reagan had run on "morning in America"; Bill Clinton had run on a "third way" eschewing partisanship; George W. Bush had run on "compassionate conservatism"; Obama ran on the terms "hope" and "change," pledging to move beyond America as a collection of "red states and blue states" and instead to unite Americans more broadly. In fact, Obama's personal story was part and parcel of this appeal: he could justifiably claim to unite the most contentious strains of America in his own background, being the child of a white mother and a black father, raised in Hawaii but ensconced in the hard-knock world of Chicago, born to a single mother and raised by grandparents but educated at Columbia and Harvard Law School. Obama was, as he himself stated, a "blank screen on which people of vastly different political stripes project their own views."[3]

By 2012, however, Obama had cast aside those ambiguities. He was the architect of Obamacare, the creator of Cash for Clunkers and "shovel-ready jobs," a critic of police departments across the country, a newfound expositor of same-sex marriage, a defense-cutting, tax-increasing, big-spending progressive. His progressivism had prompted an ardent response from the American Right: the Tea Party movement and Obama's loss of Congress in 2010. No longer could Americans of various political stripes project onto him their own views, or their hopes and desires for the nation.

Obama's personal popularity—his eloquence, camera-readiness, lovely family—certainly buoyed him. But none of that would have been enough to get him reelected. No, what Obama needed was a new strategy. That strategy—the shift away from appealing to broad bases of Americans with common themes and toward narrowcasting to fragmented audiences, cobbling together ostensibly dispossessed groups—was transformational. It pitted Americans against Americans, race against race, sex against sex. Obama domesticated the destructive impulses of authoritarian leftism in pursuit of power.

Before Barack Obama, the American Left had been split by dueling impulses: on one hand, the impulse toward top-down government control, complete with its implicit faith in the unending power of the state to solve individual problems; and on the other hand, the impulse toward destruction of America's prevailing systems, which the American Left believed were, in essence, responsible for disparities in group outcome—systems rooted in individual rights, ranging from free markets to free speech to freedom of religion. Each of these impulses—the Utopian Impulse and the Revolutionary Impulse—carries certain aspects of authoritarian Leftism. The Utopian Impulse reflects a desire for top-down censorship, and reflects anti-conventionalism; the Revolutionary Impulse believes in revolutionary aggression, and reflects a similar anti-conventionalism. But the two impulses are in conflict.

Obama rectified that split by embracing the power of government—and acting as a community organizer within the system itself, declaring himself the revolutionary representative of the dispossessed, empowered with the levers of the state in order to destroy and reconstitute the state on their behalf.

And it worked.

In building his coalition, Obama no doubt worked a certain political magic. It just so happened that Obama's brew of identity politics and progressive utopianism emboldened an authoritarian leftism that poisoned the body politic. America may not recover.

THE RISE AND FALL OF UTOPIAN GOVERNMENT IN AMERICA

The American Left has always been attracted by the promise of power.

The power of the state is an aphrodisiac: it warms the heart and fires the mind with the passion of utopian change. Utopians of the Left are generally advocates for anti-conventionalism; they believe that their moral system is the only decent moral system. They're also quite warm toward top-down censorship, designed to stymie those moral opponents.

American progressives in the early twentieth century felt the euphoric intoxication of the Utopian Impulse. The early American progressives identified the state as the solution to a variety of social ills: income inequality and exploitation of labor, under-education and even intellectual deficiency. Concerns about individual rights were secondary; the Declaration of Independence and its guarantees of natural liberty were hackneyed; the Constitution itself was a mere constraint on the possibility of utopia.

Woodrow Wilson suggested that the state was the repository of all possibility, championing the notion that "all idea of a limitation of public authority by individual rights be put out of view, and that the State consider itself bound to stop only at what is unwise or futile in its universal superintendence alike of individual and of private interests." Such a notion, Wilson thought, did not preclude democracy—after all, democracy was merely about "the absolute right of the community to determine its own destiny and that of its members. Men as communities are supreme over men as individuals." Given the challenges of modern life, Wilson asked, "must not government lay aside all timid scruple and boldly make itself an agency for social reform as well as political control?"[4]

John Dewey, perhaps the most influential early progressive, believed similarly that the state could act as the moving force behind utopian ambition. "The State," wrote Dewey, "is then the completed objective spirit, the externalized reason of man; it reconciles the principle of law and liberty, not by bringing some truce or external harmony between them, but by making the law the whole of the prevailing interest and controlling motive of the individual."[5]

Indeed, progressives reveled in the limitless nature of ambition given a powerful state. As president, Wilson activated the state to persecute his political opponents, including antiwar socialist Eugene V. Debs; Wilson's attorney general, Thomas Gregory, turned a blind eye toward the American Protective League, a vigilante group a quarter of a million strong, raiding their neighbors' mail for proof of antiwar activity.[6] Justice Oliver Wendell Holmes, a fellow progressive, explained that the state had the ability to restrict reproduction of those with Down syndrome, since "It would be strange if [the public welfare] could not call upon those who already sap the strength of the State for these lesser sacrifices, often not felt to be such by those concerned, in order to prevent our being swamped with incompetence."[7] Margaret Sanger, founder of Planned Parenthood, called for the sterilization or quarantining of some "fifteen or twenty millions of our populations" in order to prevent the supposed poisoning of the gene pool.[8]

With the end of World War I, however, America grew tired of the progressive vision of state as sovereign; the Utopian Impulse had been humored and found wanting. The triumphant election of Warren G. Harding ushered in an era of smaller government, and a return to the traditional vision of individual freedoms guarded by a constitutionally limited state. Calvin Coolidge, Harding's successor and the winner of

54 percent of the popular vote and 382 electoral votes in the 1924 election, expressed his view of business with reverence toward the free markets. "[I]f the federal government should go out of existence, the common run of people would not detect the difference in the affairs of their daily life for a considerable length of time," he stated. "We live in an age of science and of abounding accumulation of material things. These did not create our Declaration. Our Declaration created them."[9]

The restoration of constitutional normalcy did not last. With the Great Depression, the Utopian Impulse—and the crushing hand of government—once again gained the upper hand. Crisis was, as always, an excellent opportunity for a renewed love affair with democratic socialism. While today's intelligentsia likes to bask in the glow of President Franklin Delano Roosevelt's accomplishments—most obviously, the creation of massive new welfare state programs—his actual record was dismal. FDR implemented massive new regulations, manipulated the currency, and attacked private property. Individualism once again fell out of vogue, with FDR stating, "I believe in individualism in all of these things—up to the point where the individualist starts to operate at the expense of society."[10] Which, of course, meant that he didn't actually believe in individualism.

FDR declared that the fundamental freedoms guaranteed by the Constitution—free speech, freedom of the press, trial by jury, freedom of religion—were utterly insufficient. "As our Nation has grown in size and stature," FDR declared, "these political rights proved inadequate to assure us equality in the pursuit of happiness." Instead, he proposed, America had to embrace a "second Bill of Rights," which would guarantee the rights to a job, to food, to clothing, to a decent profit for farmers, to housing, to medical care, to social security, and to education. "All of these rights spell security," FDR trumpeted. He went so far as to suggest that should the economic policies of the

1920s—a time of limited government and free markets—return, "even though we shall have conquered our enemies on the battlefields abroad, we shall have yielded to the spirit of Fascism here at home."[11]

FDR combined his utopian government programs with top-down censorship, including fascistic crackdowns on dissenters. As Jonah Goldberg describes in his book *Liberal Fascism*, "it seems impossible to deny that the New Deal was objectively fascistic. Under the New Deal, government goons smashed down doors to impose domestic policies. G-Men were treated like demigods, even as they spied on dissidents. Captains of industry wrote the rules by which they were governed. FDR secretly taped his conversations, used the postal service to punish his enemies . . ." FDR aide Harry Hopkins openly suggested, "we are not afraid of exploring anything within the law, and we have a lawyer who will declare anything you want to do legal."[12]

The result of all of this government utopianism was catastrophic for everyday Americans, besotted though they were with the overpowering personal appeal of FDR. According to University of California, Los Angeles, economists Harold Cole and Lee Ohanion, FDR's policies—particularly his attempt at top-down organization of industry via cartelization, curbing free market forces in favor of centralized control—made the Great Depression great again, lengthening the depression by fully seven years. Consumption dropped dramatically; work hours dropped dramatically.[13]

With the rest of the world lying in ruins at the end of World War II, America could afford the bloat and inefficiency associated with larger government programs. But the added ambitions of the LBJ administration taxed the resources of the American democratic socialist ideal to the breaking point. President Lyndon Baines Johnson doubled down on FDR's commitments, now suggesting that America could become a "Great Society" only by launching a multiplicity of major government spending initiatives, fighting a "war on poverty."

Government encroached into nearly every arena of American life, offering subsidies and threatening prosecutions and fines. Government promised housing; it offered instead government-run projects, which quickly degraded into dystopian hellholes. Government promised welfare; it offered instead the prospect of intergenerational poverty through sponsorship of single motherhood. Government promised educational opportunity; it offered instead forced busing and lowered public schooling standards.[14]

This was a bipartisan affair—former conservative Richard Nixon, as president, re-enshrined LBJ's economic programs, including unmooring the American dollar from the value of gold and setting prices, wages, salaries, and rents.[15] And once again, as with FDR's response to the Great Depression, economic stagnation set in, with the percentage of people living in poverty stopping its decrease in 1970 and the stock market topping out in January 1966 around 8,000 . . . and dropping steadily until July 1982 in inflation-adjusted terms.[16]

By the end of the Jimmy Carter presidency, America had fallen out of love with the utopian government schemes. The Utopian Impulse had waned. "Fixing the world" through government measures had been reduced to gas lines, inflation, unemployment, and a president bemoaning an American malaise, admitting that "all the legislation in the world can't fix what's wrong with America."[17] Ronald Reagan took up that baton, declaiming in his First Inaugural Address, "government is not the solution to our problem; government is the problem. . . . It is time to check and reverse the growth of government which shows signs of having grown beyond the consent of the governed."[18]

In reality, Reagan didn't reduce the size and scope of government—government continued to grow. But in the minds of Americans, the progressive agenda had failed. By 1996, the Democratic president, Bill Clinton, was mirroring Reagan's rhetoric on the role of the government, explaining, "the era of big government is over," sounding almost Reagan-esque in his suggestion that a "new, smaller government must work in an old-fashioned American way," calling for a "balanced budget" and an end to "permanent deficit spending."[19] In his 2000 Republican National Convention acceptance speech, George W. Bush echoed that language, suggesting "big government is not the answer."[20] And in 2004, a young black Senate candidate from Illinois named Barack Obama suggested, "The people I meet—in small towns and big cities, in diners and office parks—they don't expect government to solve all their problems."[21] A consensus had formed in the minds of most Americans: government was not a panacea, the cure to all human problems. Often, government was the obstacle to human success and flourishing. Yes, Americans were happy to accept taxpayer-sponsored programs that benefited them, and reacted with anger to proposals that would implement change to those programs. But Americans now sounded more like Reagan than Wilson in terms of what they thought government could accomplish.

THE RISE AND FALL OF REVOLUTIONARY IDENTITY POLITICS

While progressives argued throughout the twentieth century that government was the solution to all of humanity's ills—and as Americans were gradually disabused of that notion—another, somewhat contradictory idea began to take root on the American Left. This idea agreed with the progressive thesis that the Declaration of Independence and Constitution were past their sell-by dates. But it went further: it suggested that virtually every system in America had to be torn to the ground in order to achieve true justice. Where progressives had believed that the power of government could be harnessed to a redistributive agenda in order to achieve utopian ends, this new brand of radicalism—animated by the Revolutionary Impulse—argued that the American governmental system was itself inherently corrupt, and that it needed to be torn out at the root. Revolutionary aggression was justified, the radicals argued, in order to tear down the hierarchies of power acting as a barrier to the triumph of moral anti-conventionalism.

An early influential form of this argument came from the scholars of the so-called Frankfurt School, European expatriates who escaped to America to avoid the Nazis. Max Horkheimer (1895–1973), one of the leaders of this school of thought, suggested that since all human beings were products of their environments, all evils in America could be attributed to the capitalist, democratic environment; as he put it, "the wretchedness of our own time is connected with the structure of society."[22] Erich Fromm, another member of the Frankfurt School, posited that American freedoms didn't make human beings free. "*The right to express our thoughts*, however, *means something only if we are able to have thoughts of our own*," he stated. American consumerism, however, had deprived Americans of that ability—and thus made them ripe for proto-fascism.[23] To liberate individuals, all systems of power had to be leveled.

This meant that traditional American freedoms would have to be curbed. Freedom of speech would have to die so that freedom of subjective self-esteem could flourish. As Herbert Marcuse explained, "Liberating tolerance, then, would mean intolerance against movements from the Right and toleration of movements from the Left . . . it would extend to the stage of action as well as of discussion and propaganda, of deed as well as of word." This held true *especially* for minority groups, who could assert their power only by striking back against the system.[24]

While the Frankfurt School thinkers were Marxist in orientation, their argument made little sense as a matter of class. After all, economic mobility has long been the hallmark of American society, and free markets grant opportunities to those of all stripes. But when the argument for American repression was translated from economic into racial terms, it began to bear fruit. America *had* allowed and fostered the enslavement of black people; America had allowed Jim Crow to flourish. While America had abolished slavery and eventually eviscerated Jim Crow—and done so, as former slave Frederick Douglass suggested in 1852, *because* of the ideals expressed in the Declaration of Independence and Constitution—the argument that America was at root racist and thus unfixable had some plausibility.

This was the contention of so-called Critical Race Theory (CRT). CRT transmuted the class-based argument that America is rigged into a race-based one. According to CRT, every institution in America is rooted in white supremacy; every institution is "structurally" or "institutionally" racist. This idea was first put forth by Stokely Carmichael, then the head of the Student Nonviolent Coordinating Committee, in 1966 (later, Carmichael would become a black separatist and the head of the Black Panther Party). Hot on the heels of the Civil Rights Act of 1965, Carmichael posited that while the federal government had barred discrimination on the basis of race, racism could not be alleviated by such action: inequality in outcome could be chalked up to historic racism and the structure of institutions built in a time of racism. Carmichael wrote, "It is white power that makes the laws, and it is violent white power that enforces those laws with guns and nightsticks." The predictable result: institutions would have to be torn down to the ground.[25]

Carmichael was not arguing that the system could be mobilized on behalf of those it had victimized. He was arguing that the *definition of racism* would have to itself change: from now on, actions would be considered prima facie racist if they produced racially disparate results, rather than if they were *actually racist* in intent or content. This made disparate impact the test of racism—a logically unsupportable proposition, since literally every policy ever crafted by humankind has resulted in disparate results for some groups. In fact, many of the Left's favorite policies—see, for example, minimum wage—exacerbate disparate outcomes rather than vitiating them. To treat disparate outcomes as a result obtained *only* through racist systems is to ignore all of human history in pursuit of a mythical utopia. Instead of arguing that some measures would have to be taken to level the playing field, Carmichael was arguing that the playing field would have to be dynamited.

This was the Revolutionary Impulse given an intellectual framework: revolutionary aggression, combined with anti-conventionalism.

Carmichael's intellectual heirs formally launched the CRT project in the late 1970s and early 1980s. Expositors Richard Delgado and Jean Stefancic set out the basic principles of CRT: first, that "racism is ordinary, not aberrational"; second, that "our system of white-over-color ascendancy serves important purposes, both psychic and material." The system, in other words, is designed to *create* racially disparate outcomes; any proof of racially disparate outcomes is evidence of the malignancy of the system.[26]

Critical Race Theory pioneer Derrick Bell wrote that "the whole liberal worldview of private rights and public sovereignty mediated by the rule of law needed to be exploded . . . a worldview premised upon the public and private spheres is an attractive mirage that masks the reality of economic and political power."[27] According to Bell, even purportedly *good outcomes* may be evidence of white supremacy implicit within the system—white people are so invested in the system that if they have to do something purportedly racially tolerant to uphold it, they will. But in the end, it's all about upholding white power. No wonder Bell posited that white Americans would sell black Americans to space aliens in order to alleviate the national debt if they could—and suggested *in 1992* that black Americans were more oppressed than at any time since the end of slavery.[28]

This argument gained little ground in the mainstream for decades. The confidence of Lyndon Baines Johnson–era progressives stymied it. LBJ believed the power of government could bridge gaps between white and black. And the government *did* engage in effort after effort to level the playing field, spending trillions on anti-poverty programs designed to act as a form of soft reparations for the evils of American racism. Because LBJ believed that the gap between identity politics and utopian progressivism could be papered over by the power of government, he created massive new governmental tools, rewriting the essential bargain between Americans and their government. As Christopher Caldwell writes, "The changes of the 1960s, with civil rights at their core, were not just a major new element in the Constitution. They were a *rival* constitution with which the original one was frequently incompatible."[29] The system of law in the United States radically changed, with the federal government given extraordinary power to end discrimination, both real and imagined, both in the public sector and the private sector. As Caldwell writes, there was a successful attempt by government to "mold the whole of society—down to the most intimate private acts—around the ideology of anti-racism."[30] And when instances of racism couldn't provide a proper pretext for government interventionism, the rubric of anti-discretion was expanded to include any supposedly victimized minority group. Coercion by government—and support for such coercion—became a sign of morality rather than a violation of freedom:

> The civil rights model of executive orders, litigation, and court-ordered redress eventually became the basis for resolving every question pitting a newly emergent idea of fairness against old traditions. . . . Civil rights gradually turned into a license for

government to do what the Constitution would not previously have permitted. It moved beyond the context of Jim Crow laws almost immediately, winning what its apostles saw as liberation after liberation.[31]

In pursuit of these liberations, trillions of dollars were spent; millions of Americans were made more dependent on government; hundreds of thousands of Americans ended up working for the government directly. Even though the programs did little overall to alleviate the standing of black Americans relative to white Americans, the programs *did* paradoxically shore up the moral credibility of the American governmental system: it was difficult to claim that systems that had now been turned *in favor* of black Americans—systems from affirmative action to anti-discrimination law—were designed to make black Americans subservient. The legitimacy of the system, ironically, had been upheld by efforts to overhaul the system in the name of race-neutral progress. The Utopian Impulse had stymied the Revolutionary Impulse.

Thus, by the early 1990s, the radical arguments had been put aside. While critical race theorists continued to blame "the system" for racial gaps, and called for race-specific discrimination on behalf of victimized groups, Americans of all stripes instead maintained the notion that race-neutral legal systems were indispensable. When hip-hop artist Sister Souljah defended the Los Angeles riots, suggesting, "I mean, if black people kill black people every day, why not have a week and kill white people?,"[32] candidate Bill Clinton called her out, comparing her to David Duke.[33] When crime rates soared out of control, particularly in minority communities, a bipartisan coalition came together in Washington, D.C., to pass a tough-on-crime bill designed to lengthen sentencing. That bill was supported by 58 percent of black Americans, including most black mayors.[34] It passed the Senate by a 94–5 vote.

In the battle over whether to utilize the government to pursue uto-pia, or to tear down the government in the name of radicalism, the utopians had won. Calls to destroy the system from within were re-jected, not merely by the political Right but by the political Left. Iden-tity politics had been roundly defeated.

In fact, in 2004, a young Barack Obama confirmed that thesis in his Democratic National Convention speech rejecting the central tenets of identity politics and Critical Race Theory. "I stand here knowing that my story is part of the larger American story, that I owe a debt to all of those who came before me, and that, in no other country on earth, is my story even possible," Barack Obama stated, to wild cheers. He would go on to chide the myth, pervasive in inner-city neighborhoods, "that says a black youth with a book is acting white." And he would conclude with his most famous dictum, one he repeated—in increasingly hollow fashion—over the course of his subsequent career:

There is not a liberal America and a conservative America—there is the United States of America. There is not a Black America and a White America and Latino America and Asian America—there's the United States of America.[35]

HOW BARACK OBAMA FUNDAMENTALLY TRANSFORMED AMERICA

This general consensus—that right or left, the government could not solve all problems, but that the American system was inherently good—held through 2008. Barack Obama campaigned on that prom-ise. He promised hope. He suggested that Americans were united by a common vision, and by a common source.

But simmering under the surface of Obamaian unity was something philosophically uglier—something deeply divisive. As it turned out, Obama was no devotee of either founding ideology, LBJ-style government utopianism, or even a Clintonian Third Way. Obama's philosophy was also rooted not in the racial conciliation of Martin Luther King Jr., but in the philosophy of Derrick Bell, a man Obama himself had stumped for during his Harvard Law School days. It was no surprise that Obama gravitated to Jeremiah Wright, attending his church for twenty years, listening to him spew bile from the pulpit about the evils of the United States. Furthermore, Obama was a believer in his own messianic myth—that he was the embodiment of everything good and decent. Michelle Obama summed up the feeling well during the 2008 campaign: she suggested that "our souls are broken in this nation," and that "Barack Obama is the only person in this race who understands that . . . we have to fix our souls."[36] Obama himself said his mission was to "fundamentally transform[] the United States of America" in the days before the 2008 election.[37]

That combination led Obama to a revised political position, after his overwhelming election in 2008: all criticism of him, it turned out, was *actually* racially motivated, because Obama—as America's first black president—represented the best hope of transforming America's systems from within. To be fair, the signs of Obama's racially polarizing stance were clear even in the 2008 race. Early on in that race, Obama explained his lack of working-class support in Rust Belt areas by referencing their supposed racism: "They get bitter, they cling to guns or religion or antipathy to people who aren't like them or anti-immigrant sentiment or anti-trade sentiment as a way to explain their frustrations."[38] Throughout his 2008 campaign, Obama made reference to his race as a sort of electoral barrier, despite the fact that but for his race, he never would have been nominated; he even said that his opponent, John McCain, was scaring voters by suggesting

Obama didn't "look like all those other presidents on those dollar bills."[39]

But that racially polarizing undertone didn't fully surface until after the election. In Obama's view, the only reason for Americans to oppose any element of his agenda was subtle—or not-so-subtle—racism. As Obama revealed in his memoir in 2020, he believed "my very presence in the White House had triggered a deep-seated panic, a sense that the natural order had been disrupted . . . millions of Americans [were] spooked by a Black man in the White House." Obama saw McCain's running mate, Sarah Palin, as an avatar for this viciously bigoted America: "Through Palin, it seemed as if the dark spirits that had long been lurking on the edges of the modern Republican Party—xenophobia, anti-intellectualism, paranoid conspiracy theories, an antipathy toward Black and brown folks—were finding their way to center stage." Obama even wrote that he deployed Vice President Joe Biden to Capitol Hill to negotiate with Senate Minority Leader Mitch McConnell (R-KY) instead of doing so directly because of his awareness that "negotiations with the vice president didn't inflame the Republican base in quite the same way that any appearance of cooperation with (Black, Muslim socialist) Obama was bound to do." Obama and Michelle both chalked up Tea Party opposition to Obamacare to racism as well.[40]

Given Obama's personal rejection of opponents as benighted racists, it was no wonder that in 2012 he charted a different course than in 2008. Instead of running a campaign directed at a broad base of support, Obama sliced and diced the electorate, focusing in on his new, intersectional coalition, a demographically growing agglomeration of supposedly victimized groups in American life.

Practically speaking, this was a strategy long used by community organizers—as Obama well knew, since he had been one. Obama was trained in the strategies of Saul Alinsky, himself the father of community organizing—and as the Marxist Alinsky wrote in 1971, "even if all the low-income parts of our population were organized—all the blacks, Mexican-Americans, Puerto Ricans, Appalachian poor whites—if through some genius of organization they were all united in a coalition, it would not be powerful enough to get significant, basic needed changes. It would have to . . . seek out allies. The pragmatics of power will not allow any alternative." But while Alinsky encouraged radical organizers to use "strategic sensitivity" with middle-class audiences in order to "radicalize parts of the middle class,"[41] newer community organizers spotted an opportunity to jettison the lower-middle class—people Alinsky himself disdained as insecure and bitter (language Obama himself echoed in 2008). They would focus instead on college graduates, on the young, as potential allies.

This coalitional strategy would eventually be elevated into a philosophy, termed intersectionality by law professor Kimberlé Crenshaw. Crenshaw posited, correctly, that a person could be discriminated against differently thanks to membership in multiple historically victimized groups (a black woman, for example, could be discriminated against differently from a black man). But she then extended that rather uncontroversial premise into a far broader argument: that Americans can be broken down into various identity groups, and that members of particular identity groups cannot understand the experiences of those of other identity groups. This granted members of allegedly victimized identity groups unquestionable moral authority.[42] Identity lay at the core of all systems of power, Crenshaw argued; the only way for those of victimized identity to gain freedom would be to form coalitions with other victimized groups in order to overthrow the dominant systems of power.

The biggest problem with the intersectional coalition, however, remained practical rather than philosophical: the coalition was itself rift by cross-cutting internal divisions. Black Americans, for example, were no fans of same-sex marriage or illegal immigration—so how could a coalition of black Americans and gay Americans and Latino Americans be held together? And how could that coalition unite with enough white voters to win a majority again?

Obama did so in his very person. Essentially, Obama used his own identity as the wedge point in favor of policies black Americans *didn't especially like*—then used his popularity with black Americans in order to glue together the coalition. Every group in the intersectional coalition would receive its goodie bag during the 2012 cycle: in May, gay Americans were thrilled to learn that Obama had flipped on his 2008 position and now supported same-sex marriage;[43] the following month, Obama announced the Deferred Action for Childhood Arrivals program, unilaterally vowing not to enforce immigration law despite his own promises not to do so;[44] Obama, along with a compliant press, labeled Republican policies a "war on women" and vowed to fight for women's rights. As for the black community, Obama largely took it for granted that he would earn their support—and, as it turned out, he was right.[45]

To hold together his intersectional coalition, Obama had to raise the specter of something powerful and dangerous. That "something powerful" couldn't be the government, since Obama was the head of that government. Instead, Obama would unify the coalition against the past. Obama's brilliant slogan was the simple mandate, "FORWARD." Biden suggested to a black audience that opponent Mitt Romney wanted to put black Americans "back in chains."[46] Obama stated that Romney would "turn back the clock 50 years for women, gays and immigrants," stating that he would instead "move us forward."[47] Attacks on Barack Obama's political program wasn't a mere difference of opinion—it was now an attack on the *identities* of blacks, women, gays, Latinos.

The new Obama coalition successfully squared the circle: it knit together the Utopian Impulse, which put ultimate faith in government, and the Revolutionary Impulse, which saw tearing down the system as the answer. Obama united these two ideas with one simple notion: perpetual revolution from *within the government*. Democrats would campaign on revolutionary aggression designed to tear down hierarchies of power, both external to government and within the government itself; top-down censorship of all those who would oppose that agenda; and an anti-conventionalism designed to castigate opponents as morally deficient—indeed, as bigots.

And the strategy worked.

The election of 2012 marked the victory of the Obama coalition. Dan Balz of *The Washington* Post observed that Obama's campaign relied heavily on demographic change: "against the obstacles in Obama's path was a belief in Chicago in the glacial power of demographic change. . . . Obama's advisers were certain that the electorate would have fewer white voters." Obama received the same level of white support as Michael Dukakis in 1988—but won the election because of changing demographics, since he won 80 percent of nonwhite voters. In fact, as Balz observed, Obama's team "invested in what it called Operation Vote, which was aimed exclusively at the key constituencies that make up Obama's coalition: African Americans, Hispanics, young voters and women (particularly those with college degrees)." The campaign communicated directly with these groups, targeting specific gathering places and advertising to niches.[48]

The Obama coalition strategy was forged. And progressives cheered wildly. As Ruy Teixeira and John Halpin wrote for the Center for American Progress (CAP), "Obama's strong progressive majority—built on a multi-racial, multi-ethnic, cross-class coalition in support of an activist . . . is real and growing and it reflects the face and beliefs of the United States in the early part of the 21st Century. The GOP must face the stark reality that its voter base is declining and its ideology is too rigid to represent the changing face of today's country." As CAP noted, the Obama coalition "marks the culmination of a decades-long project to build an electorally viable and ideologically coherent progressive coalition in national politics."[49]

Democrats had long hoped for that culmination. All the way back in 2002, Teixeira penned a book with journalist John Judis titled *The Emerging Democratic Majority*, positing that an increased number of minority Americans could come together to bring forth a permanent progressive utopia.[50] In 2016, NPR championed "the browning of America," suggesting that the country "is at a demographic inflection point," with Democrats reliant on their intersectional coalition buttressed by a majority of college-educated whites. "The Democratic Party," NPR concluded, "has adapted to this demographic change, and is more diverse, more urban, and more liberal than at any time in its history."[51]

Then came 2016. Trump shocked the world, winning a slim majority in the swing states. This created a choice for Democrats in 2020: either they could rethink the Obama intersectional coalition that Hillary Clinton had been unable to replicate or they could double down on it. They chose to try to remake the Obama coalition. As *Politico* noted during the Democratic primaries, "The rhetoric has shifted the debate about electability from an ideological plane—where moderates and more progressive Democrats argued for months over policy—to one based more on identity, and which candidate is best positioned to reassemble the Obama coalition of young people, women and non-white voters that proved instrumental to Democratic successes in the 2018 midterm elections."[52]

Biden successfully mobilized that coalition against Trump, largely by suggesting that Trump presented a unique historic threat to identity groups within the coalition. In his victory speech, Biden name-checked the identity groups in his coalition: "Gay, straight, transgender. White. Latino. Asian. Native American." He pledged, especially, support for the "African-American community" who "stood up again for me." "They always have my back," Biden stated, "and I'll have yours."[53] In homage of his coalition, Biden then doled out cabinet positions based on intersectional characteristics. This was overt racial pandering. The coalition was back in power. And that coalition had learned the main lesson of the Obama era: uniting the Utopian Impulse of progressivism with the Revolutionary Impulse of identity politics could achieve victory.

USING THE SYSTEM TO TEAR DOWN THE SYSTEM

In July 2020, in the midst of the George Floyd protests alleging widespread and systemic American racism, the National Museum of African American History and Culture—a project of the Smithsonian Museum, a taxpayer-funded entity—put up an online exhibit condemning "whiteness." The exhibit, titled "Aspects & Assumptions of Whiteness & White Culture in the United States," explained that Americans had internalized aspects of white culture. What were these terribly white cultural barriers posing challenges to nonwhites? According to the exhibit, "rugged individualism" was a white concept, rooted in nasty ideas like "the individual is the primary unit," "independence & autonomy highly valued + rewarded," and "individuals assumed to be in control of their environment." "Family structure" represented another white concept, with "the nuclear family" condemned as an aspect of whiteness, along with the notion that children "should be independent." Other irrevocably white ideas included an "emphasis on scientific method," complete with "cause and effect relationships"; a focus on history, including "the primacy of Western (Greek, Roman) and Judeo-Christian tradition"; a belief that "hard work is the key to success" and encouragement of "work before play"; monotheism; placing emphasis on "delayed gratification" and following "rigid time schedules"; justice rooted in English common law and intent and private property; "decision-making" and "action orientation"; and, of course, "be[ing] polite."[54]

One moment's thought would betray the fact that assuming that such commonsense pathways to success as delayed gratification, being on time, being polite, and forming stable family structures has nothing to do with racism—and that to call such excellent notions "white" actually degrades nonwhite Americans by assuming them incapable of making decent life decisions. The NMAAHC exhibit was a textbook case of the soft bigotry of low expectations. To find it in a taxpayer-funded exhibit was indeed shocking.

But not all that shocking. The argument put forth by the new intersectional coalition—the argument that any failures within the American system are due to the inherent evils of the system, not to individual failures within that system—now predominates throughout instruments of politics, government, and law. Joe Biden's unity agenda with Bernie Sanders pledged, "On day one, we are committed to taking anti-racist actions for equity across our institutions, including in the areas of education, climate change, criminal justice, immigration, and health care, among others." By anti-racist policy, of course, Biden means policy designed to level all outcomes, no matter the individual decision making at issue. The 2020 Democratic Party platform makes that point even clearer: "Democrats are committed to standing up to racism and bigotry in our laws, in our culture, in our politics, and in our society, and recognize that race-neutral policies are not sufficient to rectify race-based disparities. We will take a comprehensive approach to embed racial justice in every element of our governing agenda."[55]

The federal government controversially was, until ordered to cease, inculcating Critical Race Theory inside the executive branch, with training sessions telling participants that "virtually all White people contribute to racism," and in which employees were required to explain that they "benefit from racism."[56] Companies have been threatened with loss of federal contractor status for failure to abide by woke ideological standards. Anti-discrimination law has been radically extended to include everything from transgender identification to same-sex marriage, clashing dramatically with freedom of association and freedom of religion; it remains an unsettled legal question whether failure to use a proper biological pronoun could be considered a violation of federal anti-discrimination law. Parents now have to fear the predations of state and local governments seizing control of their child rearing; churches fear loss of tax-exempt status; police departments are cudgeled into non-enforcement.

Advocates of this perverse ideology are dedicated to using the revolutionary tools of government created in the 1960s not to fix the system, but to tear it down. The tools of the system will be turned against the system. There is a reason that Ibram X. Kendi, ideological successor to Derrick Bell and Stokely Carmichael, has openly called for a federal Department of Anti-Racism, empowered with the ability to preclear "all local, state and federal public policies to ensure they won't yield racial inequality, monitor those policies, investigate private racist policies when racial inequality surfaces, and monitor public officials for expressions of racist ideas." The DOA would have the ability to punish "policymakers and public officials who do not voluntarily change their racist policy and ideas."[57] This is as pure an expression of fascism as it is possible to imagine.

We're not there yet. But the battle is under way.

WILL THE AUTHORITARIAN LEFTIST COALITION HOLD?

For progressives, the importance of the Obama coalition lies in its purported ability to cram down policy on a large minority—or even a majority—of Americans. By cobbling together supposedly dispossessed minorities and woke white Americans desperate for psychological dissociation from America's alleged systemic bigotry, Democrats hope to leave behind the era of broad public appeals and simply renormalize the American political system. Mainstream Democrats hope to cement the Obama coalition through concessions to "anti-racist" philosophy; in return, they demand fealty to a traditional progressive set of policy proposals.

The new governing power in America, so the theory goes, will be the intersectional-progressive coalition. This coalition is authoritarian in orientation: it promotes revolutionary aggression against the system itself, from both within and without; it seeks top-down censorship of those who disagree; and it sets itself up as an unquestionable moral system, superior to its predecessors.

Democrats banked on that strategy in 2020. They claimed that Donald Trump was a unique, shocking, and direct threat to black Americans, to women, to Latino Americans, to gay Americans. Trump represented all that was worst about America, and it was up to the intersectional coalition and their goodhearted allies to strike a blow on behalf of a new, transformed, *better* America.

Just three weeks after the 2020 election, Professor Sheryll Cashin of Georgetown University called on Democrats to continue to double down on the Obama coalitional strategy. She called on Democrats to ignore Trump voters, silence them, and focus on appeasing all the other members of the intersectional coalition. "A more viable strategy for progressives than trying to win over Trump's supporters right away would be to continue to win elections powered by energized majorities of Black Americans in critical states, in coalitions with other energized people of color rightfully taking their place in American politics and the critical mass of whites willing to see and resist racism," Cashin wrote. Progressive priorities could be allied to "anti-racist" priorities in order to solidify a coalition of the woke.[58]

But, as it turned out, things are not quite that simple.

First, demographics are not destiny. Trump's gains among various identity groups demonstrate that Americans think for themselves, and will not be relegated over time to the boundaries of racial, ethnic, or sexual orientation–based solidarity.

More pressingly, however, the practical problems of intersectionality remain: not all members of the coalition get along. The more radical members of the coalition are unlikely to sit idly by while the more moderate members shape policy. The tension between the Utopian Impulse and the Revolutionary Impulse has not dissipated. And without Barack Obama to paper over those differences—or, just as important, to wave the wand of race and magically deem friends anti-racist and foes the opposite—the coalition cannot hold. Moderate members are unlikely to watch their jobs disappear because radicals have taken the reins. In the aftermath of Biden's 2020 victory, moderate Democrats in Congress fretted that they'd nearly lost their House majority, and were unable to gain a Senate majority. Those moderates blamed radicals pushing idiotic positions for the tenuous Democratic grip on power: Representative Abigail Spanberger (D-VA) lit into her radical colleagues for their sloganeering about "defunding the police" and "socialism," pointing out that Democrats had "lost good members" because of such posturing.[59] Meanwhile, radical members of Congress—members such as Representative Alexandria Ocasio-Cortez (D-NY), Representative Ayanna Pressley (D-MA), Representative Rashida Tlaib (D-MI), and Representative Ilhan Omar (D-MN)—joined forces to savage Democrats like Spanberger, arguing in an open letter to colleagues, "The lesson to be learned from this election cannot and should not be to lean into racist resentment politics, or back away from the social movements that pushed Democrats to power."[60]

Because the Democratic coalition *is* so fragile, representing at best a large minority or bare majority of Americans, it can be fractured. The most obvious way to fracture the Democratic coalition is through generalized resistance to individual elements of the intersectional agenda. And each element of the intersectional agenda is becoming increasingly more radical. During the 2020 election cycle, Democrats, afraid of alienating black Americans, ignored the rioting and looting associated with Black Lives Matter protests; embraced the ideological insanity of CRT; indulged mass protests against police in the middle of a global pandemic; and fudged on whether they were in favor of defunding the police as crime rates spiked. Afraid of alienating LGBT Americans, Democrats embraced the most radical elements of gender theory, including approval of children transitioning sex; they pressured social media companies to punish Americans for "misgendering"; they vowed to crack down on religious practice in the name of supposed LGBT rights. Afraid of alienating Latino Americans, Democrats began treating the term *Latino* itself as insulting, instead embracing the little-known and little-used academic terminology, *Latinx*; more broadly, they advocated decriminalizing illegal immigration itself.

As each intersectional demand grows more radical, however, the Democrats' coalition is threatened. The renormalization of American politics that Democrats seek can only occur in the absence of majoritarian backlash. If, for example, a majority of Americans—including members of the Democratic coalition—said no to the radical transgender agenda, the coalition would have to choose between jettisoning transgender interest groups (perhaps fracturing the coalition) or losing the soft moderates who join their coalition (probably losing its slim majority in the process).

In order to solve these problems, the Left can't rely on pure renormalization through democratic means. It must stymie its opponents in order to prevent the fracture of its coalition. The Left must increase the size of its coalition by intimidating its opponents into inaction, or by browbeating them into compliance. The Left must engage in institutional capture, and then use the power of those institutions in order to compel the majority of Americans to mirror their chosen political priorities. Without control of the commanding cultural heights, the leftist coalition cannot win. That is why they've focused all their energies on taking those commanding heights.

CHAPTER 3

THE CREATION OF
A NEW RULING CLASS

On March 12, 2019, federal prosecutors revealed a bombshell case involving at least fifty defendants, a case spanning from 2011 to 2018. Dozens of the defendants were extraordinarily wealthy; many were preternaturally famous. The two biggest names were Lori Laughlin, star of *Full House*, and Felicity Huffman, Oscar-nominated actress. Their crime: trying to bribe their children's way into college, by either paying someone to cheat on tests, paying someone to create fake résumé enhancers and bribe college administrators, or other means. Laughlin, according to prosecutors, "agreed to pay bribes totaling $500,000 in exchange for having their two daughters designated as recruits to the USC crew team—despite the fact that they did not participate in crew";[1] Huffman paid $15,000 to inflate her daughter's test score by paying a proctor to correct her answers.[2]

College officials involved in the scheme hailed from some of the most prominent schools in the country: Yale, Stanford, UCLA, and USC, among others.[3] For her crime, Laughlin did two months in prison, two years of probation, 100 hours of community service, and paid a $150,000 fine; Huffman did 14 days in prison, 250 hours of community service, and paid a $30,000 fine.[4]

The scandal made national headlines. Those on the political Left suggested that the story smacked of white privilege—after all, these were all people of means, paying hundreds of thousands of dollars to game the system on behalf of their children. Those on the political Right suggested that the story was just more evidence that the college system itself had become a scam.

All of this missed the real point: why in the world did rich, famous parents—millionaires and billionaires—feel the need for their children to go to "good schools"? That question was particularly pressing with regard to Laughlin's daughter, Olivia Jade, already a social media celebrity with millions of followers. And after the scandal broke, Jade lost sponsorships with makeup companies like Sephora.[5] So why, exactly, was it vital for Laughlin and her husband, Mossimo founder Mossimo Giannulli, to drop half a million dollars to send their daughter to the second-best school in Los Angeles?

The question becomes even more puzzling when we reflect that Jade had no great aspirations for college. It's not as though she was looking forward to a career in genetic engineering. In fact, Jade drew outsized criticism when she posted a social media video describing her hopes for her university career to her 2 million followers, explaining, "I don't know how much of school I'm gonna attend. But I'm gonna go in and talk to my deans and everyone, and hope that I can try and balance it all. But I do want the experience of like game days, partying . . . I don't really care about school, as you guys all know."[6]

But here's the thing: Jade was right.

The real reason many Americans go to college—particularly Americans who aren't majoring in science, technology, engineering, and math fields—is either pure credentialism, social cachet, or both. College, in essence, is about the creation of a New Ruling Class. It's an extraordinarily expensive licensing program for societal influence.

Americans simply don't *learn very much* if they're majoring in the liberal arts. Yes, Americans may have a higher career earnings trajectory if they attend a good college and major in English than if they stop their educational career after high school. But that's because employers typically use diplomas as a substitute for job entrance examinations, and also because college graduates tend to create social capital with other college graduates. College, in other words, is basically a sorting mechanism. That's why Olivia Jade's massively wealthy parents would risk jail time and spend hundreds of thousands of dollars to get her into a good-but-not-great school like USC.

Begin with credentialism. In 1950, only 7.3 percent of American men and 5.2 percent of American women had gone to college; in 1980, that number was 20.9 percent of men and 13.6 percent of women, a nearly threefold increase. As of 2019, 35.4 percent of men had gone to college, and so had 36.6 percent of women.[7] This trend, which relies on the simple fact that Americans on average earn more with a college degree than without, has led to tremendous inflation in the credential market: where you could get a job as a dental lab technician or medical equipment operator just a few years ago without a college degree, that's no longer true. You now have to outcompete others who have graduated from college for the same job—and this means that colleges have an interest in churning out as many degrees as possible, given that employer demand for college graduates continues to increase.

One October 2017 study from Harvard Business School professors Joseph Fuller and Manjari Raman found that "degree inflation is undermining US competitiveness and hurting America's middle class." Fuller and Raman explained that "[p]ostings for many jobs traditionally viewed as middle-skills jobs (those that require employees with more than a high school diploma but less than a college degree) in the

United States now stipulate a college degree as a minimum education requirement. . . . Our analysis indicates that more than 6 million jobs are currently at risk of degree inflation." Damage from degree inflation particularly targets those who disproportionately don't go to college—namely, low-income students, many of whom are minority. During economic downturns, those trends are only exacerbated as newly unemployed college graduates crowd out those who don't have college degrees in middle-skills professions.[8]

Naturally, the demand for college graduates has led to a massive increase in the number of Americans pursuing postgraduate degrees. According to the Census Bureau, the number of Americans over twenty-five with a master's degree *doubled* between 2000 and 2018, and the number of Americans with a doctorate increased 125 percent. Overall, while only 8.6 percent of Americans had a postgraduate degree in 2000, 13.1 percent did in 2018.[9]

Degree inflation doesn't necessarily mean that Americans are better qualified for work than they were when they didn't go to college— nothing about a queer studies theory bachelor's degree will make anyone ready for an entry-level position as a dental assistant. In fact, top high school graduates who don't attend college tend to do just as well as college graduates. As a recent Manhattan Institute study found, high schoolers who graduate within the top 25 percent of their class but don't go on to college routinely outperform college graduates who finish in the bottom 25 percent of their class. And as the study authors point out, "more than 40 percent of recent college graduates wind up in jobs that do not require a degree . . . on top of the roughly half of college attendees who fail to earn a degree at all."[10]

College, then, may grant an undue advantage to graduates based on credentials. But that's not the only advantage. The other advantage is access to a new class hierarchy.

In *Hillbilly Elegy*, J. D. Vance writes of his ascension from growing up poor in Appalachia to graduation from Yale Law. For Vance, the transition wasn't merely economic or regional—it was cultural. As Vance writes, "that first year at Yale taught me most of all that I didn't know how the world of the American elite works." Vance was embarrassed to find at a formal dinner that he didn't know what sparkling water was, how to use three spoons or multiple butter knives, or the difference between chardonnay and sauvignon blanc. But this was all part of a test: "[law firm] interviews were about passing a social test—a test of belonging, of holding your own in a corporate boardroom, of making connections with potential future clients."[11]

That test of belonging separates college graduates from everyone else. As Charles Murray notes in his seminal 2012 work, *Coming Apart*, Americans—he focuses on white Americans particularly—have separated into two classes: an elite, "the people who run the nation's economic, political and cultural institutions," those who "are both successful and influential within a city or region" . . . and everyone else.[12] Murray calls the former group the new upper class, "with advanced educations, often obtained at elite schools, sharing tastes and preferences that set them apart from mainstream America." They are better termed the New Ruling Class, given that economic strata are not the main divider.

The members of the New Ruling Class have almost nothing in common with the "new lower class, characterized not by poverty but by withdrawal from America's core cultural institutions." Members of the New Ruling Class are more likely to be married, less likely to engage in single parenthood, less likely to be victimized by crime. They are also more likely to be political liberal. Murray describes their viewpoint as "hollow"—meaning that they refuse to promulgate the same social standards they actually practice. They stand firmly against propagating and encouraging adherence to the life rules they have followed to success. Left-leaning historian Christopher Lasch says the New Ruling Class (he calls them the "new elites) "are in revolt against 'Middle America,' as they imagine it: a nation technically backward, politically reactionary, repressive in its sexual morality, middlebrow in its tastes, smug and complacent, dull and dowdy. . . . It is a question whether they think of themselves as Americans at all."[13]

The ticket to membership in the New Ruling Class is often credential-based. Members of the New Ruling Class know this. In December 2020, Joseph Epstein, who taught at the University of Chicago, wrote a column pointing out that incoming first lady Jill Biden was not in fact a doctor—her doctorate was in education from the prestigious University of Delaware. "A wise man once said that no one should call himself 'Dr.' unless he has delivered a child," Epstein wrote. "Think about it, Dr. Jill, and forthwith drop the doc."[14] The media reacted with unmitigated scorn and fury. Dr. Jill, they said, was not merely a doctor—she was the greatest doctor since Jonas Salk.

Michelle Obama posted in umbrage on Instagram: "All too often, our accomplishments are met with skepticism, even derision. We're doubted by those who choose the weakness of ridicule over the strength of respect. And yet somehow, their words can stick—after decades of work, we're forced to prove ourselves all over again." Second Gentleman Douglas Emhoff tweeted that Biden "earned her degrees through hard work and pure grit. She is an inspiration to me, to her students, and to Americans across this country." Dr. Jill herself went on Stephen Colbert's propaganda hour, where he cloyingly read from her book and nodded along as she intoned, "One of the things I'm most proud of is my doctorate. I've worked so hard for it."[15]

There is only one problem. Dr. Jill is not a doctor in any meaningful sense. That's not just because her supposed hard work amounted to receiving a degree for a dissertation from a university with a public policy school named after her husband in a state represented by her husband for decades (although one could make the case that such a degree is a tad . . . well . . . unearned). It has to do with the fact that only actual doctors—you know, people you'd call if your kid had an ear infection—should be called doctor. I have a juris doctor from Harvard Law School. I am not a doctor. My wife has a medical degree from UCLA. She is a doctor. There is, in fact, a terribly simple test of whether someone ought to be called doctor in daily life: if you're on a plane and the pilot asks if there is a doctor available, do you raise your hand? (Note: if you raise your hand because you have a doctorate in education, your fellow passengers should be allowed by law to send you through the exit door at 30,000 feet.)

So, what was the big deal? Why, in fact, does Dr. Jill insist that everybody call her doctor, when she is about as much of a doctor as Dr. J, and boasts a significantly lower lifetime PPG average? (Dr. J does have an honorary doctorate from the University of Massachusetts.) She insists on being called "doctor" because it's a mark of membership in the New Ruling Class. As Dr. Jill once told her husband, Joe Biden, "I was so sick of the mail coming to Sen. and Mrs. Biden. I wanted the mail addressed to Dr. and Sen. Biden."[16]

This is, technically speaking, the height of obnoxious silliness. My wife—again, an actual doctor—is frequently referred to as Mrs. Shapiro. And as she told me, she doesn't care one whit, since she knows what she does for a living, and her identity isn't wrapped up in whether others know her degrees.

Credentialism, in other words, isn't generally about recognition of merit. It's a way of signaling commonality with the patricians of our society.

But something has happened since Murray's book came out that has deepened cultural divides even further: members of the New Ruling Class aren't merely constituted by educational history. They must now *speak the language of social justice.* There is a parlance taught at America's universities and spoken only by those who have attended it, or adopted by those who aspire to membership in the New Ruling Class. That parlance is foreign both to non—college graduates and to those who graduated from college years ago. It sounds like gobble-dygook to those who haven't attended universities; it's illogical when rigorously examined. But the more time you spend in institutions of higher learning, the better you learn the language.

Quibbling with that language earns you a ticket to the social leper colony. While from the 1990s to the 2008 election, the voting gap between high school and college graduates was "small, if not negligible," it opened wide between 2008 and 2012. As Adam Harris of *The Atlantic* observes, "white voters without a college degree were distinctly more likely to vote Republican than those with college degrees." In 2016, 48 percent of white college graduates voted for Trump, compared with 66 percent of those who didn't graduate from college.[17] In 1980, the 100 counties with the highest share of college degrees went Republican, 76 to 24; in 2020, Democrats won top college-graduate counties 84 to 16.[18]

Naturally, leftist commentators attribute this emerging voting gap to both Republican stupidity and Republican racism. But that's not the story. The story is the creation of an elitist group of Americans who speak the Holy Tongue of Wokeness—a language built for internal solidarity and designed for purgation of unbelievers.

LEARNING THE WOKABULARY

Wokeism, of course, is rooted in identity politics. It takes cues from intersectionality, which suggests a hierarchy of victimhood in which you are granted credibility based on the number of victim groups to which you belong. But it doesn't stop there. Wokeism takes identity politics to the ultimate extreme: it sees *every structure of society* as reflective of deeper, underlying structures of oppression. Reason, science, language, and freedom—all are subject to the toxic acid of identity politics.[19] To stand with *any* purportedly objective system is to endorse the unequal results of that system. All inequality in life can be chalked up to systemic inequity. And to defend the system means to defend inequity.

This argument, which fell out of favor over the course of the 1970s and 1980s, suddenly roared back in full force in the 2010s in the universities. To be fair, the philosophy had never truly disappeared—even when I attended UCLA in the early 2000s, calls for mandatory "diversity courses" steeped in intersectionality were commonplace. But in the 2010s, wokeism moved from a prominent but minority philosophy to the dominant philosophy of America's major universities. Suddenly, discredited theories of inherent American evil sprang back to the forefront.

But these theories don't constitute another mere trend. They represent an entire *religious*, unfalsifiable worldview. To deny that an inequality means an inequity has taken place became sinful and dangerous: by suggesting that perhaps inequality resulted from luck, natural imbalances, or differential decision making, you are a *threat* to others, a victim-shamer. As Boston University professor of history Ibram X. Kendi, perhaps the most popular of the woke thinkers, states, "Racial inequality is evidence of racist policy and the different racial groups are equals."[20] Robin DiAngelo, Kendi's white woke counterpart and a professor at the University of Washington, summarizes: "if we truly believe that all humans are equal, then disparity in condition can only be the result of systemic discrimination."[21] In other words, all decisions should create the same result—and if you disagree, you are racist.[22]

"Social justice" dictates that you sit down and shut up—that you listen to others' experiences, refrain from judgment, and join in the anarchic frenzy at destroying prevailing systems.

And it is a cult. It is a moral system built on anti-conventionalism—on the belief that its expositors are the sole beacons of light in the moral universe, and therefore justifiable in their revolutionary aggression and top-down censorship.

To be deemed anti-racist, for example, one must take courses with Robin DiAngelo, participate in Maoist struggle sessions, and always—*always*—mirror the prevailing woke ideas. To fail to do so is to be categorized as undesirable. All "microaggressions" must be spotted. All heresies must be outed. And all logical consistency—even basic decency itself—must be put aside in the name of the greater good. As Kendi puts it, "The only remedy to racist discrimination is antiracist discrimination. The only remedy to past discrimination is present discrimination. The only remedy to present discrimination is future discrimination."[23]

Repeat and believe. Or be labeled evil. For Ibram X. Kendi, America has two souls. One is the soul of justice, which "breathes life, freedom, equality, democracy, human rights, fairness, science, community, opportunity, and empathy for all." The other is those who disagree, who breathe "genocide, enslavement, inequality, voter suppression, bigotry, cheating, lies, individualism, exploitation, denial, and indifference to it all."[24] Notice the inclusions of the terms "individualism" and "denial" in Kendi's litany of evil. If you believe that individuals have rights, that in a free country you are largely responsible for your own fate, or if you deny the clearly false proposition that all inequality is evidence of inequity, you are inhabited by the soul of evil.

If this sounds cultish, that's because it is. "Social justice" has indeed become a cult. As Helen Pluckrose and James Lindsay, both liberal scholars, write:

Social Justice Theorists have created a new religion, a tradition of faith that is actively hostile to reason, falsification, disconfirmation,

and disagreement of any kind. Indeed, the whole postmodern-
ist project now seems, in retrospect, like an unwitting attempt to
have deconstructed the old metanarratives of Western thought—
science and reason along with religion and capitalist economic
systems—to make room for a wholly new religion, a post-modern
faith based on a dead God, which sees mysterious worldly forces in
systems of power and privilege and which sanctifies victimhood.
This, increasingly, is the fundamentalist religion of the nominally
secular left.[25]

The religion of wokeism requires more than adherence. It requires
fluency in the wokabulary. This isn't an attribute unique to wokeness—
all religions contain elements of signaling, the use of unique signifiers
to identify members of the group. Social groups often rely on signifiers in order to create solidarity, thus forming bonds across larger
numbers of people: religious Jews wear yarmulkes, for example, not
only to symbolize fealty to something higher, but in order to signal to
other religious Jews a level of commitment to the religion. As evolutionary anthropologists Richard Sosis and Candace Alcorta write, this
sort of activity is true even in the animal kingdom: "Ritual signals, by
allowing clear communication of intent, were seen as promoting coordination and reducing the costs of agonistic encounters, thus laying
the foundation for the development and stability of social groups." In
order to deter those trying to imitate group signals in order to gain
improper social entry, groups often require sacrifice—signaling that
becomes costly to fake. The most effective signaling includes an aspect of the sacred: "The ability of religious ritual to elicit emotions
makes it difficult for nonbelievers to imitate and renders it a powerful
tool for social appraisal."[26]

This is what the wokabulary is all about. It is not about convincing
others. It is about demonstration of belief in the cult. As Lasch writes:

The culture wars that have convulsed America since the sixties are best understood as a form of class warfare, in which an enlightened elite (as it thinks of itself) seeks not so much to impose its values on the majority (a majority perceived as incorrigibly racist, sexist, provincial, and xenophobic), much less to persuade the majority by means of rational public debate, as to create parallel or "alternative" institutions in which it will no longer be necessary to confront the unenlightened at all.[27]

Membership in the New Ruling Class comes with clear cultural signifiers—it is easy to tell whether someone is an initiate into the New Ruling Class. Do they use pronouns in their public bio to show solidarity with the transgender agenda, nodding gravely at patent linguistic abominations like ze/hir, ze/zem, ey/em, per/pers— ridiculous terms meant to obscure rather than enlighten? Do they use the word *Latinx* rather than *Latinos* in order to show sensitivity to Latinas, despite the gendered nature of Spanish? Do they talk about "institutional" or "systemic" or "cultural" discrimination? Do they attach modifiers to words like *justice*—"Environmental justice," "racial justice," "economic justice," "social justice"—modifiers that actually undercut the nature of individual justice in favor of communalism? Do they worry about "microaggressions" or "trigger warnings"? Do they use terms like "my truth" rather than "my opinion"? Do they "call out" those who ask for data by castigating them for "erasure" or "destruction of identity," or dismiss their beliefs by referencing their opponents' alleged "privilege"? Do they talk about "structures of power," or suggest that terms like "Western civilization" are inherently bigoted? Do they speak of the "patriarchy" or "heteronormativity" or "cisnormativity"?

It's a complex language. Adherence requires constant attention to the changing dictionary of norms. What was absolutely inoffensive yesterday can become deeply offensive today, without warning—and ignorance is no defense. There is no set system for changing the wokabulary—changes can emerge, fully formed, nearly instantaneously.

The wokabulary is facially absurd. Two decades ago, New York University mathematician Alan Sokal published a gobbledygook word salad of deconstructionism in a postmodern academic journal. Its title: "Transgressing the Boundaries: Towards a Transformative Hermeneutics of Quantum Gravity." In 2018, scholars James Lindsay, Helen Pluckrose, and Peter Boghossian repeated the feat, but on a far larger scale. The left-liberal scholars submitted a series of hilariously farcical articles to prestigious academic journals—and a bevy of those articles were accepted. Of the twenty papers submitted, seven were accepted and four were published. Only six were rejected outright.[28] *Gender, Place, and Culture* published a paper titled, "Human Reaction to Rape Culture and Queer Performativity at Urban Dog Parks in Portland, Oregon." The journal *Fat Studies* published a paper titled, "Who Are They to Judge? Overcoming Anthropometry and a Framework for Fat Bodybuilding." *Sex Roles* approved a paper titled, "An Ethnography of Breastaurant Masculinity: Themes of Objectification, Sexual Conquest, Male Control, and Masculine Toughness in a Sexually Objectifying Restaurant."

The content of these papers was no less absurd. One of the articles argued against "western astronomy," since that field of inquiry was allegedly rooted in bigotry; instead, the authors suggested "[o]ther means superior to the natural sciences . . . to extract alternative knowledges about stars," which would include such wonders as "modern feminist analysis" of "mythological narratives" about stars and perhaps "feminist interpretative dance (especially with regard to the movements of the stars and their astrological significance)." Another accepted paper took on the important topic of whether masturbation while thinking about someone makes you a sexual abuser, since the object hasn't given her consent.[29] Yet another paper discussed whether transphobia and homophobia from straight males could be overcome through "receptive penetrative sex toy use." One paper was a rewrite of a section of *Mein Kampf* using women's studies terminology.

The hoax worked because Lindsay, Pluckrose, and Boghossian were fluent in the wokabulary: they understood that simply by characterizing every problem as a critique of societal victimization, they owned the skeleton key to academia. The professors themselves explained, "Scholarship based less upon finding truth and more upon attending to social grievances has become firmly established, if not fully dominant" in many areas of higher education.[30]

It is this language—the wokabulary—that universities now teach. Outside of the sciences, universities no longer exist in order to train you for a job. They exist to grant you a credential and usher you into the broader world of the New Ruling Class via your new bilingualism in the wokabulary. David Randall of the National Association of Scholars notes that over the last twenty years a new generation of academics and administrators has taken power, seeking to "transform higher education itself into an engine of progressive political advocacy, subjecting students to courses that are nothing more than practical training in progressive activism." So dominant is the wokeism that in many major university departments, not a single conservative can be identified on the staff. Professors leverage social justice into their curricula, into their research, into their writings; administrators use their power to push social justice in all aspects of both academic and social life, from residential life to public events.

To that end, the New Ruling Class in charge of our universities aims at maximizing the budgets allocated to social justice–oriented courses; overall, colleges spend tens of billions of dollars on such pursuits.[31] One of the not-accidental by-products of wokeism is the dramatic increase in college budgets directed toward useless fields—diversity studies directed not toward broadening minds but narrowing them. As Heather Mac Donald writes in *The Diversity Delusion*, "Entire fields have sprung up around race, ethnicity, sex, and gender identity. . . . A vast administrative apparatus—the diversity bureaucracy—promotes the notion that to be a college student from an ever-growing number of victim groups is to experience daily bigotry from your professors and peers." Even departments supposedly disassociated from social justice activism are often rife with it. Wokeism completely dominates our institutions of higher education.[32]

HOW UNIVERSITIES WERE RENORMALIZED

The universities represented the first line of attack for cultural radicals. In the 1960s, a liberal consensus still prevailed, a belief in the freedoms guaranteed by the Constitution, as well as a commitment to the very notion of truth-seeking itself. By the end of the 1960s, that consensus had completely collapsed on campus. The renormalization of the universities occurred because that liberal consensus was hollow—because enlightenment ideals of open inquiry and the pursuit of truth are not self-evident, and die when disconnected from their cultural roots.

The soft underbelly for Enlightenment liberals lay in an inability to rebut what Robert Bellah termed "expressive individualism." Expressive individualism is the basic idea that the goal of life and government ought to be ensuring the ability of individuals to explore their own perception of the good life, and to express it as they see fit.[33] Enlightenment liberalism was still unconsciously connected to old ideas about reason and virtue. By contrast, expressive individualism obliterated all such limits. If you found meaning in avoiding responsibility for others, including children, that was part and parcel of liberty; if you found meaning in defining yourself in a way directly contrary to reality or decency, that was simply liberty, too.

What's more, according to philosopher Charles Taylor, expressive individualism requires the *approval* of others. As O. Carter Snead of the University of Notre Dame relates, Taylor "identified a new category of harm that emerges in a culture of expressive individualism, namely, the *failure to receive, accept, and appreciate* the expression of others' inner depths. . . . To fail to recognize the expression of other selves is a violation and a harm to them." We must all cheer for others' ideas, decisions, and proclamations, no matter how bad, how perverse, or how untrue.[34]

The critique provided by deconstructionism was, at heart, merely a radical version of expressive individualism. Where Enlightenment liberalism had taken for granted certain ideas about human rights, the value of objective truth, and the ability for human beings to understand the world around them—ideas borrowed from Judeo-Christianity—and then built on those ideas by questioning long-held but unproven axioms about science and power, deconstructionism bathed *everything* in the acid of questioning, hence "deconstructing" everything. The postmodernists made the case that all knowledge was the result of pre-existing narratives that had to be questioned, and that none of those narratives could rebut any other narratives. Postmodernism could be used to tear down any attempt to establish truth—even scientific facts could be rebutted by critiquing the way we define truth based on our cultural context.

Postmodernism carved the heart out of the liberal project. Enlightenment liberalism pushed reason and logic to the center of discourse; postmodernism dismissed reason and logic as just, like, your opinion, man.

The resulting hollowness spelled disaster for the universities, where postmodernism had become heavily influential. Colleges were ripe for the picking. Instead of dedicating themselves to teaching the long-held truths of Western civilization, they dedicated themselves to "thinking critically"—which, in practice, meant critiquing Western civilization while asking "who are we to judge?" about other cultures. While pure deconstructionism, however, would have pointed out the frailty of *all* cultural structures, the deconstructionism adopted in American universities applied *only* to the West. To apply deconstructionism to others would violate the tenets of expressive individualism. Identity groups quickly took advantage of this weakness, suggesting that membership in a victimized group lent special knowledge and status to their critiques of the prevailing ideological systems. And those in charge of the universities—crippled by their inability to rebut criticisms of Western systems of inquiry and knowledge, and too "nice" to use the tools of deconstructionism against other cultures—simply collapsed.[35]

In practical terms, the universities imploded because in the name of the Cordiality Principle, those who should have fought back did not; because in the name of liberalism, those who should not have tolerated illiberalism did; because the radicals were simply intransigent, and built coalitions large enough to hold institutions hostage. The authoritarian leftists took over the university because they successfully renormalized the institutions themselves.

To take but one example, the 1964 Berkeley Free Speech Movement (FSM), now championed as a glorious American moment of liberty, was actually a mere pretense designed at gaining power and control. As author Roger Kimball notes, the controversy began when students began using a strip of university-owned land for political purposes. The university objected, pointing out that the students had plenty of areas designated for such activity. Nonetheless, the students rallied to the call—and that call went far beyond time and place restrictions on political activity. One 1965 FSM pamphlet pointed out that "politics and education are inseparable," and that the university should not be geared toward "passing along the morality of the middle class, nor the morality of the white man, nor even the morality of the potpourri we call 'western society.'"[36]

During the same period, Harvard students seized buildings; Columbia students held a dean hostage and occupied the president's office. At Cornell, armed students took professors hostage, invaded college buildings, and forced the faculty to reverse its own penalties placed on offending students. The president of the university then proceeded to call the incident "one of the most positive forces ever set in motion in the history of Cornell." Professors with spines, including Walter Berns and Allan Bloom, resigned. Later, one of the ringleaders of the entire affair, Tom Jones, would be appointed to the Cornell board of trustees. Bloom wrote that students now knew that "pompous teachers who catechized them about academic freedom could, with a little shove, be made into dancing bears."[37]

The students knew it. Shelby Steele, who would later become conservative, recalls attending college in the late 1960s, leading black students into the president's office with a list of demands. As Steele narrates, "with all the militant authority I could muster, I allowed the ashes from my lit cigarette to fall in little grey cylinders onto the president's plush carpet. This was the effrontery, the insolence, that was expected in our new commitment to militancy." Steele fully expected the college president, Dr. Joseph McCabe, to chastise him. But, says Steele, it simply didn't happen:

I could see that it was all becoming too much for him. . . . There was no precedent for this sort of assault on authority, no administrative manual on how to handle it. I saw something like real anger come over his face, and he grabbed the arms of his chair as if to spring himself up. . . . But his arms never delivered him from his seat. I will never know what thought held him back. I remember only that his look turned suddenly inward as if he were remembering something profound, something that made it impossible for him to rise up. Then it was clear that the cigarette would be overlooked. . . . In that instant we witnessed his transformation from a figure of implacable authority to a negotiator empathetic with the cause of those who challenged him—from a traditional to a modern college president.

As Steele states, it was McCabe's understanding of the evils of racism that allowed such outrageous behavior by students. His own "vacuum of moral authority," springing from knowledge of American sins, stopped him cold.[38] Authoritarian leftists, relying on an anti-conventionalism that castigated traditional liberalism as morally deficient, silenced McCabe, as they did most college administrators.

Liberalism's separation from its values-laden roots left it unable to defend itself. The dance of renormalization had occurred. First, they silenced those in power. Then they forced them to publicly repent. Then they cast them aside. That's the authoritarian Left's process in every country and in every era.

THE PURGE

The universities have now become factories for wokeism. There are few or no conservatives in the faculty and staff of most top universities; a 2020 *Harvard Crimson* survey found that 41.3 percent of the faculty members identified as liberal, and another 38.4 percent as very liberal; moderates constituted just 18.9 percent of the faculty, and 1.46 percent said they were conservative.[39] A similar *Yale Daily News* survey of faculty in 2017 found that 75 percent of faculty respondents identified as liberal or very liberal; only 7 percent said they were conservative, with just 2 percent labeling themselves "very conservative." In the humanities, the percentages were even more skewed, with 90 percent calling themselves liberal; overall, 90 percent of all faculty said they opposed Trump.[40] One liberal Yale professor told *The Wall Street Journal*, "Universities are moving away from the search for truth" and toward "social justice."[41]

Overall, for over 2,000 college professors spanning thirty-one states and the District of Columbia who donated to political candidates from 2015 to 2018, contributions to Democrats outpaced those to Republicans by a 95:1 ratio.[42] Another study published in *Econ Journal Watch* in 2016 found that of the 7,243 professors registered to vote at forty leading universities, Democrats outnumbered Republicans 3,623 to 314.[43] The Carnegie Foundation surveyed professors about their political affiliations in 1969, and found 27 percent were conservative; by 1999, just 12 percent were. Samuel Abrams of the Higher Education Research Institute suggested that since 1984, the ratio of liberals to conservatives on college faculty has increased 350 percent. By one study, just 2 percent of political science professors were estimated to be conservative; just 4 percent of philosophy professors; just 7 percent of history professors; and just 3 percent of literature professors.[44] These are political identification numbers that would make Fidel Castro blush in envy.

It's not only that conservatives have been weeded out at America's top universities. It's that even old-school, rights-based liberals have now been marginalized. Former head of the American Civil Liberties Union Ira Glasser recently told *Reason* about visiting one of America's top law schools:

[T]he audience was a rainbow. There were as many women as men. There were people of every skin color and every ethnicity . . . it was the kind of thing we dreamed about. It was the kind of thing we fought for. So I'm looking at this audience and I am feeling wonderful about it. And then after the panel discussion, person after person got up, including some of the younger professors, to assert that their goals of social justice for blacks, for women, for minorities of all kinds were incompatible with free speech and that free speech was an antagonist. . . . For people who today claim to be passionate about social justice to establish free speech as an enemy is suicidal.[45]

But the suicide of the academy is well under way. Even moderate liberals now find themselves on the chopping block. When liberal professor Bret Weinstein refused to leave the Evergreen State College campus after black radicals demanded that white teachers not teach on a particular day—and when he added to that sin by stating that faculty jobs should be rooted in merit rather than skin color—authoritarian leftist students called him racist and took over campus buildings.[46] Students walked out on a class taught by his wife, evolutionary biologist Heather Heyer, when she pointed out that men are, on average, taller than women.[47] Professor Nicholas Christakis and his wife, Erika, were shouted out of their positions as Yale faculty-in-residence at Yale's Silliman College after Erika committed the grave sin of asking students to be less sensitive about Halloween costumes. Students confronted Nicholas on the quad and screamed at him. "Who the f*** hired you?" screamed one black female student. "You should step down! . . . It is not about creating an intellectual space! It is not! Do you understand that? . . . You are disgusting!"[48]

Such incidents have terrified dissenters into silence or, worse, compliance. But it's not just student intimidation at issue. It's the self-perpetuating nature of the New Ruling Class at our universities. According to sociologist George Yancy, 30 percent of sociologists openly admitted they would discriminate against Republican job applicants, as well as 24 percent of philosophy professors; 60 percent of anthropologists and 50 percent of literature professors said they would discriminate against evangelical Christians. But just as important, once wokeism has been enshrined as the official ideology of higher education, conservatives self-select out of that arena. How often will a dissertation adviser take on a PhD student in political science who posits that individual decision making rather than systemic racism lies at the root of racial inequalities? How often will a college dean hire an associate professor who maintains that gender ideology is a lie? As Jon Shields, himself an associate professor of government at Claremont McKenna College, notes at *National Affairs*, "the leftward tilt of the social sciences and humanities is self-reinforcing."[49]

CONCLUSION

The religion of the New Ruling Class—as well as the ritualistic pagan activities surrounding it—is an intellectual virus. And it has infected broad strains of American life. In fact, wokeism is so incredibly virulent that in February 2021, French president Emmanuel Macron stated that the country's unity was threatened by "certain social science theories imported from the United States." Macron's education minister warned that the "intellectual matrix from American universities" should not be imported.[50]

For decades, conservatives scoffed at the radicals on campus. They assumed that real life would beat the radicalism out of the college-age leftists. They thought the microaggression culture of the universities would be destroyed by the job market, that paying taxes would cure college graduates of their utopian redistributionism, that institutions would act as a check on the self-centered brattishness of college indoctrination victims.

They were wrong.

Instead, wokeism has been carried into every major area of American life via powerful cultural and governmental institutions—nearly all of which are composed disproportionately of people who graduated from college and learned the wokabulary. Growth industries in the United States are industries dominated thoroughly by college graduates. In fact, between December 2007 and December 2009, the Great Recession, college graduates actually *increased* their employment by 187,000 jobs, while those with a high school degree or less lost 5.6 million jobs. Over the course of the next six years, high school graduates would gain a grand total of just 80,000 jobs during the so-called Obama recovery, compared to 8.4 million jobs for college graduates.[51]

Instead of postgraduation institutes shaping their employees, employees are shaping their institutions. It turns out that corporate heads and media moguls are just as subject to renormalization as colleges ever were. As we will see, corporate titans are now afraid of their woke staff, and have turned to mirroring their priorities; old-school liberals in media have turned over their desks to repressive wokescolds; even churches have turned over their pulpits, increasingly, to those who would cave to the new radical value system.

One area of American life, though, should have been immune to the predations of authoritarian leftism: science. After all, science has a method, a way of distinguishing truth from falsehood; science is designed to uncover objective truths rather than to wallow in subjective perceptions of victimization. Science should have been at the bleeding edge of the pushback.

Instead, science surrendered, too. Next, we'll take a look at why.

CHAPTER 4

HOW SCIENCE™ DEFEATED ACTUAL SCIENCE

Two thousand twenty was a banner year for science.

In the midst of a global pandemic caused by a novel coronavirus, scientists in laboratories across the world stepped into the breach. They researched the most effective methods of slowing the virus's spread. They developed new therapeutics designed to reduce death rates, and researched new applications of already-existent drugs. Most incredibly, they developed multiple vaccines for Covid-19 within mere months of its exponential spread across the West. Most of the West didn't shut down until March 2020. By December, citizens were receiving their first doses of vaccine, immunizing the most vulnerable and flattening the infection curve.

Meanwhile, in hospitals, doctors and nurses labored in perilous conditions to care for waves of the sick. Physicians were called upon to be resourceful with limited resources; nurses were called upon to brave danger to themselves to treat others. As they learned more about the nature of the disease, those medical workers saved tens of thousands of lives.

And the public took measures, too. Across the West, citizens socially distanced and masked up; they closed their businesses and took their children out of school and told their parents to stay home in order to protect others.

The historic scourge of disease challenged humankind. Science emerged victorious.

And yet.

While laboratory scientists did unprecedented work creating solutions for an unprecedented problem, while doctors worked in dangerous conditions to preserve the lives of suffering patients, public health officials—the voices of The Science™, the politically driven perversion of actual science in the name of authoritarian leftism—proceeded to push politically radical ends, politicize actual scientific research, and undermine public trust in science itself. Unfortunately, because science is such an indispensable part of Western life—it is perhaps the only arena of political agreement left in our society, thanks to the fact that it has heretofore remained outside the realm of the political—it is too valuable a tool to be left unused by the authoritarian Left. And so the authoritarian Left has substituted The Science™ for science.

Science itself is a process of gathering knowledge through painstaking trial and error, through gradual development of a body of knowledge through observation and data collection, through falsification. Science requires that we believe in objective truths about the world around us, and that we believe in our own capacity to explore the unknown to uncover those truths. Most of all, science provides the final word where it speaks.

The Science™ is a different story. The Science™ amounts to a call for silence, not investigation. When members of the New Ruling Class insist that we follow The Science™, they generally do *not* mean that we ought to acknowledge the reality of scientific findings. They mean that we ought to abide by their politicized interpretation of science, that we ought to mirror their preferred solutions, that we ought to look the other way when they ignore and twist science for their own ends. The Science™ is never invoked in order to convince; it is invoked in order to cudgel. The Science™, in short, is politics dressed in a white coat. Treating science as politics undermines science; treating politics as science costs lives. That's precisely what the authoritarian Left does when it invokes The Science™ to justify itself.

We saw The Science™ prevail over science itself repeatedly during the pandemic, to ugly effect.

Perhaps the most robust finding with regard to Covid—a finding replicated across the globe—was that large gatherings involving shouting and singing were inherently more dangerous than sparsely populated, socially distanced situations. The media quickly seized on this fact, for example, to chide anti-lockdown protesters for their irresponsibility, claiming that even outdoor protests could be unsafe.[1] Meanwhile, local officials in many areas went beyond the science itself, closing beaches, hiking trails, and even public parks—areas that were in no way chief vectors for transmission.[2] Republicans who refused to close beaches in largely unaffected areas, like Governor Ron DeSantis of Florida, were heavily criticized.[3] All of the pro-lockdown policy and rhetoric was justified with appeals to science.

As it turned out, public health officials weren't concerned about science. They were merely using science as a tool to press for their preferred policies. They were, in short, more interested in The Science™ than in science itself.

That became perfectly clear at the end of May.

On May 25, George Floyd, a forty-six-year-old black man, died in the custody of Minneapolis police. Floyd was a career criminal with a serious record; the police were called because he had passed a counterfeit twenty-dollar bill while buying cigarettes; his autopsy found that he had a "fatal level" of fentanyl in his system. Selectively edited tape of Floyd on the ground for nearly nine minutes, saying he couldn't breathe as a police officer put his knee on the back of Floyd's neck, went viral. The officer restraining Floyd was charged with second-degree murder.

Floyd's death generated massive protests and riots around the country. Those protests and riots were driven by the false notion that police across the nation routinely murdered black men—an evidence-free untruth.[4] Led by the radical Black Lives Matter movement, these "racial justice" gatherings—in the midst of a deadly pandemic—were unprecedented in size and scale. According to polling, somewhere between 15 and 26 million people in the United States attended a protest.[5] The protests were certainly not socially distanced; some wore masks, but certainly many did not. Often, the protests devolved into violence, including mass looting and property destruction; major cities across America were forced to declare curfew for the law-abiding. More often, the protests turned into party-like atmospheres, including dancing and singing and shouting.

And the same public health professionals who decried anti-lockdown protests, who urged Americans to do their part to socially distance, who cheered as businesses were told to close and schools to board up, ecstatically endorsed the mass gatherings. Apparently, the virus was itself woke: it would kill Republicans who opposed economy-crippling lockdowns, but would pass over anyone chanting trite slogans about defunding the police.

Politicians from the Left—devotees of wokeism—appeared in the midst of mass protests personally. Governor Gretchen Whitmer (D-MI) attended a civil rights march in Highland Park with hundreds of others, standing "shoulder-to-shoulder with some march participants." She did so just days after explaining that protests could in fact endanger lives.[6] Even as the National Guard policed Los Angeles in the wake of widespread rioting and the law-abiding were confined to their homes, Mayor Eric Garcetti took a knee with the Black Lives Matter crowd and "pulled down his blue Los Angeles Dodgers face mask to speak."[7] Speaking on CNN, New York mayor Bill de Blasio openly stated that only BLM marches would be allowed in his city: "This is a historic moment of change. We have to respect that but also say to people the kinds of gatherings we're used to, the parades, the fairs—we just can't have that while we're focused on health right now."[8]

Leaving aside the First Amendment implications of such statements, none of this could be remotely justified by the science itself. But authoritarian leftist politicians could count on members of the public health establishment to back their play, manufacturing anti-scientific narratives in the name of science. More than one thousand "public health specialists" signed an open letter supporting the largest protests in American history *in the middle of a global pandemic*, claiming that such protests were "vital to the national public health," and adding, "This should not be confused with a permissive stance on all gatherings, particularly protests against stay-at-home orders." Infectious-disease expert Ranu S. Dhillon of Harvard Medical School told *The New York Times*, "Protesting against systemic injustice that is contributing directly to this pandemic is essential. The right to live, the right to breathe, the right to walk down the street without police coming at you for no reason . . . that's different than me wanting to go to my place of worship on the weekend, me wanting to take my kid on a roller coaster, me wanting to go to brunch with my friends."[9]

The social science simply does not support the contention that the police are, writ large, targeting Americans of color based on racial animus. But even if such a wild accusation could be substantiated, it is absolutely absurd to suggest that mass protests over such a systemic issue—protests capable of spreading a highly transmissible deadly disease—represent a net positive for public health. Yet precisely that contention became commonplace in the world of The Science™.

Julia Marcus, epidemiologist at Harvard Medical School, and Gregg Gonsalves, epidemiologist at Yale School of Public Health, penned an article at *The Atlantic* claiming, "Public-health experts are weighing these same risks at a population level, and many have come to the conclusion that the health implications of maintaining the status quo of white supremacy are too great to ignore, even with the potential for an increase in coronavirus transmission from the protests."[10]

The University of California, San Francisco, hospital gave doctors of color a day off after Floyd's death; many of those doctors joined protests. One, Dr. Maura Jones, explained, "I would argue that, yeah I'm a doctor and I encourage you to social distance and I care about coronavirus and I know that it's a real threat, but racism is, to me to my family, the bigger threat right now and it has been for hundreds of years." Dr. Jasmine Johnson joined a protest by the University of North Carolina Student National Medical Association with a sign reading, "Racism is a pandemic too!" She claimed that racism was the root cause of racial disparities in death statistics from Covid—and therefore suggested that protest was actually a public health *good*.[11] Ashish Jha, dean of the Brown University School of Public Health, made the most insane case of all: that the protests would fuel Covid spread, but that this didn't matter. "Do I worry that mass protests will fuel more cases? Yes, I do. But a dam broke, and there's no stopping that," he stated.[12] Based on The Science™, liberal figures in government began promoting declarations that racism represented a "public health crisis."[13]

The science said that gathering in large numbers was a bad idea. To that end, thousands of Americans watched from afar as parents, brothers and sisters, family and friends died alone in hospitals; funerals were held by Zoom. Businesses shut by the hundreds of thousands.

The Science™ said that health concerns were secondary, and political concerns were primary.

And then our scientific establishment wonders why Americans have trust issues.

As it turned out, we may never know whether the mass protests spread Covid. We do know that the summer saw radical increases in viral transmission—increases the media quickly chalked up to Memorial Day gatherings, which occurred the same week protests broke out. But cities like New York actually told their contact tracers *not to ask* whether those diagnosed with Covid had attended a protest.[14]

The public health community's willingness to extend its area of supposed expertise to problems of alleged racial injustice highlights one very serious problem for the scientific establishment: the Ultracrepidarian Problem. Ultracrepidarianism is weighing in on matters outside one's area of expertise, or pretending that one's area of expertise extends to questions in different subject areas. Suffice it to say, our public health experts—and the doctors who weigh in on the political matter of policing and race relations—are certainly operating in uncharted waters for them. Simply slapping the label "science" on a political opinion doesn't make that opinion scientific any more than calling a man a woman makes that man a biological woman. The Ultracrepidarian Problem extends the reach of science into areas of pseudo-science, claiming the mantle of the objective and verifiable on behalf of subjective conjecture.

There is a second related, perhaps even more serious problem for scientific institutions in the United States, however: what we can call the Bleedover Effect. Whereas the Ultracrepidarian Problem comes from the scientific community speaking outside its area of expertise, the Bleedover Effect occurs when outside political viewpoints bleed over into scientific institutions themselves. This, predictably, restricts the actual reach of science, supplanting anti-scientific ruling ideologies for scientific inquiry.

Take another example from the world of Covid policy: the decision making surrounding vaccine distribution. Now, this would seem to be a simple scientific question: who is most vulnerable to Covid? The most vulnerable obviously ought to be given the Covid vaccine first. And, as it turns out, that question has an obvious answer: the elderly, who are most susceptible to multiple preexisting conditions. Covid risk is heavily striated by age: according to the Centers for Disease Control, the death rate of Covid for those above the age of eighty-five is 630 times the death rate for those between the ages of eighteen and twenty-nine; for those between seventy-five and eighty-four, the death rate is 220 times higher; for those between sixty-five and seventy-four, the death rate is 90 times higher.[15] So it should have been an easy call for the Centers for Disease Control to set out vaccine distribution guidelines based on age.

That, however, was not what happened. Instead, wokeism bled into the scientific process, turning science into The Science™.

On November 23, 2020, CDC public health official Kathleen Dooling presented her recommendations for tranching out the vaccine to the Advisory Committee on Immunization Practices. Dooling explained that essential workers—some 87 million people—should receive the vaccine *before* the elderly. Yes, Dooling's modeling acknowledged, this would increase the number of deaths somewhere between 0.5 percent and 6.5 percent. But such differences were "minimal," Dooling stated, when compared with the fact that racial equity could be pursued through her recommended policy. After all, Dooling pointed out, "racial and ethnic minority groups are underrepresented among adults > 65." Because white people have a longer life expectancy than black and

Hispanic Americans, Dooling was arguing, there were too many old white people. Why not prioritize younger black and Hispanic people *at lower risk of dying from the disease* as a sort of reparative measure?

This proposal was not merely morally idiotic. It was evil. Statistically speaking, even if white people are overrepresented as a percentage of the population among those over sixty-five, placing that group after essential workers would kill *more black people*—it would tranche black Americans more likely to die (those over age sixty-five) behind black Americans who were less likely to die (twenty-year-old grocery workers, for example). Thus, even if fewer black Americans would die as a percentage, more black Americans would die in *absolute numbers*.[16]

This perspective was not fringe. It was well respected and well reported. On December 5, *The New York Times* reported that the committee had unanimously supported Dooling's proposal. At least eighteen states had decided to take into account the CDC's "social vulnerability index" in tranching out vaccines. As the *Times* acknowledged, "Historically, the committee relied on scientific evidence to inform its decisions. But now the members are weighing social justice concerns as well, noted Lisa A. Prosser, a professor of health policy and decision sciences at the University of Michigan." The *Times* quoted one Harald Schmidt, an alleged expert in ethics and health policy at the University of Pennsylvania, expressing himself in blatantly eugenic terms: "Older populations are whiter. Society is structured in a way that enables them to live longer. Instead of giving additional health benefits to those who already had more of them, we can start to level the playing field a bit."[17] All it would take to level that playing field was to bury some disproportionately white bodies in the low-lying areas.

Public blowback to the CDC's standards led them to revise—but only somewhat. After medical workers were treated, the CDC recommended that the elderly and frontline workers be placed in the same tranche. This approach, too, will cost lives. As Yascha Mounk, a liberal thinker who often writes for *The Atlantic*, points out, "America's botched guidance on who gets the vaccine first should, once and for all, put the idea that the excesses of wokeness are a small problem that doesn't affect important decisions to bed." Furthermore, as Mounk pointed out, the *Times*—which was so eager to cheer on the infusion of wokeism into scientific standards—barely reported that the committee had changed its recommendations based on public pressure. "A faithful reader of the newspaper of record would not even know that an important public body was, until it received massive criticism from the public, about to sacrifice thousands of American lives on the altar of a dangerous and deeply illiberal ideology," Mounk wrote.[18]

When science becomes The Science™, Americans rightly begin to doubt their scientific institutions. They begin to believe, correctly, that the institutions of science have been hijacked by authoritarian leftists seeking to use white coats to cram down their viewpoints in top-down fashion.

"LISTEN TO THE EXPERTS"

The Ultracrepidarian Problem crops up regularly in the realm of policy making, when scientists determine that they are not merely responsible for identifying data-driven problems and providing data-driven answers, but for answering all of humanity's questions. The Ultracrepidarian Problem is nothing new in the realm of science. Indeed, it is an integral part of Scientism, the philosophy that morality can come from science itself—that all society requires is the management of experts in the scientific method to reach full human flourishing. Scientism says that it can answer ethical questions without resort to God; all that is required is a bit of data, and a properly trained scientist.

The history of Scientism is long and bleak—it contains support for eugenics, genocide, and massively misguided social engineering—but the popularity of Scientism hasn't waned. Modern Scientism is a bit softer than all of that, but maintains the same premise: that science can answer all of our moral questions, that it can move us easily from the question of what is to the question of what *ought* to be done.

Steven Pinker, a modern Scientism advocate, writes, "The Enlightenment principle that we can apply reason and sympathy to enhance human flourishing may seem obvious, trite, old-fashioned . . . I have come to realize that it is not."[19] The phrase "human flourishing" comes up a lot in the philosophy of Scientism. But the question of what "human flourishing" constitutes is indeed a moral question, not a scientific one. The debate over whether a human being should live a socially rich life filled with commitment to others or a hedonistic life filled with commitment to self-fulfillment is literally as old as philosophy.

On a less philosophical level, the Ultracrepidarian Problem undermines science by undercutting the credibility of scientists who insist on speaking beyond their purview. Take, for example, the problem of climate change. In the scientific community, there is a set of well-established facts and well-accepted principles: first, that climate change *is* happening, and that the world has been warming; and second, that human activity, particularly carbon emissions, are contributing significantly to that warming. There is serious debate over how much the world will warm over the course of the next century—the Intergovernmental Panel on Climate Change estimates that the global climate will warm somewhere between 2°C and 4°C above the mean temperature during the 1850–1900 period. That's a rather large range.[20] There is also significant uncertainty about sensitivity of the climate to carbon emissions; as NASA's Goddard Institute of Space Studies director Gavin Schmidt explains, climate sensitivity "has quite a wide uncertain range, and that has big implications for how serious human-made climate change will be."[21] Furthermore, there is wide uncertainty about the *impact* with regard to climate change—will human beings be able to adapt? How many "shock" events will occur?

These uncertainties lie at the heart of climate change policy. How much should we sacrifice current economic well-being and future economic growth for the sake of stabilizing the environment? What level of probable future risk justifies real-world, real-time policy making in the present?

True scientists are modest about their recommendations on such questions. They speak in terms of risk assessments and quantifiable metrics. William Nordhaus, for example, who won the Nobel Prize in Economics for his work on climate change, has suggested that people ought to accept that a certain amount of global warming is baked into the cake, and that we will be able to adapt to it—but that we ought to work on curbing global warming outside of that range.[22]

Experts in The Science[TM], however, have no problem proposing radical solutions to climate change that just coincidentally happen to align perfectly with left-wing political recommendations. Those who disagree are quickly slandered as "climate deniers," no matter their acceptance of IPCC climate change estimates. Thus the media trot out Greta Thunberg, a scientifically unqualified teenaged climate activist who travels the world obnoxiously lecturing adults about their lack of commitment to curbing climate change, as an expert; they ignore actual scientific voices on climate change. After all, as Paul Krugman of *The New York Times* writes, "there are almost no good-faith climate-change deniers . . . when failure to act on the science may have terrible consequences, denial is, as I said, depraved." He then lumps together those who deny outright the reality of global warming with those who "insist that nothing can be done about it without destroying the economy."[23]

But here's the thing: very little can be done about climate change in terms of regulation without seriously harming the economy. To abide by the Paris Agreement guidelines would cost, by Heritage Foundation estimates, at least $20,000 income loss per family by 2035 and a total aggregate GDP loss of $2.5 trillion.[24] And as even the UN Environment Programme found in 2017, if every major country kept to its pledges under the much-ballyhooed Paris Agreement, the earth will *still* warm at least 3°C by 2100.[25] In fact, even if the United States were to cut its carbon emissions 100 percent, the world would be 0.2°C cooler by 2100. To reach net zero carbon emissions worldwide by 2050 via Representative Alexandria Ocasio-Cortez's (D-NY) infamous Green New Deal would cost the typical family of four $8,000 *every single year.*[26]

This is not to suggest that nothing can be done about climate change. We should be investing in adaptive measures like seawalls, and be looking to new technologies like geoengineering. We should be cheering on America's fracking industry, which has redirected energy use from more carbon-intensive industries; we should be pushing for the use of nuclear energy; we should be promoting capitalism, which increases living standards around the globe, thus making people in poverty less vulnerable to the ravages of climate change. Yet those who promote these policies are treated as "deniers"; those who shout that the world is ended and the only solution is massive economic redistributionism are treated as truth speakers.

Behind closed doors, those who truly know about climate change understand the complexity of the problem and the foolishness of many of the publicly proposed solutions. Several years ago, I attended an event featuring world leaders and top scientific minds. Nearly all acknowledged that climate change was largely baked into the cake, that many of the most popular solutions were not solutions at all, and that the alternatives to carbon-based fossil fuels, particularly in developing countries, were infeasible. Yet when one actress then stood up and began cursing at these prominent experts, screaming that they weren't taking climate change seriously enough, they all stood and applauded.

That wasn't science. That was The Science™.

But the attempt to claim solutions for all problems in the name of science—the Ultracrepidarian Problem—quickly shades over into an even deeper problem: the Bleedover Effect, in which those with the politically correct opinions are deemed experts, and in which science finds itself at the mercy of these so-called experts.

THE BLEEDOVER EFFECT

Perhaps the greatest irony of the Ultracrepidarian Problem is that by enabling scientists to speak outside their area of expertise—to allow them to engage in the business of politics while pretending at scientific integrity—scientists create a gray area, in which politics and science are intermingled. This gray area—the arena of The Science™—then becomes the preserve of leftist radicals, who promptly adopt the masquerade of science in order to actively prevent scientific research.

In recent years, postmodernism has entered the world of science through this vector, endangering the entire scientific enterprise. Postmodernism claims that even scientific truths are cultural artifacts—that human beings cannot truly understand anything like an "objective truth," and that science is merely one way of thinking about the world. In fact, science is a uniquely Western (read: racist, sexist, homophobic, transphobic, etc.) way of thinking about the world, since it is a theory of knowledge that has historically perpetuated systems of power.[27] Again, this is nothing new in human history—the Nazis rejected "Jewish science" just as the Soviets rejected "capitalist science." But the fact that the Western world, enriched to nearly unimaginable heights by science and technology, has even countenanced the post-modern worldview is breathtakingly asinine.

This philosophy obviously hasn't infused all of our scientific institutions, but it doesn't have to do so in order to endanger the enterprise. Renormalization must merely occur in terms of *setting boundaries* to research—science must be curbed in the most sensitive areas when it conflicts with authoritarian leftist thought. That is precisely what has happened. Where the Ultracrepidarian Problem widens the boundaries of science beyond the applicable, the Bleedover Effect narrows the boundaries of science to the "acceptable." By infusing social justice into science, science must now meet with the approval of the New Ruling Class. Those who speak in contravention of established left-wing theology are outed and ousted, in truly authoritarian fashion. As theoretical physicist Lawrence Krauss writes, "academic science leaders have adopted wholesale the language of dominance and oppression previously restricted to 'cultural studies' journals to guide their disciplines, to censor dissenting views, to remove faculty from leadership positions if their research is claimed by opponents to support systemic oppression."[28]

That left-wing theology dictates that all groups ought to achieve equal results in every area of human life; if science suggests differently, science must be silenced. Thus, conversations about IQ and group differences will be met with exorbitant outrage, as Sam Harris found out, even when the participants explicitly denounce racism in all of its forms;[29] conversations regarding differences between men and women in terms of aptitudes and interests must be punished, as Lawrence Summers found out;[30] studies questioning whether women do better with male mentors in academia rather than female mentors are retracted, based not on faulty research but on "the dimension of potential harm." In fact, *Nature*—perhaps the most prestigious science publication on the planet—quickly issued a policy stating that editors would be seeking outside opinions on the "broader societal implications of publishing a paper," an open invitation for political interference into the scientific process.[31] This means the death of scientific inquiry at the hands of the woke.

The overt politicization of science is most obvious with regard to gender dysphoria. Gender dysphoria is a condition characterized by the persistent belief that a person is a member of the opposite sex; it is an exceedingly rare phenomenon. Or, at least, it was—rates of reported gender dysphoria have been increasing radically in recent years, particularly among young girls, a shocking phenomenon given that the vast majority of those diagnosed with gender dysphoria have historically been biologically male. That unexplained phenomenon became the subject of research from Brown University assistant professor Lisa Littman, who released a study on "rapid-onset gender dysphoria," documenting the fact that teenage girls were becoming transgender in coordination with others in their peer group. Brown pulled the study, with Brown School of Public Health dean Bess Marcus issuing a public letter denouncing the work for its failure to "listen to multiple perspectives and to recognize and articulate the limitations of their work."[32] Something similar happened to journalist Abigail Shrier: when she wrote a book on rapid-onset gender dysphoria, Amazon refused to allow her to advertise it,[33] and Target temporarily pulled the book from its online store. Chase Strangio, the ACLU's deputy director for transgender justice, suggested "stopping the circulation of this book"—a fascinating take from an organization literally named for its defense of civil liberties.[34]

There is no evidence whatsoever that gender is disconnected from biological sex. Yet scientists have given way to gender theorists, whose pseudo-science is inherently self-contradictory. This leads directly to absurdity. Doctors have claimed that gender identity is "the only medically supported determinant of sex," despite the fact that biology clearly exists.[35] In 2018, the American Medical Association announced that it would oppose any definition of sex based on "immutable biological traits identifiable by or before birth," instead favoring language stating that doctors "assign" sex at birth—a laughable assertion.[36] The AMA even outlined legislation that would ban therapists from suggesting to children that they ought to become more comfortable with their biological sex rather than acting in contravention to it.[37]

The *New England Journal of Medicine*, likely the most prestigious scientific journal in America, printed an article in December 2020 recommending that sex designations on birth certificates be moved below the line of demarcation, since they "offer no clinical utility."[38] Despite the lack of longitudinal data on transgender surgeries and the high rate of desistance from gender dysphoria over time from young people, much of the scientific community has rejected "watchful waiting" as somehow transphobic; blacklisted doctors and journalists who refuse to encourage gender transition for those who are underage; and stated without evidence that the solution to gender dysphoria is a radical redefinition of sex itself, whereby children ought to be taught that they can freely choose their own gender, and adults ought to be socially cudgeled into using biologically inapposite pronouns. "Your truth" now matters more than objective scientific truth. And those who know better are forced to denounce the objective science, engaging in top-down censorship of other viewpoints while proclaiming their adherence to the new moral code.

Scientific inquiry is forbidden. Now authoritarian leftism, citing The Science™, rules.

How far has this insanity gone? In June 2020, the American Physical Society, an organization of 55,000 physicists, closed down its offices as part of a "strike for black lives," recommitting itself to "eradicate systemic racism and discrimination, especially in academia, and science."

Nature put out an article titled "Ten simple rules for building an anti-racist lab." Princeton faculty—more than one thousand of them—issued a letter to the president proposing that all scientific departments create a senior thesis prize for research that "is actively anti-racist or expands our sense of how race is constructed in our society."[39]

In December 2020, a group of professors of computer science felt it necessary to write an open letter to the Association for Computing Machinery—the world's largest computing society—decrying cancel culture. "We are a group of researchers, industry experts, academics, and educators, writing with sadness and alarm about the increasing use of repressive actions aimed at limiting the free and unfettered conduct of scientific research and debate," the group of professors wrote. "Such actions have included calls for academic boycotts, attempts to get people fired, inviting mob attacks against 'offending' individuals, and the like. . . . We condemn all attempts to coerce scientific activities into supporting or opposing specific social-political beliefs, values, and attitudes, including attempts at preventing researchers from exploring questions of their choice, or at restricting the free discussion and debate of issues related to scientific research."[40]

The fact that such a letter was necessary in *computer science* demonstrates the depth of the problem. But it was necessary: earlier in 2020, NeurIPS, the most prestigious AI conference on the planet, required authors to submit papers only with a statement explaining how the research could impact politics—a question decidedly outside the bounds of science, but firmly within the bounds of The Science™.[41]

THE "DIVERSIFICATION" OF SCIENCE

If science is supposed to be about the pursuit of truth via verification and falsification, the scientific community is supposed to be a meritocracy: those who do the best research ought to receive the most commendations. But when wokeism infuses science, the meritocracy falls by the wayside: the composition of the scientific community becomes subject to the same anti-scientific demand for demographic representation. To prove the point, in 2020, the Association of American Medical Colleges hosted professional racists Ibram X. Kendi and Nikole Hannah-Jones to explain that the standards for entrance into the scientific community ought to be changed in order to achieve demographic parity. Hannah-Jones explained to the annual meeting of the AAMC that when she requires a doctor, she tries to "seek out a black doctor"; Kendi explained that the lack of black doctors overall is a result of "stage 4 metastatic racism." Kendi told the AAMC—which administers the Medical College Admissions Test—that standardized tests are racist, because standardized tests tend to weed out black and Latino students. "Either there's something wrong with the test, or there's something wrong with the test-takers," Kendi said. And of course to suggest that not all individuals perform equally well on tests is to suggest that there is something wrong with some of the test takers—which would make you racist. All of this supposedly "anti-racist action," Hannah-Jones agreed, is part and parcel of choosing "to undo the structures that racism created."[42]

This is insulting tripe. It's insulting to those who achieve in the meritocracy; it's even more insulting to those who are assumed victims of the system. More than insulting, however, such ridiculous race-based thinking is *dangerous*. After all, if the alternative to a meritocracy is wokeism, wouldn't that necessarily mean the admission of less-than-qualified people to the highest ranks of science?

Yes. But it's happening nonetheless. According to Claremont McKenna professor Frederick Lynch, between 2013 and 2016, medical schools "admitted 57 percent of black applicants with a low MCAT of 24 to 26, but only 8 percent of whites and 6 percent of Asians with those same low scores." Meanwhile, the National Science Foundation, a federal funding agency for science, says that it wants to pursue a "diverse STEM workforce"—not the best scientists of all races, but a specifically diverse group.[43]

There is no evidence that a more diverse demographic research body should impact the findings of science. Science is not literature; personal experience should be of little relevance in chemistry. But to point this out is to meet with the rage of the mob. In June 2020, Brock University chemist Tomáš Hudlický printed an essay in Wiley's *Angewandt Chemie*, a prominent chemistry journal. He argued that the push for diversity over merit in chemistry had damaged the standards of the field, stating that diversity training had "influenced hiring practices to the point where the candidate's inclusion in one of the preferred social groups may override his or her qualifications." He also explained the patently obvious truth that "hiring practices that suggest or even mandate equality in terms of absolute numbers of people in specific subgroups is counter-productive if it results in discrimination against the most meritorious candidates."[44] Chemists emerged from the woodwork to condemn the essay and its author; the Royal Society of Chemistry and the German Chemical Society penned a statement calling the essay "outdated, offensive and discriminatory," adding "We will not stand for this. Diversity and equality are fantastic strengths in workplaces, in culture and in wider society. This is not only demonstrated by overwhelming evidence from decades of research, but we also hold it is morally the only acceptable position."

What overwhelming evidence suggests that prioritizing racial diversity over scientific ability is a fantastic strength? The statement cited no such evidence. But the moral statement—an unscientific statement, to be sure—was clear. The journal deleted the article, and added a statement: "Something went very wrong here and we're committed to do[ing] better." Two editors were suspended. Sixteen board members, including three Nobel Prize winners, resigned. They put out a joint statement lamenting the "journal's publishing practices," which they said had "suppressed ethnic and gender diversity." Fellow scientists called for Hudlický to be fired.[45]

CONCLUSION

In October 2020, the politicization of science—and its replacement with The Science™—became more obvious than ever before. *Scientific American*, perhaps the foremost popular science publication in America, issued the first presidential endorsement in its 175-year history. Naturally, they endorsed Joe Biden. "We do not do this lightly," the editors intoned. "The evidence and the science show that Donald Trump has badly damaged the U.S. and its people— because he rejects evidence and science." Joe Biden, by contrast, was providing "fact-based plans to protect our health, our economy and the environment." Those fact-based plans were, of course, simply liberal policy prescriptions, open to debate. But *Scientific American* spoke in the name of The Science™.[46] Not to be outdone, *Nature* similarly endorsed Joe Biden. "We cannot stand by and let science be undermined," the editorial board explained. Among their reasons: Trump's rejection of the Iran nuclear deal, a decidedly ultracrepidarian concern.[47] The *New England Journal of Medicine*, another prominent medical journal, suggested that Trump be booted from office for his Covid response. Yes, Trump's Covid rhetoric was wild and inconsistent. But even Trump's most ardent critics, were they honest, would recognize that Biden provided no actual Covid plan of his own. "Reasonable people will certainly disagree about the many political positions taken by candidates. But truth is neither liberal nor conservative," *NEJM* stated.[48]

No, science is neither liberal nor conservative. But The Science™—the radicalized version of science in which scientists speak their politics, and in which political actors set the limits of science—is certainly a tool of authoritarian leftists. And it predominates across the scientific world. Americans still trust their doctors to tell them the truth; they still trust scientists to speak on issues within their purview. But increasingly, they reject the automatic institutional legitimacy of the self-described scientific establishment. And they should. We can only hope that scientists realize that scientific credibility relies not on membership in the New Ruling Class but in the pure legitimacy of the scientific process before the entire field—a field that has transformed the world in extraordinary ways—collapses.

CHAPTER 5

YOUR AUTHORITARIAN BOSS

I n December 2020, I received an email from a fan. The fan explained that she worked at a Fortune 50 company—a company that had "quotas on who they want to hire and put into position of leadership based solely on skin color." At a company meeting, this fan voiced her opinion that the company should not support programs rooted in racial composition. "All 5 of the participants in the meeting immediately called my manager and their managers to voice deep concerns," she related. "My manager asked if I was still a good fit and I came close to losing my job." Her question, she wrote, was simple: "Should I immediately start looking for another role outside the company?"

I receive these sorts of emails daily. Multiple times a day, in fact. Over the past two years, the velocity of such emails has increased at an arithmetic rate; whenever we open the phone lines on my radio show, the board fills with employees concerned that mere expression of dissent will cost them their livelihood.

And they are right to be worried.

America's corporations used to be reliably apolitical. If anything, the business world trended toward conservatism. From 2000 to 2017, executives at the biggest public companies gave overwhelmingly to Republicans: according to the National Bureau of Economic Research, 18.6 percent of CEOs routinely donated to Democrats, while 57.7 percent donated to Republicans. Yet over time, while the percentage of Republican CEOs remained far higher than that of Democratic CEOs, more and more CEOs began preferring political neutrality to Republican giving. And the disparity between Republicans and Democrats in the West and Northeast—read California and New York—is far lower than in other regions of the country, with those who are neutral comprising a heavy percentage.[1]

Now, today's corporations are bastions of authoritarian leftism. During the Black Lives Matter summer, nearly every major corporation in America put out a statement decrying systemic American racism, mirroring the priorities of the woke Left. What's more, nearly all of these corporations put out internal statements effectively warning employees against dissent. Walmart, historically a Republican-leaning corporation, put out a letter from Doug McMillon pledging to "help replace the structures of systemic racism, and build in their place frameworks of equity and justice that solidify our commitment to the belief that, without question, Black Lives Matter." McMillon pledged more minority hiring, "listening, learning and elevating the voices of our Black and African American associates," and spending $100 million to "provide counsel across Walmart to increase understanding and improve efforts that promote equity and address the structural racism that persists in America."[2] The fact that Walmart had to close hundreds of stores due to the threat of BLM looting went unmentioned.[3]

Major corporations tripped over themselves to issue public statements denouncing racism—and, more broadly, America's supposed systemic racism. Many of the corporations pledged to fund their own quasi-religious indulgences, which would alleviate their supposed complicity in the racist system. Tim Cook of Apple issued a letter stating that America's racist past "is still present today—not only in the form of violence, but in the everyday experience of deeply rooted discrimination," and offered funding for the Equal Justice Initiative,[4] a progressive organization that blames historic racism for nearly every modern ill. Satya Nadella, CEO of Microsoft, issued a letter stating, "It's incumbent upon us to use our platforms, our resources, to drive systemic change";[5] the company stated that it would spend $150 million on "diversity and inclusion investment," aiming to "double the number of Black and African American people managers, senior individual contributors, and senior leaders in the United States by 2025."[6] Netflix issued a statement commanding, "To be silent is to be complicit," and pledged $100 million to build "economic opportunity for Black communities." That commitment followed CEO Reed Hastings announcing he would donate $120 million to black colleges.[7]

Even the most tangential and irrelevant companies chimed in. Ice cream company Ben & Jerry's issued a statement: "We must dismantle white supremacy. . . . What happened to George Floyd was not the result of a bad apple; it was the predictable consequence of a racist and prejudiced system and culture that has treated black bodies as the enemy from the beginning."[8] And it would be remiss not to mention that Gushers partnered with Fruit by the Foot to fight systemic racism, trumpeting, "We stand with those fighting for justice."[9]

These statements and actions weren't merely meaningless public breast-beating. Corporations began taking internal actions to cram down the radical Left's viewpoint on American systemic racism. Corporation after corporation mandated so-called diversity training for employees—training that often included admonitions about the evils of whiteness and the prevalence of societal white supremacy. Dissent from this orthodoxy could be met with suspension or firing. Employees at Cisco lost their jobs after writing that "All Lives Matter" and that the phrase "Black Lives Matter" fosters racism;[10] Sacramento Kings broadcaster Grant Napear lost his job for tweeting that "all lives matter";[11] Leslie Neal-Boylan, dean of University of Massachusetts Lowell's nursing school, lost her job after stating, "BLACK LIVES MATTER, but also, EVERYONE'S LIFE MATTERS"—which, after all, is the hallmark of nursing;[12] an employee at B&H Photo lost his job for writing, "I cannot support the organization called 'Black Lives Matter' until it clearly states that all lives matter equally regardless of race, ethnicity, religion or creed, then denounces any acts of violence that is happening in their name. In the meantime, I fully support the wonderful organization called 'America' where EVERY life matters. E pluribus unum!"[13]

Even corporate heads weren't immune from the pressure: CrossFit CEO Greg Glassman was forced to resign from his company after controversial comments about George Floyd; two officials from the Poetry Foundation stepped down after their pro-BLM statement was considered too mealy-mouthed; the editor in chief of *Bon Appétit* was forced out after an old photograph circulated of him dressed in Puerto Rican garb.[14]

To be clear, none of these corporations—all beneficiaries of a free market in hiring, firing, and customer base—actually believe that America is "systemically racist" in the same way the authoritarian leftists mean. These corporations merely mirror what most Americans think when they hear the term "systemic racism"—that racism still exists. And they say that "black lives matter" because, of course, black lives *do* matter. But the very term "black lives matter" is semantically overloaded: it's unclear, when used, whether it signifies a belief in the value of black lives (undeniable), the evils of the American system that supposedly devalues black lives today (an extreme notion lacking serious evidence), or support for the Black Lives Matter organization (which pushes actual Marxist radicalism).

Corporations, then, merely do what they do in order to make money. As always.

And herein lies the problem.

As we've examined, the authoritarian Left believes that America's systemic racism is evident in *every aspect of American society*—that all inequalities in American life are traceable to fundamental inequities in the American system. That means that for the authoritarian leftists who promote the "systemic racism" lie, systemic racism is evidenced by the *simple presence of successful corporations*. Successful corporations, in supporting the notion that America is systemically racist, are chipping away at the foundations of their own existence.

There is something undeniably ironic about corporations pretending support for a worldview that sees their very presence as evil. Black Lives Matters cofounder Patrisse Cullors infamously proclaimed, "We do have an ideological frame. Myself and Alicia [Garza], in particular, are trained organizers; we are trained Marxists. We are superversed on, sort of, ideological theories. And I think what we really try to do is build a movement that could be utilized by many, many Black folks." Black Lives Matter DC openly advocated for "creating the conditions for Black Liberation through the abolition of systems and institutions of white supremacy, capitalism, patriarchy and colonialism."[15]

Yet corporate employees fear speaking up about the decency of America, against racial preferences, against racial separatism. When corporations began posting black squares on Instagram to signify support for BLM, employees often did the same, seeking safety in symbolic virtue signaling. Failure to abide by the increasingly political diktats of the corporate overlords may risk your job.

What's more, everyone lives in fear of retroactive cancellation. It's not merely about you posting something your employer sees. It's about a culture of snitching, led by our media, that may out a ten-year-old Facebook post and get you canned from your job. In internet parlance, this has become known as "resurfacing"—the phenomenon whereby a person who doesn't like you very much finds a Bad Old Tweet and then tells your employer, hoping for a firing. It works. Resurfacing has become so common that NBC News ran a piece in 2018 guiding Americans on how to "delete old tweets before they come back to haunt you."[16]

All of which is a recipe for silence.

The nature of the business world requires adherence to top-down rules, the threat of expulsion, and fear of external consequences. Counterintuitively, then, the institutional pillar thought to guard most against the excesses of authoritarian leftism crumbled quickly and inexorably once the stars aligned.

And align they did.

THE CONFLUENCE OF INTERESTS

To understand the corporate embrace of authoritarian leftism, it's necessary to first understand a simple truth: corporations are not ideologically geared toward free markets. Some CEOs are pro-capitalism; others aren't. But all corporations are geared toward profit seeking. That means that, historically, corporate heads have not been averse to government bailouts when convenient; they've been friendly toward regulatory capture, the process by which companies write the regulations that govern them; they've embraced a hand-in-glove relationship with government so long as that relationship pays off in terms of dollars and cents. Government, for its part, loves this sort of stuff: control is the name of the game.

What's more, corporations are willing to work within the confines provided by the government—in particular, in limiting their own liability. Since the 1960s, the framework of civil rights had been gradually extended and expanded to create whole new categories of legal liability for companies. The Civil Rights Act and its attendant corpus of law didn't merely outlaw governmental discrimination—it created whole new classes of established victim groups that had the power to sue companies out of existence based on virtually no evidence of discrimination. Those companies, fearful of lawsuits and staffed increasingly by members of the New Ruling Class—people who agreed with the idea that society could be engineered in top-down fashion by a special elect—were all too happy to comply with the de rigueur opinions of the day. As Christopher Caldwell writes in *The Age of Entitlement*:

> Corporate leaders, advertisers, and the great majority of the press came to a pragmatic accommodation with what the law required, how it worked, and the euphemisms with which it must be honored. . . . "Chief diversity officers" and "diversity compliance officers," working inside companies, carried out functions that resembled those of twentieth-century commissars. They would be consulted about whether a board meeting or a company picnic was sufficiently diverse.[17]

Second, it's important to note that businesses cater to their customer base—and, in particular, their most passionate customer base. This provides a catalyst for renormalization via market forces: if enough customers can form an intransigent core, dedicated to one ideology, they can direct corporate resources toward appeasing them. Studies show that as we've become more polarized, more and more Americans now say they want their brands to make political stands. One research group found that 70 percent of American consumers say they want to hear brands' stands on social and political issues—this despite the fact that a bare majority of consumers say that brands only do so for marketing purposes. Some 55 percent of respondents claimed they would stop shopping with brands that didn't mirror their political preferences; another 34 percent said they would cut their spending to such brands.[18]

Such desire for politics from corporations resides almost solely with the Left. One study found that survey participants dinged a fake company, Jones Corporation, 33 percent for conservative politics, and said they were 25.9 percent less likely to buy its products, 25.3 percent more likely to buy from a competitor, and 43.9 percent less likely to want to work there. For companies perceived as liberal, no penalty accrued. As James R. Bailey and Hillary Phillips observed in *Harvard Business Review*, "That a company engaged in conservative or liberal political activity did not affect Republicans' opinions of that company, but it did for Democrats . . . the 33 percent drop in opinion with Jones Corps engaged in a conservative agenda was entirely driven by participants who identified as Democrats." In the end, consumers thought that companies being liberal was "merely normal business." Being conservative? That was punishable activity.[19]

Third, corporations seek regularity in their day-to-day operations. They seek to avoid controversy at nearly all costs—whether via legal liability, frustrated consumers, or even staffers. Concerns about troublesome staffers used to manifest in what was called "the company man"—the man in the gray flannel suit, rigid in his outlook, cookie-cutter in his type. Conservatives and liberals alike used to fret about the enforced conformity of corporate life. But corporations have now discovered the magic of quaffing from the well of wokeism: by following the diktats of political correctness in hiring, they can escape censure for the "corporate culture." After all, they have Diversity™—an amalgamation of various people of different races, genders, heights, ages, and hair colors . . . all of whom think precisely the same way, and who raise holy hell if anyone different is discovered among them.

Corporate heads are now petrified of their own woke staffers, and cater to their every whim. Where old-style bosses used to tell quarrelsome, peacocking employees to sit down at their desks or find themselves standing on the bread lines, today's bosses seek to comply with every woke demand, up to and including days off for mental health during politically fraught times.

Finally, all three of the aforementioned factors—the legal structures that provide liability for violating the tenets of political correctness; a motivated and politicized customer base; and authoritarian staffers unwilling to countenance dissent—mean that the true power inside corporations doesn't lie in their own hands at all: it lies with the media, which can manipulate all of the above. All it takes is one bad headline to destroy an entire quarter's profit margin. Corporations of all types are held hostage to a media dedicated to the proposition that the business world is doing good only when it mirrors their priorities. It isn't hard for a staffer to leak a lawsuit to *The New York Times*, which will print the allegations without a second thought; it isn't difficult to start a boycott campaign on the back of a clip cut out of context, and propagated through the friends of Media Matters; it isn't tough to generate governmental action against corporations perceived to violate the standards of the authoritarian Left.

And so corporations live in fear.

THE SECRET COWARDICE OF CORPORATE DO-GOODERISM

That corporate fear used to manifest as unwillingness to court controversy. But as the authoritarian Left moved from "silence is required" to "silence is violence," corporations went right along. They declared themselves subject to the authoritarian Left structure—and were consolidated by the Borg. That's most obvious in corporate America's willingness to engage in every leftist cause, from climate change to nationalized health care to pro-choice politics to Black Lives Matter, on demand.

In fact, corporate leaders have determined that they will clap loudest and longest for the authoritarians, in the hopes that they will be lined up last for the guillotine. They know that capitalism is on the menu. They just hope that they'll be able to eke out a profit as the chosen winners of the corporatist game. Centuries ago, governments used to charter companies and grant them monopolies. Today, corporations compete to be chartered by the authoritarian Left, to be allowed to do business, exempted from the usual anti-capitalism of the Left. The only condition: mirror authoritarian leftist priorities.

Thus, in December 2020, NASDAQ, a stock exchange covering thousands of publicly traded companies, announced that it would seek to require those listed on its exchange to fulfill diversity quotas on their boards. According to the *Wall Street Journal*, NASDAQ told the Securities and Exchange Commission that it would "require listed companies to have at least one woman on their boards, in addition to a director who is a racial minority or one who self-identifies as lesbian, gay, bisexual, transgender or queer." Any company that did not do so would be called on the carpet by NASDAQ and made to answer for its lack of diversity or be subjected to delisting. Smaller companies would be hardest hit by the requirements, of course, but NASDAQ had no problem putting its boot on their neck. The New York Stock Exchange similarly set up an advisory council to direct "diverse" board candidates toward publicly traded companies. Goldman Sachs stated it would not help roll out initial public offerings for companies without a "diverse" board member. The civil rights movement that once sought to treat people by individual merit rather than group identity has been turned completely on its head—and corporations, which supposedly used to stand for the meritocracy, are pushing that moral inversion.[20]

Many are doing so under the guise of so-called stakeholder capitalism. In late 2020, Klaus Schwab, founder and executive chairman of the World Economic Forum, laid out his support for what he called "the Great Reset." Schwab explained in *Time* that the Covid pandemic had pushed forward a key question: "Will governments, businesses and other influential stakeholders truly change their ways for the better after this, or will we go back to business as usual?" Now, this was truly an odd question. Prior to the pandemic, the world economy was in the midst of a boom time. Unemployment rates in the United States had dropped to record lows; economic growth was strong. What, then, was the impetus for corporations "changing their ways for the better"? Indeed, what did "the better" even *mean*?

According to Schwab, the problem was free markets. "Free markets, trade and competition create so much wealth that in theory they could make everyone better off if there was the will to do so," wrote Schwab. "But that is not the reality we live in today." Free markets, he said, were "creating inequality and climate change"; international democracy "now contributes to societal discord and discontent." Yes, the time had come to move beyond the "dogmatic beliefs" that "government should refrain from setting clear rules for the functioning of markets," that "the market knows best."

Instead, Schwab recommended a "better economic system" rooted not in doing the bidding of shareholders, but in acting in the interest of "stakeholders"—acting "for the public good and the well-being of all, instead of just a few." What would metrics of success look like? Not profitability. Oh no. The success of companies would revolve around their "gender pay gap," the diversity of their staff, the reduction of greenhouse gas emissions, the amount of taxes paid. Corporations would no longer be so low-minded as to focus on producing goods and services at the best possible price for the most possible consumers. Now corporations would be in the do-gooding business.[21]

This commitment to "stakeholder capitalism" versus "shareholder capitalism" has become increasingly popular in the business world. That's because it allows business leaders to retain control over the levers of power—they're Platonic philosopher-kings, sitting atop vast empires but acting for the benefit of the masses—without being answerable to lowly shareholders, those greedy investors who have actually put their own savings and faith into the company. Such nonsense is also pleasant to the ears of the authoritarian Left, which can now—with the permission of the business community, no less!—dump regulations and commitments on corporations in the name of the so-called public good. No wonder Joe Biden has called for "an end to the era of shareholder capitalism," suggesting his antipathy for the dreaded stock market.[22] And the US Business Roundtable agrees—in an August 2019 statement, they explained, "While each of our individual companies serves its own corporate purpose, we share a fundamental commitment to *all* of our stakeholders."

Putting shareholders second sounds kind and nice. It isn't. It's sinister. It's placing unnamed, uninvested interests in charge of corporations, and placing corporate heads in positions of untrammeled power—so long as they please the *true* powers that be: members of government, members of the press, and their politically like-minded peers. Capitalism creates wealth and prosperity for all because it is rooted in a fundamental truth: your labor belongs to you, and you have no right to demand the products of my labor without giving me something I want in return. Stakeholder capitalism doesn't create wealth or prosperity. It just traffics in unearned moral superiority, turning the engine of growth into a second quasi-government, unanswerable to those it is supposed to represent in the first place—and it simultaneously forwards the lie that corporations that *do* seek to do business alone are somehow morally suspect.

DESTROYING DISSENTERS

In October 2020, CEO David Barrett of Expensify, a corporation that specializes in expense management, sent a letter to all of the company's users. That letter encouraged them all to vote for Joe Biden. "I know you don't want to hear this from me," Barrett wrote, quite correctly. "And I guarantee I don't want to say it. But we are facing an unprecedented attack on the foundations of democracy itself. If you are a US citizen, anything less than a vote for Biden is a vote against democracy. That's right. I'm saying a vote for Trump, a vote for a third-party candidate, or simply not voting at all—they're all the same, and they all mean: 'I care more about my favorite issue than democracy. I believe Trump winning is more important than democracy. I am comfortable standing aside and allowing democracy to be methodically dismantled in plain sight.'"[23]

What were Expensify employees supposed to think of the letter? If they signaled their support for Trump, certainly they could expect to lose their jobs. But Barrett obviously didn't care. His politics were the right politics. His opponents were wrong.

Yet few concerns about the power imbalance between Barrett and his employees materialized. Instead, praise came pouring from the rafters.

In reality, Barrett wasn't taking a business risk in issuing this letter. He was doing the opposite. He was signaling that he and his company were members of the righteous coterie of right-thinking corporations.

Such signaling isn't merely done via external public relations. It's enforced in rigorous fashion internally. Employees are subjected to bouts of "diversity training" with "experts" like Robin DiAngelo, who maintain that white supremacy pervades all of American life; that it is impossible for members of victimized groups to be racist; that meritocracies are themselves representative of racist hierarchical thinking; that believing you aren't racist is excellent evidence that you're racist; that white women's tears are a form of racism; that racist intent is absolutely unnecessary in order to label action racist, since only impact and harm matter.[24] All it costs them is $20,000 a pop to both indoctrinate their workers into the requisite politics and to ensure against the possibility of a discrimination lawsuit![25]

This garbage is wildly ineffective. A controlled study of one diversity training course found that there was "very little evidence that diversity training affected the behavior of men or white employees overall—the two groups who typically hold the most power in organizations and are often the primary targets of these interventions."[26] Actually, diversity training tends to drive *more* anger and discrimination, because people don't like being told they are racists or that they must follow a set of prescribed rules in order to alleviate their supposed racism.[27]

But effectiveness isn't the point. Preventing blowback is the point—and creating an environment of conformity on controversial issues. And corporations pour billions into doing both. As of 2003, corporations were spending $8 billion per year on diversity efforts. And in America's biggest companies, the number of "diversity professionals" has increased dramatically over the past few years—by one survey, 63 percent between 2016 and 2019. Nearly everyone now has to sit through some form of indoctrination designed by the authoritarian Left—indoctrination that requires struggle sessions, public compliance with the new moral code, and kowtowing to false notions of racial essentialism. All of this is designed to cram down false notions of systemic privilege and hierarchy.[28]

Meanwhile, for those corporations that refuse to comply, the cudgel is available.

When Goya CEO Robert Unanue appeared at a Trump White House event to tout his work during the pandemic, leftists began a nationwide boycott. Something similar happened when LGBT activists targeted Chick-fil-A over founder Dan Cathy's support for traditional marriage, encouraging local Democratic politicians to try to stop the chain's expansion into their cities.[29] When billionaire investor Stephen Ross held a fund-raiser for Trump in 2019, leftists launched a boycott against Equinox and SoulCycle, both companies in which Ross had investments. Chrissy Teigen tweeted, "everyone who cancels their Equinox and Soul Cycle memberships, meet me at the library. Bring weights."[30]

No one would want to be Goya or Equinox. So when, in June 2020, leftist organizations including Color of Change, NAACP, ADL, Sleeping Giants, Free Press, and Common Sense Media called for Facebook advertisers to pause their spends to pressure Facebook into restricting content on its platform, more than a thousand companies complied. Those companies included the brands REI, Verizon, Ford, Honda, Levi Strauss, and Walgreens.[31]

And that's the goal for the authoritarian Left: to cow everyone into silence, except those who agree with them. Corporations generally survive boycotts—statistics demonstrate that most boycotts are wildly unsuccessful at removing revenue. But boycotts can impact the overall health of a brand, and can certainly generate sleepless nights for the companies targeted. As Northwestern Institute for Policy Research professor Braydon King argues, "The no. 1 predictor of what makes a boycott effective is how much media attention it creates, not how many people sign onto a petition or how many consumers it mobilizes."[32] Companies *hate* media attention they can't control. Which is why they so frequently apologize, back down, and beg for mercy.

Which, of course, only starts the cycle anew.

The purging of the public square has now reached epidemic proportions. All it takes is one bad story about your business to put you squarely in the authoritarian leftist cultural crosshairs. And it's now easier than ever to manufacture and spotlight such stories. In October 2020, Yelp—a site that allows members of the public to review businesses—announced that it would place an alert on a business if "someone associated with the business was accused of, or the target of, racist behavior." That means that if someone resurfaced a Trump-supporting post from a janitor, you could find yourself on the wrong end of a Yelp alert. And if there was "resounding evidence of egregious, racist actions from a business owner or employee, such as using overtly racist slurs or symbols," such evidence being "a news article from a credible media outlet," the business would be hit with a "Business Accused of Racist Behavior Alert." Yelp had now created a Stalinesque system of woke snitching, in which all it would take to forever destroy a business would be an account of racism about an employee, a twenty-two-year-old reporter looking for clicks, and an email address. Between May 26 and September 30, more than 450 alerts were placed on business pages accused of racist behavior related to Black Lives Matter alone.[33]

THE DEATH OF BUSINESS NEUTRALITY

The final consequence of corporate America going woke isn't merely internal purges—it's corporate America's willingness to direct its own resources against potential customers guilty of such heresy. As the authoritarian Left flexes its power, wielding pusillanimous corporations as its tool, those corporations will increasingly refuse to do business with those who disagree politically. The result will be a complete political bifurcation of markets.

In fact, this is already happening. In 2016, North Carolina passed a bill that would ensure separate bathroom facilities for men and women throughout the state, in contravention of a local Charlotte ordinance that would allow transgender people to access the bathroom of their choice. The business world reacted with universal outrage, and big business vowed not to do business *at all* in the state: PayPal dumped plans for a facility, as did Deutsche Bank; Adidas decided to hire in Atlanta rather than Charlotte; the NCAA vowed to cancel championship games; Bank of America CEO Brian Moynihan stated, "Companies are moving to other places, because they don't face an issue that they face here." According to the Associated Press, North Carolina was slated to lose some $3.75 billion over a dozen years if the state didn't dump the bathroom bill.[34] In March 2017, the bathroom bill was duly repealed.

The same pattern has held true in a variety of states. In 2010, businesses began boycotting Arizona after the passage of a law that allowed local law enforcement to enforce federal immigration law.[35] After Georgia passed a pro-life law, Hollywood production companies announced they wouldn't do business in the state—even while doing business in human-rights-abusing China.[36]

And corporations are beginning to target private citizens based on political belief, too. In August 2017, Visa and Discover announced they would not allow "hate groups" to process their credit card payments; PayPal, too, announced its app would be barred from use for those groups. MasterCard, by contrast, said it doesn't ban merchants "based on our disagreement with specific views espoused or promoted."[37] In February 2018, the First National Bank of Omaha dropped its National Rifle Association credit card, stating, "Customer feedback has caused us to review our relationship with the NRA."[38] That same month, American Airlines and United Airlines announced they would pull all discount benefits for NRA members.[39]

In March 2018, Citigroup announced it would limit retail clients' firearm sales; one month later, Bank of America announced the bank would no longer give loans to manufacturers of guns for civilians. Leftist interest groups immediately began pressuring other major banks to do the same: American Federation of Teachers president Randi Weingarten said the union would not recommend Wells Fargo's mortgage lending program to its members because of ties to the gun industry.[40] In May 2019, Chase Bank began closing bank accounts for customers deemed radical, including Enrique Tarrio of the Proud Boys and radical activist Laura Loomer. Jamie Dimon, CEO of Chase Bank, said, "Very directly, we have not and do not debank people because of their political views."[41] For now, presumably.

This threat extends beyond the financial services industry. When Amazon Web Services, whose sole job is to provide cloud services, decides to deplatform Parler, that's polarizing. When Mailchimp, an email delivery service, refuses to do business with the Northern Virginia Tea Party, that's polarizing.[42] When PayPal announces that it uses slurs from the Southern Poverty Law Center to determine which groups to ban, that's polarizing.[43] When Stripe announces it will not process funds for the Trump campaign website after January 6, that's polarizing.[44]

The question here isn't whether you like any of these groups. The question is whether neutral service providers should be removing access to their business based on political viewpoint. The hard Left demands that religious bakers violate their religious scruples and bake cakes for same-sex weddings . . . and then turn around and cheer when credit card companies decide not to provide services for certain types of customers. There's a solid case to be made that private businesses should be able to discriminate against customers based on their right to association. But our corpus of law has now decided that such freedom of association is largely forbidden, unless it targets conservatives. Anti-discrimination law in most states bars discrimination on the basis of sex, sexual orientation, gender identity, religion, race, medical disability, marital status, gender expression, age, and a variety of other categories. But there is no anti-discrimination protection for politics. Since the Left is particularly litigious, this means that businesses are wary of avoiding business with anyone of the Left—but when it comes to the right, businesses have acted to protect themselves from rearguard attacks by the woke authoritarians.

The result will be two separate systems of commerce in the United States. We won't eat at the same restaurants. We won't go to the same hotels, theme parks, or movies. We won't use the same credit cards.

All of which makes it rather difficult to share a country.

THE MONOLITH

The chances are that you, the reader, know all of this already. That's because the chances are quite good that if you work, you're working for a giant company that's part of the authoritarian monolith. Decades ago, you probably would have worked for a company with fewer than 100 workers; today, you likely work for a massive company with rigorous, top-down policies that mirror the prevailing political notions of the day. According to *The Wall Street Journal*, nearly 40 percent of Americans now work for a company with more than 2,500 employees, and about 65 percent work for companies with more than 100 employees.

And the big companies are growing. The arenas in which big companies thrive—the services sector, finance, the retail trade—are also the fastest-growing areas in the American economy.[45] Unsurprisingly, these are also the areas in which employers are most likely to lean to the Left, or at least to mirror leftist priorities.

The Covid-19 pandemic has only exacerbated the advantage for large companies. Between March 2020 and September 2020, more than 400,000 small businesses closed. Meanwhile, big companies got bigger. As economist Austan Goolsbee wrote in *The New York Times*, "Big Companies Are Starting to Swallow the World."[46]

Small businesses are generally tied to the communities in which they exist—they know the locals, they trust the locals, and they work with the locals. Large companies cross boundaries of locality—they're national in scope and orientation. This means that they are far more concerned with enforcing a culture of compliance than in preserving the local diversity that typically characterizes smaller outfits. Large companies have huge HR departments, concerned with the liability that innately accrues to deep pockets; they have legislative outreach teams, concerned with the impact of government policy; they have corporate CEOs who are members of the New Ruling Class.

And there's something else, too. Entrepreneurs believe in liberty, because they require liberty to start their businesses. But as those businesses grow, and as managers begin to handle those businesses, managers tend to impose a stifling top-down culture. Managers prefer order to chaos, and rigidity to flexibility. And these managers are perfectly fine with the rigid social order demanded by the authoritarian Left.

Which means that our corporations aren't allies of free markets—or of the ideology that undergirds free markets, classical liberalism. They've now become yet another institutional tool of an ideology that demands obeisance. And so long as their wallets get fatter, they're fine with it. Better to lead the mob, they believe, than to be targeted by it.

There's only one problem: sooner or later, the mob will get to them, too.

CHAPTER 6

THE RADICALIZATION
OF ENTERTAINMENT

In September 2020—in the midst of the supposed racial "reckoning" sweeping the nation after the death of George Floyd—the Academy Awards announced it would shift the standards for its golden statuettes. No longer would films be selected on the basis of quality. Instead, studios would be given a choice of fulfilling one of four criteria. First, the film could itself contain certain woke prerequisites: either a lead or significant supporting actor from an "underrepresented racial or ethnic group"; or at least 30 percent of all actors in secondary roles would have to be from such a victim group or a woman or LGBTQ or have a disability; or the main story line would have to center on such an underrepresented group. Second, the film could be staffed by members of those underrepresented groups. Third, the film company could provide paid apprenticeship and internship opportunities for such victimized groups. Finally, those participating in the marketing could be from one of those victimized groups. Academy president David Rubin and CEO Dawn Hudson explained, "We believe these inclusion standards will be a catalyst for long-lasting, essential change in our industry."[1]

The standards were superfluous: Hollywood has long dedicated itself to the simple proposition that prestige pictures must fulfill leftist messaging requirements, and moneymakers must please the public. Sometimes prestige pictures *are* moneymakers. Generally, they aren't: superhero movies bring in the dollars, and *Moonlight* brings the critical plaudits. The last four Best Pictures winners are, in reverse chronological order, a morality tale about the evils of income inequality (*Parasite*); a morality tale about racism and homophobia (*Green Book*); a morality tale about the evils of the military, and discrimination against the disabled, blacks, homosexuals, communists, and fish (*The Shape of Water*); and a morality tale about racism and homophobia (*Moonlight*). None of this means all these movies are necessarily bad (although *The Shape of Water* is indeed one of the worst movies ever committed to film). It just means that Oscar voters aren't typical representatives of the American entertainment audience. It isn't difficult to handicap the odds of Oscar victory by tallying woke talking points beforehand.

But the Academy's new standards weren't about a change of heart. They were about ass covering. In 2015, on the back of massive racial unrest after the shooting of Michael Brown in Ferguson, Missouri, and the death of Freddie Gray in Baltimore, Hollywood's woke contingent began complaining that Hollywood had marginalized black creators. In 2015, the Academy hadn't nominated a single black actor in any of its categories. This, obviously, meant that Hollywood had to get woke. Thus the hashtag #OscarsSoWhite was born. Cheryl Boone Isaacs, president of the Academy, said that as soon as she saw the nominations, "my heart sank." Spike Lee later commented, "When black Twitter gets on your black ass . . . ooh, it ain't no joke." Ana Duvernay, who directed *Selma*—which was indeed nominated for Best Picture that year—said, "It was a catalyst for a conversation about what had really been a decades-long absence of diversity and inclusion."

Decades-long. Never mind that literally the year before, in 2014, *12 Years a Slave* had won Best Picture, Chiwetel Ejiofor had been nominated for Best Actor, Barkhad Abdi had been nominated for Best Supporting Actor, and Lupita Nyongo had won Best Supporting Actress. Never mind that *Selma* is, in fact, a rather mediocre movie. *Selma*'s lack of awards attention meant that discrimination had reared its ugly head.

And no dissent would be brooked. As Duvernay said, "I would do it all again. If you cannot be respectful of our alignment with that cause, with that protest, with that rallying cry, then there was nothing I wanted from you anyway."

Naturally, the Academy responded the next year with an emergency meeting and sought to radically shift the Academy membership through affirmative action directed at women and minorities. When other members of the Academy complained that political correctness had taken control of the institution—when, for example, Dennis Rice, a member of the Academy's public relations branch, explained that he was "color- and gender-blind when it comes to recognizing our art," and added, "You should look purely and objectively at the artistic accomplishment"—Boone Isaacs shot back, "Are you kidding me? We all have biases. You just don't see it if it doesn't affect you."

In 2017, *Moonlight*, a little-known film among audiences, revolving around a black gay man growing up in gang-infested Miami, won Best Picture. As Barry Jenkins, director of the film, said, "If *Moonlight* had come out three years earlier, I'm not sure how many people would have picked up that screener."[2]

Hollywood had embraced woke politics as the sine qua non for art. And Hollywood would continue to chest-thump its own wokeness in spite of the evidence that Hollywood is, in many ways, insanely regressive.

Later that year, sexual abuse allegations against mega-producer Harvey Weinstein began to resurface. Hollywood celebrities began hashtagging #MeToo, pointing out the exploitation of women that ran rife through the industry. And they weren't wrong. The Hollywood casting couch—the sexist and disgusting practice by which females were subjected to sexual harassment and assault by powerful men in Hollywood in exchange for job advancement—had been a feature of the industry since the very beginning: the intersection of Hollywood and Highland featured, for years, a fiberglass structure widely known as the "casting couch" in town. But it was Hollywood's decision not to look internally but to pronounce judgment on the *rest of America* that spoke to the new wokeness. Instead of recognizing its own complicity in #MeToo, Hollywood celebrities began lecturing the rest of America about the country's inherent sexism.

The cause quickly morphed from the universally praised attempt to end sexual harassment and assault into broader left-wing talking points: criticism of the supposed gender pay gap, for example, or attempts to lecture Americans about heteronormativity. At the Oscars, Jimmy Kimmel—who used to star on a television show, *The Man Show*, featuring women bouncing on a trampoline, and who infamously wore blackface on Comedy Central—lectured America, "the truth is if we are successful here, if we can work together to stop sexual harassment in the workplace, if we can do that, women will only have to deal with harassment all the time at every other place they go." Magically, Hollywood was transformed from moral pariah to moral leader.[3]

It was merely an ironic shock, then, when the Oscars ended up canceling a black host, Kevin Hart, for violating woke tenets. After Hart was named the host of the 2019 Oscars, the woke internet went to work, digging up Bad Old Tweets™—in this case, a tweet from 2011 suggesting, "Yo if my son comes home & try's 2 play with my daughers doll house I'm going 2 break it over his head & say n my voice 'stop that's gay.'" In 2010, it turns out, Hart did a routine about how he would prefer his son not to be gay, too. Hart responded to the burgeoning scandal correctly: "Our world is becoming beyond crazy, and I'm not gonna let the craziness frustrate me . . . if you don't believe people change, grow, evolve as they get older, [then] I don't know what to tell you."[4] Within a few days, Hart announced he would be stepping down from the Oscars gig. He then kowtowed to the mob: "I'm sorry that I hurt people. I am evolving and want to continue to do so. My goal is to bring people together not tear us apart." When Ellen DeGeneres tried to encourage Hart to come back and do the show in January, even Ellen was slammed by the woke Left.[5]

With all that controversy, it was no shock when the Academy moved to formalize woke standards, largely as a preventative measure designed at buying time and space from the woke mob. Just as in the universities, the liberals gave way to the radicals.

HOLLYWOOD'S LONG HISTORY OF PREENING

More broadly, the Academy's move to formalize its heretofore-voluntary politics was merely the culmination of a long-lasting movement in Hollywood to propagandize on behalf of leftism, slap at flyover country, undercut traditional values, and excise those who disagree. Hollywood has been the preserve of political liberals for decades: the artistic community in the United States has typically leaned to the Left, a phenomenon that can be attributed to the counterculturalism that characterizes art itself. Pushing the envelope is often the name of the game in art, and in the United States—a traditional values country with a solid religious streak—the artistic community has historically bucked hard against traditional values. And when it comes to film and television, artistic media predominantly located in the echo chambers of New York and Hollywood, such attitudes are amplified radically. That echo chamber routinely reflects the self-absorbed notion of liberal elites that they have a monopoly on decency. As Allan Burns, co-creator of *The Mary Tyler Moore Show*, told me years back, "Writers have always had a social conscience. That's no surprise. I don't mean to sound arrogant about it, because I don't consider myself to be an intellectual, but I do consider myself to be a person who empathizes and thinks about what's going on in the world."[6]

Hollywood has long believed itself better than the common rabble.

That disconnect was evident early. The Hollywood films of the 1920s were so racy, for example, that local authorities began passing laws censoring theaters. Hollywood responded with the so-called Production Code, a set of standards meant to prevent films from promoting sundry moral no-nos of the time. The Production Code held, "No picture shall be produced which will lower the moral standards of those who see it. Hence, the sympathy of the audience should never be thrown to the side of crime, wrongdoing, evil or sin. . . . Law, natural or human, should not be ridiculed, nor shall sympathy be created for its violation."[7] By the 1960s, the American people had stopped boycotting films on the basis of Code violations, and adherence quickly collapsed. Television made a similar move during the 1960s, moving away from more values-oriented programming like *Bonanza* and toward politically oriented material like *All in the Family*. Hollywood both reflected and drove forward America's generalized move toward liberal causes. And as that liberalism set in, Hollywood closed itself to outside voices and creators: As Michael Nankin, producer on *Chicago Hope* and *Picket Fences*, told me, "People generally like to work with people they've worked with before or with whom they're comfortable. . . . And that mindset, which is entirely appropriate, makes it hard for new people to get in."[8] Fred Silverman, former head of NBC, ABC, and CBS, was blunter when I spoke with him a decade ago: "Right now, there's only one perspective. And it's a very progressive perspective."[9]

Hollywood is the land of liberal renormalization, the chief outlet for a political minority making emotional appeals to a broader country. As television's top creator Shonda Rhimes stated in her book, *Year of Yes*:

> I am NORMALIZING television. You should get to turn on the TV and see your tribe. . . . If you never see openly bisexual Callie Torres stare her father down and holler (my favorite line ever), "You can't pray away the gay!!!" at him . . . If you never see a transgender character on TV have family, understand, a Dr. Bailey to love and support her . . . If you never see any of those people on TV . . . What do you learn about your importance in the fabric of society. What do straight people learn?[10]

In 2017, she added, "I get really offended at the concept that what came out of the [2016] election was that—how do I say this?—impoverished people who are not of color needed more attention. . . . I don't think any [of the audience that watches my shows] are [Trump supporters], because I'm a black, Planned Parenthood–loving, liberal feminist."[11] So perhaps Rhimes should have explained that you should be able to turn on the TV and see your tribe . . . unless your tribe disagrees with Rhimes. In that case, your tribe will be represented by stand-ins for John Lithgow in *Footloose*, glowering at the joy and wonder of liberal moral culture.

That attitude toward conservatives in both movie and television content is nothing new. Conservatives exist in dramas as foils for more open-minded and tolerant liberals; in comedies, they generally take the form of wrong-thinking incompetents. Occasionally, a stray libertarian may be portrayed as a cynical life guide (see, for example, Ron Swanson in *Parks and Recreation* or Jack Donaghy in *30 Rock*), but it is an absolute certainty that no mainstream television show or movie will ever portray an advocate for traditional marriage as anything but a bigot, or a thoroughly pro-life woman as anything but a sellout.

Why does this matter? It matters because, as my old mentor Andrew Breitbart used to say, culture is upstream of politics. Americans engage with the culture *far more* than with politics: political feeling is just the manifestation of underlying feelings people have about compassion and justice, about right and wrong. And *those* feelings are shaped by the cultural sea in which we all swim.

Netflix has 195 million global subscribers; Disney+ has over 70 million; Hulu has another 32 million. HBO Max has in excess of 30 million subscribers. Apple TV has over 42 million subscribers. Amazon Prime has over 140 million.[12] According to Nielsen, Americans over the age of eighteen spend at least four hours per day watching TV; they spend more than twelve hours a day on average engaged with TV.[13]

And that cultural sea is dominated by the Left, from top to bottom. There is a reason Netflix has green-lit a multiyear slate of projects from Barack and Michelle Obama;[14] that Obama administration alum and now Biden staffer Susan Rice was on the Netflix board;[15] that 98 percent of all donations from Netflix employees went to Democrats in 2016, and 99.6 percent in 2018;[16] that Netflix announced it would not invest in making film or television in Georgia if the state's pro-life law stood[17] (Netflix has no problem doing business with China, of course).[18] There is a reason Disney said it would have a tough time doing business in Georgia, too[19] (and yes, *Mulan* was filmed in Xinjiang, where the Chinese government has been stuffing Muslim Uighurs in concentration camps).[20] There is a reason that during the Black Lives

Matters riots of summer 2020, Amazon Prime recommended left-leaning films and television to those who chose to log on. Hollywood is thoroughly leftist, and that is reflected from top to bottom. Its bias is inescapable.

The product is obvious: more people thinking along leftist lines. A study from the Norman Lear Center found that conservatives watch far less television than either "blues" or "purples," and are also "least likely to say they have learned about politics and social issues from fictional movies or TV"; both "blues" and "purples" are more likely to discuss politics based on entertainment and to take action based on entertainment; 72 percent of all political shift measured since 2008, not coincidentally, was toward liberal perspectives. Naturally, the Lear Center concluded that television creators should place "more emphasis on raising awareness of discrimination and its profound social impact."[21]

But Hollywood's progressivism isn't enough. Not anymore. Not for the authoritarian Left. The Hollywood Left used to decry McCarthyism. Now they are its chief practitioners.

THE CANCEL CULTURE COMES FOR EVERYONE

Cancel culture is the order of the day in Hollywood. And you need not be a conservative to be canceled. The mere passage of time may subject you to the predations of the authoritarian leftist mob. It's become a truism to state that classics of the past simply wouldn't be made today—movies like *Airplane!* and shows like *All in the Family* would never make the cut. And that's obviously true. Hollywood studios regularly prescreen their shows for activist groups like the Gay and Lesbian Alliance Against Defamation; GLAAD brags that its media team "work closely with TV networks, film studios, production companies, showrunners, scriptwriters, casting directors, ad agencies, and public relations firms" to ensure "fair and accurate representation" of LGBT people. By "fair and accurate," GLAAD presumably means reflective of GLAAD's agenda.[22] It's unlikely that GLAAD would let slide any joke about sexual orientation.

In fact, most jokes are now off-limits. *The Office* retconned its own content, removing a scene in Season 9 in which a character wore blackface (never mind that the scene was about how insane and inappropriate it was to wear blackface). Executive producer Greg Daniels intoned, "Today we cut a shot of an actor wearing blackface that was used to criticize a specific racist European practice. Blackface is unacceptable, and making the point so graphically is hurtful and wrong. I am sorry for the pain that caused." Meanwhile, *Community* cut an entire episode from the Netflix library because an Asian character dressed in blackface, prompting a black character to fire back, "So, we're just gonna ignore that hate crime, uh?" Even *condemning* blackface is offensive now. Episodes of *Scrubs* and *30 Rock* were also disappeared.[23]

Movies of the past have been taken down to provide "context," most famously when HBO Max removed *Gone with the Wind* from its library, explaining that the film was "a product of its time" that contained "ethnic and racial prejudices" that were "wrong then and are wrong today."[24] Never mind that Hattie McDaniel, who was accused of embodying that prejudice in playing Mammy, became the first black actress to win an Oscar for her role. Disney+ has now updated old movies with a warning: "This program includes negative depictions and/or mistreatment of people or cultures. These stereotypes were wrong then and are wrong now. Rather than remove this content, we want to acknowledge its harmful impact, learn from it and spark conversation to create a more inclusive future together. Disney is committed to creating stories with inspirational and aspirational themes that reflect the rich diversity of the human experience around the globe." Movies tagged with this pathetic mewling include *Aladdin*, *Fantasia*, *Peter Pan*, *Lady and the Tramp*, *The Jungle Book*, and *Swiss Family Robinson*.[25]

And if content is perceived as un-woke—no matter how apolitical—it may be targeted for cancellation as well. In the midst of the Black Lives Matter protests and riots of 2020, the reality series *Cops* was canceled from Paramount Network after a thirty-one-year run—all because of fears that the show might show police officers in a positive context. The leftist activist group Color of Change cheered the decision, stating, "Crime television encourages the public to accept the norms of over-policing and excessive force and reject reform, while supporting the exact behavior that destroys the lives of Black people. *Cops* led the way. . . . We call on A&E to cancel *Live PD* next."[26] Days later, it was.[27]

It's not a matter of merely canceling shows or movies, either. Artists who cross the woke mob find themselves targeted for destruction. In July 2018, Scarlett Johansson dropped out of production on a movie titled *Rub and Tug*, about a transgender man. The radical Left suggested that *only* a transgender man could play a transgender man—a biological woman who did not identify as a man could not. Now, this is one of the most absurd contentions in human history: actors literally act like other people. And verisimilitude shouldn't have been an issue here: a biological human female was playing a biological human female who believes she is male. Yet the woke community decided it was better that the film, starring one of Hollywood's biggest stars, be canceled outright rather than starring a non-transgender person. Johansson duly performed her penance: "I am thankful that this casting debate . . . has sparked a larger conversation about diversity and representation in film."[28] This illogical proposition creates some awkward moments: when Ellen Page announced she was a transgender man, the series in which she stars, *Umbrella Academy*, announced it would be fine for "Elliot Page," a transgender man, to continue to play a non-transgender woman.

This puritanism regarding woke standards represents a serious career threat to comedians, who make their money off willingness to mock hard-and-fast rules. Hilariously, this has led to the specter of top comics tearing into the woke. After Sarah Silverman, a radical leftist, revealed that she had lost a film role thanks to a blackface sketch from 2007 (again, the sketch was about racism faced by black Americans), she tore into cancel culture: "Without a path to redemption, when you take someone, you found a tweet they wrote seven years ago or a thing that they said, and you expose it and you say, 'this person should be no more, banish them forever.' . . . Do we want people to be changed? Or do we want them to stay the same to freeze in a moment we found on the internet from 12 years ago."[29] Dave Chappelle has slammed cancel culture, calling it "celebrity-hunting season."[30] Bill Burr ranted on *Saturday Night Live*, "You know, how stupid is that 'canceled' thing? They're literally running out of people to cancel. They're going after dead people now."[31] Rowan Atkinson recently and correctly compared the cancel culture to the "digital equivalent of the medieval mob, roaming the streets, looking for someone to burn." He added, "It becomes a case of either you're with us or against us. And if you're against us, you deserve to be 'canceled.'"[32]

HOW HOLLYWOOD GOT RENORMALIZED

All of this raises a serious question: if woke culture quashes compelling entertainment, wrecks comedy, and generally makes entertainment worse, why cave to it? Why not simply make entertainment for the broadest possible swath of Americans?

The answer lies, once again, in renormalization. All it takes to renormalize an institution is a solid minority of intransigent, inflexible people: catering to that base, while preying on the innate compliance of the majority, can lead to a complete reorientation. That's precisely what's happened in Hollywood. Where Hollywood used to broadcast—emphasis on *broad*—searching for the biggest possible audience, they now narrowcast in order to appease the inflexible leftist coalition. Practically, this means catering to critics, who are near universal in their reflection of woke priorities; it also means superserving intransigent subsets of the audience, then counting on the rest of the audience to go along.

Hollywood critics are monolithically adherents to authoritarian leftism. This authoritarian leftism has infused film criticism to an extraordinary extent: films, if perceived as political, are no longer judged broadly on their merits. Instead, they're judged on checking woke boxes. RottenTomatoes—the one-stop-shop for movie criticism—demonstrates a clear bias in favor of leftist films.[33] For critics, RottenTomatoes' aggregation of opinion also exacerbates confirmation bias: critics don't want to stand out from the crowd. As Owen Gleiberman of *Variety* writes, "The sting of the pressure to conform is omnipresent."[34] When one *Variety* critic recently had the temerity to suggest that Carey Mulligan was miscast in the left-wing-oriented *Promising Young Woman*, *Variety* went so far as to tar its own critic as a crypto-misogynist and offer an *apology* for his review.[35] The top-down censorship of the authoritarian Left is in full swing among the critics. The goal isn't just silencing dissent, but forcing public confession and repentance.

There's a reason critics are, all too often, wildly out of touch with movie audiences. It's not rare for audiences to reject a film based on its lack of quality, but for critics to praise it to the skies for political reasons. For example, *Ghostbusters* (2016), the female-cast reboot of the original Bill Murray classic, met with tepid audience response—a 50 percent positive score among audiences on RottenTomatoes, and a brutal box-office run that cost the studio $70 million. That's because the film happens to be a mediocre piece of annoying crap. But according to critics, the movie was *important*—and it was important because it supplanted male leads with female leads. Megan Garber of *The Atlantic* wrote, "For a moment, it seemed, the future of women in Hollywood—and the future of feminism itself—would be riding on the shoulders of Paul Feig, Ivan Reitman, Melissa McCarthy, and some CGI-ed ghosts." And—surprise!—Garber found the movie to be "pretty great," balancing "ghosts and guns and gags and girl power."[36]

When critics come into conflict with audiences, there can be only one explanation: Americans are a bunch of bigots. So naturally, *Ghostbusters'* failure became evidence that Americans simply couldn't handle powerful females. And the film's failure was laid at the feet of these fans, who were merely frustrated manbabies incapable of expressing a thought about a mediocre film.

This phenomenon has been invoked over and over again to explain just why critics like movies the public often doesn't. If fans think that *Star Wars: The Last Jedi* was an incoherent mishmash of bad plotting, destruction of beloved and iconic characters, addition of new and boring characters, with a side plot of animal rights silliness, that's not because maybe they're right—it's because they are "toxic fans." If, in particular, *Star Wars* fans found Rose (Kelly Marie Tran) to be an absolutely superfluous and soporific character (she was), that was because they were racist and sexist. The critics spoke, and loved *The Last Jedi* (90 percent fresh); the audience spoke and hated it (42 percent fresh). Obviously, the audience was wrong. As Matt Miller of *Esquire* put it, *Star Wars* fans "have tragically become synonymous with hate, bigotry, and pervasive assholeness in 2018. . . . *The Last Jedi* inspired the worst impulses of a far-right movement that's taking hold of the internet and extending its influence into the real world."[37] Toxic fans can be used as a constant excuse for the fact that critics are out of touch with the unwashed masses.

Meanwhile, critics can be as toxic as they like with reference to work they perceive as insufficiently woke. Dave Chappelle's *Sticks and Stones* comedy special took on cancel culture and wokescolding—so critics excoriated it, giving it a 35 percent fresh score, complaining that Chappelle had become "a man who wants it all—money, fame, influence—without much having to answer to anyone."[38] When Chappelle reverted to rants about the nature of systemic American racism, the critics reverted to type: "Can a comedy set win a Pulitzer? . . . theater at its most powerful,"[39] "not funny . . . but the comedian was in top form."[40] (Chappelle, it should be noted, survived in large measure because his entire shtick had been built around opposition to cancel culture.) When *Hillbilly Elegy* premiered, the critics savaged it (27 percent fresh)—not primarily because of its moviemaking, but because between 2016 and 2020, it became un-woke to take seriously impoverished white protagonists, or to champion the power of individual decision making. The movie review for *The Atlantic*, which deemed the film "one of the worst movies of the year," found it worthy of note that the original book, which sold several million copies, "often appears uninterested in interrogating deeper systemic issues."[41] Audiences, by the way, loved the film—the audience rating was 86 percent fresh on RottenTomatoes.

Critics help kill entertainment projects they oppose politically. But most Americans don't sit around waiting for takes from the critics. The biggest factor cutting in favor of the woking of Hollywood, ironically enough, is the fragmentation of the market itself. For decades, the rule in Hollywood was to try to cater to the largest available audience—to *broad*-cast. The biggest tent-pole movies—think of the

Marvel Universe—still do. But as the distribution mechanisms for entertainment fracture, it becomes more plausible to narrowcast toward particular audiences, or to cater to the most intransigent audiences. Narrowcasting automatically breeds renormalization.

Hollywood relies on conservative or apolitical Americans to ignore being offended, and superserves those most likely to raise a stink—or to consume products enthusiastically based on ideology. That's why Netflix has categories like "Black Lives Matter Collection" alongside "Drama," and announced just before launching the "Black Lives Matter" genre, "To be silent is to be complicit."[42] The industry is no longer about producing blockbuster films geared toward drawing massive audiences. It's about pleasing the loudest, cudgeling everyone else, and hoping nobody will tune out. Most of the time, that hope is justified. After all, it's not as though there are tons of conservative-friendly alternatives out there. Even if you're offended by Netflix mirroring the woke dictates of BLM, you can't exactly switch over to Hulu or Amazon: those companies put up their own propagandistic film categories designed to respond to America's racial "reckoning," and announced their own solidarity with Black Lives Matter.[43] Renormalization of Hollywood, combined with closing the door to dissent, has created an entertainment monolith.

HOW SPORTS WENT WOKE, THEN WENT BROKE

The radicalization of entertainment is most obvious in the context of sports. Sports is the ultimate broadcasting entertainment: it is designed to hit all subgroups. It's pure competition, merit against merit, winners and losers. The narratives are generally apolitical and the plot lines perfectly simple. Sports is about taking on the competition, muscling through adversity, working with teammates. Sports unifies.

Or at least it used to. Yes, politics played a crucial role in sports narratives—from Jackie Robinson breaking the color line in Major League Baseball to Muhammad Ali giving up his boxing career for refusing the Vietnam draft to the American Olympic hockey team defeating the Soviets. But once the game began, all exterior conflict was telescoped *into the sport*. Americans had strong rooting interests, often politically oriented, but the primary concern was the exhibition of skill *on the field*.

Sports leagues worked to keep politics off the field or court entirely. When Denver Nuggets star Mahmoud Abdul-Rauf refused to stand for the national anthem in 1996, NBA commissioner David Stern, a committed liberal, suspended him without pay. Rauf had violated a league policy requiring players and trainers to "stand and line up in a dignified posture."[44] When asked why he had remained apolitical in a contentious 1990 North Carolina Senate race, Michael Jordan explained, "Republicans buy sneakers, too." Years later, he explained, "I wasn't a politician when I was playing my sport. I was focused on my craft."[45]

This sentiment was considered relatively uncontroversial. But then something changed.

What changed was the renormalization along racial and political lines.

ESPN, the top sports channel on the planet by a vast margin, began losing money hand over fist. The network cleared cash in two ways: through advertising, which was viewer-reliant, and through carriage fees. Fully 75 percent of ESPN's money comes from cable and satellite subscribers; cable and satellite companies pay ESPN to carry the network. ESPN takes that money and pays sports leagues in order to carry *their* content.

Now, the vast majority of cable and satellite subscribers don't watch the vast majority of content on ESPN. So as people cut their cable and carriage fees dropped, and as other sports cable competitors got into the business and bid up the price of sports programming, ESPN found itself in a world of hurt. As sports journalist Clay Travis describes, "Its business model was under attack on two fronts. The cost of sports it rented and put on the air was surging just as its subscriber revenue was collapsing. . . . In 2011, at the height of its business, ESPN had 100 million subscribers. [By 2018], they'd lost 14 million subscribers."[46] ESPN responded by putting more hot talk, more cheap-to-produce, guaranteed-to-create-controversy hot takes on the air. As Travis points out, ESPN "was elevating the talent that most fervently connected left-wing politics and sports. Jemele Hill, Max Kellerman, Sarah Spain, Bomani Jones, Michelle Beadle, Pablo Torre—the more left-wing your politics, the more you got on television."[47]

This was a reflection of both the political culture of the sports journalists themselves, who voted overwhelming Democrat, and the desire to superserve a customer base that skewed disproportionately to the Left. Demographic composition of fan bases varies widely based on the sport. NBA fans are disproportionately black, for example; NHL fans are disproportionately white. And ESPN spends a disproportionate amount of time on sports viewed by minority audiences. As of 2012, according to Deadspin, *SportsCenter* spent 23.3 percent of its coverage on the NFL, 19.2 percent of its time on the NBA, and just 2.1 percent of its time on NASCAR. Yet according to a 2015 Harris poll, just 5 percent of Americans said that basketball was their favorite sport, compared to 6 percent who said auto racing.[48] ESPN isn't skewing its coverage out of a weird sense of diversity, however—they're doing so because black Americans watch more TV than white Americans,[49] and have historically spent more money per capita on "visible goods" like footwear, clothes, cars, and jewelry.[50]

And superserving a disproportionately left-leaning population means catering to their political belief system—which just happens to reflect the values held by the higher-ups at ESPN. By catering to a small sub-section of the population—a population that preferred its sports with a heavy dose of politics—the sports world renormalized itself around woke propositions.

Sports leagues began catering to their political audiences, allow-ing politics to spill over onto the field. In 2014, a white police officer shot to death eighteen-year-old Michael Brown; Brown had assaulted the officer, attempted to steal his gun, fired it in the officer's car, and then charged the officer. Members of the media repeated the lie that Brown had surrendered to the officer with his hands raised. The slo-gan "Hands Up, Don't Shoot" became shorthand for the accusation that Brown had been murdered, and for the broader proposition that police across America were systematically targeting black Americans. And the sports world followed suit: five players on the St. Louis Rams walked out during the pregame introductions with their hands raised in the "Hands Up, Don't Shoot" pose.[51] The NFL quickly announced there would be no consequences, with NFL vice president Brian Mc-Carthy explaining, "We respect and understand the concerns of all individuals who have expressed views on this tragic situation."[52] This wasn't out of a generalized respect for free speech values, however—it was about catering to wokeness. In 2016, after a Black Lives Matter supporter shot to death five police officers, the NFL rejected the Dal-las Cowboys' request to wear a decal paying tribute to the victims.[53]

Over the course of the ensuing years, sports media's and leagues' embrace of on-field wokeness only increased. When Abdul-Rauf pro-tested the national anthem, it was utterly uncontroversial for David Stern to suspend him. When Colin Kaepernick, after being benched as starting quarterback for the San Francisco 49ers in favor of the immor-tal Blaine Gabbart, decided to kneel for the national anthem in protest at the police shooting of armed stabbing suspect Mario Woods,[54] the media rushed to his defense. ESPN covered the millionaire Kaepernick as a hero, blanketing its network in worshipful praise for the benched QB, even as he declared that he would not "stand up to show pride in a flag for a country that oppresses black people and people of color."[55] The sports media then spent years propping him up as a civil rights icon. Eventually the quarterback, who had once donned socks depicting police officers as pigs, was given millions of dollars by Nike— also attempting to superserve leftist populations—in order to sell shoes with the slogan, "Believe in something. Even if means sacrificing everything." In reality, Kaepernick sacrificed nothing—he had already been benched when he made his protest, would later avoid even the most basic preconditions for rejoining an NFL team, and has cleared millions of dollars in advertising. Nonetheless, Kaepernick is now treated as a hero in the sports world; in 2020, the NFL itself tried to leverage a team into signing him. For good measure, EA Sports named Kaepernick a "starting-caliber" quarterback in its *Madden NFL 21* game, despite the fact that Kaepernick hadn't played for years and wasn't very good the last time he did.[56]

The politicization of sports had dire ramifications for its audience numbers. Ratings, which were already in recession, went into steep decline. The most popular league in America, the NFL, saw ratings declines of nearly 10 percent during the 2017 regular season.[57] ESPN saw such dramatic drop-off that ESPN president John Skipper, who had overseen the politicization of his network, admitted in late 2016, "ESPN is far from immune from the political fever that has afflicted so much of the country over the past year. Internally, there's a feeling among many staffers—both liberal and conservative—that the company's perceived move leftward has had a stifling effect on discourse inside the company and has affected its public-facing product. Consumers have sensed that same leftward movement, alienating some." Jemele Hill, an outspoken and censorious leftist, immediately shot back, "I would challenge those people who say they feel suppressed. Do you fear backlash, or do you fear right and wrong?"[58]

In 2018, Skipper was replaced by Jimmy Pitaro, chairman of its consumer products. He quickly admitted that ESPN had strayed from its core mission: "uniting people around sports." Pitaro stated, "We have to understand we're here to serve sports fans. All sports fans." ESPN's internal research showed that all fans, liberal and conservative, didn't want to hear politics on ESPN.[59]

But the network—and the leagues—had already been renormalized. It was simply too late to pull out of the tailspin. By 2020, after the killing of George Floyd in police custody resulted in nationwide protests, virtually every sports league *mandated* wokeness. The NBA festooned its sidelines with the phrase "BLACK LIVES MATTER"—a semantically overloaded phrase suggesting that America was irredeemably bigoted against black Americans. That was in and of itself a rather shocking contention coming from an 80 percent black league[60] in which the average salary is $7.7 million per season.[61] NBA players were told they could emblazon woke slogans on the back of their jerseys, limited to: Black Lives Matter, Say Their Names, Vote, I Can't Breathe, Justice, Peace, Equality, Freedom, Enough, Power to the People, Justice Now, Say Her Name, Si Se Puede, Liberation, See Us, Hear Us, Respect Us, Love Us, Listen, Listen to Us, Stand Up, Ally, Anti-Racist, I Am a Man, Speak Up, How Many More, Group Economics, Education Reform, and Mentor. Thus, it became a common sight to see Group Economics blocking Justice, and I Can't Breathe throwing up an alley-oop to Enough.[62] How any of this had anything to do with sports was beyond reasonable explanation. (The NBA's newfound commitment to political issues apparently stopped at calling America systemically racist—Houston Rockets general manager Daryl Morey was forced to apologize for tweeting "Free Hong Kong" as the Chinese

government subjected that formerly free city to complete subservi-
ence. LeBron James, the most celebrated politically oriented athlete in
America, called Morey "misinformed." After all, LeBron, Nike, and
the NBA make bank in the Chinese market.)[63]

Major League Baseball opened its season with "BLM" stamped
onto pitchers' mounds, universal kneeling before the national anthem,
and Morgan Freeman voicing over, "Equality is not just a word. It's
our right." The Tampa Bay Rays tweeted out, "Today is Opening
Day, which means it's a great day to arrest the killers of Breonna Taylor"[64] (Taylor was accidentally killed during crossfire when police
knocked on her apartment door to serve a no-knock warrant and were
met by gunfire from her boyfriend inside). The NFL followed suit,
with Roger Goodell admitting he was "wrong" by not overtly siding
with Kaepernick in 2016,[65] and the league painting social justice warrior slogans in the end zones during games—phrases like "It Takes
All of Us" and "End Racism."[66]

Racism, as it turns out, was not ended. But at least the leagues had
pleased their most ardent customers.

Unfortunately for the leagues, there weren't that many of them
anymore. The NFL's ratings dropped 10 percent in 2020;[67] the NBA
Finals declined 51 percent year-on-year;[68] MLB's World Series was
the least watched of all time.[69] To be sure, not all of that decline had
to do with politics. Sports viewership dropped across the board due
to the pandemic. But the long downward trend of sports as a unifying
factor in American life continued at record rates in 2020.

CONCLUSION

When it comes to the politics of our entertainment, many Americans
prefer to remain in the dark; better not to think about politics being

pushed than to turn off the TV. The result: large-scale emotional indoctrination into wokeism, courtesy of censorious, authoritarian leftists in our New Ruling Class. Americans now float atop a tsunami of cultural leftism, from movies to television shows, from streaming platforms to sports games. And all of this has an impact. It removes an area of commonality and turns it into a cause for division. It turns the water cooler into a place of abrasive accusation rather than social fabric building.

We are told by our New Ruling Class that worrying about culture is a sign of puritanism. Meanwhile, they practice witch burning, insist that failure to abide by certain woke standards amounts to heresy, and use culture as a propaganda tool for their ideology and philosophy, renormalizing our entertainment in order to renormalize us. Our entertainment can reflect our values, but it can also shape them. Those in positions of power know this. And they revel in it.

If entertainment is where Americans go to take a breath—and if the authoritarian Left seeks to suck all the oxygen out of the room—we begin to suffocate. America is suffocating right now. And as our entertainment becomes more and more monolithic, less and less tolerant, more and more *demanding*, we become a less fun, less interesting, and less tolerant people.

CHAPTER 7

THE FAKE NEWS

Authoritarian Leftism pushes revolutionary aggression; it calls for top-down censorship; it establishes a new moral standard whereby traditional morals are considered inherently immoral.

If there is one institution that has, more than any other, engaged in the cram-downs of the authoritarian Left, it is our establishment media. That media often cheers revolutionary aggression; participates in censorship of dissenting views, and seeks to have it cemented by powerful institutions; and promotes the notion that there is only one true moral side in American politics.

In the summer of 2020, that truth became crystal clear.

In response to the death of George Floyd while in police custody, massive protests involving millions of Americans broke out in cities across America. Never mind that even the circumstances surrounding Floyd's death were controversial—the police had been called to the scene by a shop owner after Floyd passed a counterfeit bill, was heavily drugged on fentanyl, resisted arrest, asked not to be placed in the police vehicle, and was in all likelihood suffering from serious complicating health factors.[1] Never mind that there was no evidence of racism in the actual Floyd incident itself. The impetus for the protests was rooted in a false narrative: the narrative that America was rooted in white supremacy, her institutions shot through with systemic racism, that black Americans are at constant risk of being murdered by the police (grand total number of black Americans, out of some 37 million black Americans, shot dead by the police while unarmed in 2020, according to *The Washington Post*: 15).[2] That narrative has been pushed by the media for years, in incidents ranging from the shooting of Michael Brown (the media pushed the idea that Brown had surrendered while shouting "hands up, don't shoot," an overt lie) to the shooting of Jacob Blake (the media portrayed Blake as unarmed even though he was armed with a knife).

The narrative didn't just result in protests. It resulted in violence, rioting, and looting. In Los Angeles, my hometown, the city shut down its iconic Rodeo Drive at 1 p.m. in the aftermath of looting.[3] Melrose Avenue was systematically looted as well, and police cars were left to the tender mercies of rioters, who promptly set them on fire and spray-painted them with the slogan "ACAB"—All Cops Are Bastards.[4] Looters attempted to break into the Walgreens a few blocks south of our home; a few blocks north of us, the Foot Locker was looted. For days on end, in the middle of a pandemic, the authorities informed law-abiding citizens to lock themselves in their homes at 6 p.m. Santa Monica and Long Beach saw looting as well. The *Los Angeles Times* labeled the events "largely peaceful."[5] Similar scenes took place in Washington, D.C., Chicago, and New York, where days of rioting resulted in "jarring scenes of flaming debris, stampedes and looted storefronts," according to *The New York Times*. Police officers were injured and hundreds were arrested. The *Times* labeled the events "largely peaceful."[6] So did *The Washington Post*, which used the hilarious phraseology "mostly peaceful displays punctuated by scuffles with police."[7] The media's desperate attempts to downplay the violence reached comical proportions, with reporter after reporter explaining that the protests were "mostly peaceful." Ali Velshi of MSNBC stood in front of a burning building while intoning, "This was mostly a protest, it is not generally speaking unruly, but fires have been started."[8] All of this came to its sadly hilarious culmination during riots in Kenosha, Wisconsin, in August: a CNN reporter stood in front of a flaming background, the chyron reading, "FIERY BUT MOSTLY PEACEFUL PROTESTS AFTER PO-LICE SHOOTING."[9]

Overall, the protests were "mostly peaceful" only in the sense that many protests took place that didn't break into explicit violence. But riots and looting related to the BLM movement cost somewhere up to $2 billion, making them the most expensive riots and civil disorder in American history.[10] The rioting hit some 140 cities.[11] At least 14 Americans died in violence linked to the BLM unrest[12]; more than 700 police officers were injured; at least 150 federal buildings were damaged.[13]

Many in the media went further than merely downplaying the violence: they fully excused it, cheered it, and justified it. They indulged their own Revolutionary Impulse. Now was a time to celebrate the revolutionary aggression inherent in their left-wing authoritarianism.

Nikole Hannah-Jones of *The New York Times* explained, "Destroying property, which can be replaced, is not violence."[14] She also cheered that some had termed the riots the "1619 Riots," in honor of her pseudo-history of the United States, *The 1619 Project*.[15] "Nobody should be destroying property and that sort of thing, but I understand the anger," explained CNN's Don Lemon. "Our country was started . . . The Boston Tea Party, rioting. So do not get it twisted and think that 'Oh this is something that has never happened before, and this is so terrible, and these savages,' and all of that, that's how this country was started."[16] Fellow CNN anchor Chris Cuomo wondered,

"Now, too many see the protests as the problem. No, the problem is what forced your fellow citizens to take to the streets: persistent, poisonous inequities and injustice. And please, show me where it says protesters are supposed to be polite and peaceful. Because I can show you that outraged citizens are what made the country what she is."[17] Harvard associate professor Elizabeth Hinton explained to *Time* that "rioting" didn't really capture the essence of the events—instead, the mob violence should have been termed an "uprising," since it "really captures the fact that the violence that emerges during these incidents isn't meaningless, that it is a political expression, and it is communicating a certain set of demands." *USA Today* printed an article tendentiously explaining, "'Riots,' 'violence,' 'looting': Words matter when talking about race and unrest, experts say."[18] NPR printed the commentary of Marc Lamont Hill, who declared the riots "acts of rebellion."[19]

And the media didn't stop with mere rhetorical flourishes. The overall narrative—that America was evil, and that its police were systemically racist—led to practical efforts across the country to defund the police, cheered on by the media. Police officers, realizing that even a proper arrest, if effectuated by a white officer against a black suspect, could result in a media-led crusade against them and their departments, stopped proactively policing. As a result, thousands of Americans died in 2020 who simply wouldn't have died in 2019. As Heather Mac Donald observed in *The Wall Street Journal*, "The year 2020 likely saw the largest percentage increase in homicides in American history. . . . .Based on preliminary estimates, at least 2,000 more Americans, most of them black, were killed in 2020 than in 2019."[20]

The media's desperate attempts to portray the Black Lives Matter movement as both legitimate and nonviolent led them to legitimize both untruth and violence. So when the media—quite properly—expressed outrage at the insanity of the January 6 Capitol invasion,

Americans with an attention span longer than that of a guppy could see the hypocrisy and double standard a mile off. The media, it seems, is fine with political violence when it is directed at one side.

When asked about their perfectly obvious shift from riot-cheerleaders to riot-chastisers, members of the media have reacted with pure outrage. To even compare the media's tolerance for BLM violence rooted with their rage over January 6 meant that you were engaging in intellectual hypocrisy. Anyone who pointed out the double standard was hit with the charge of "whataboutism," even though the entire basis for the double standard accusation was *condemnation of violence across the board*—condemnation in which the media had refused to engage itself.

CNN's Lemon, for example, sputtered, "I'm sick of people comparing, you can't compare what happened this summer to what happened at the Capitol. It's two different things. One was built on people, on racial justice, on criminal justice, right, on reform, on police not beating up—or treating people of color differently than they do Whites. OK? That was not a lie. Those are facts. Go look at them."[21] Lemon presented no such facts. But his opinion was good enough. After all, Lemon says that he has "evolved" as a journalist:

Being a person, a black man—let's put it this way: being an American who happens to be Black, who happens to be gay, from the south, I have a certain lens that I view the world through and that's not necessarily a bias. That's my experience . . . if I can't give my point of view, and speak through the experiences that I have had as a man of color who has lived on this earth for more than 50 years, who happens to have this platform, then when am I going to do it? I'd be derelict in my duty as a journalist and derelict in my duty as an American if I didn't speak to those issues with honesty. . . . I think, in this moment, journalists realize that we have to step up and we have to call out the lies and the BS and it has nothing to do with objectivity.[22]

Lemon's statement encapsulates the media's breathtaking dishonesty. On the one hand, media members want to be free to express their politics in their journalism, which would cut directly against their purported objectivity. On the other hand, they want to maintain the patina of objectivity so as to maintain an unearned moral superiority over supposed partisan hacks on the other side. How can today's pseudo-journalism—or those who engage in Journalisming™, as I often term it—square this circle? They simply do what Lemon does: they suggest that their opinions are actually reflections of fact, that those who disagree are dishonest, and that objectivity doesn't require you to listen to other points of view or report on them. Journalists make themselves the story—and if you doubt them, you are anti-truth and anti-journalism.

This skewing of journalism makes its purveyors, quite literally, Fake News. They pretend to be news outlets but are actually partisan activists. It would be difficult to find a single bylined staffer at *The New York Times* who voted for Donald Trump. The same holds true at *The Washington Post*. Certainly, CNN, MSNBC, ABC News, CBS News, the *Los Angeles Times*, the Associated Press—none of them are hotbeds of Republican activity. According to a 2020 report in *Business Insider*, a survey of political donations from establishment media members found that 90 percent of their donated money went to Democrats (the survey included names from Fox and the *New York Post*).[23] In 2013, a survey of journalists showed that just 7 percent identified as Republican. And by 2016, according to *Politico*, "more than half of publishing employees worked in counties that Clinton won by 30 points or more," with just 27 percent of employees working in a red district. As Jack Shafer and Tucker Doherty acknowledged, "On such subjects as abortion, gay rights, gun control and environmental regulation, the *Times*' news reporting is a pretty good reflection of its region's dominant predisposition. . . . Something akin to the *Times* ethos thrives in most major national newsrooms found on the Clinton coasts." Our Journalisming™ superiors don't just occupy a bubble. They occupy an isolation tank.[24]

Americans aren't blind. They distrust the media for a reason. Members of the media frequently blame Trump for endemic American mistrust of the fourth estate. They neglect the simple fact that Americans, particularly on the right, had justified trust issues long before Trump ever rose to prominence in politics. In 2013, for example, only about 52 percent of Americans trusted traditional media. Today, that number is 46 percent; only 18 percent of Trump voters trust the media, compared with 57 percent of Biden voters. Six in ten Americans believe "most news organizations are more concerned with supporting an ideology or political position than with informing the public."[25]

They happen to be correct. The only real question is why four in ten Americans still believe in the veracity of a media that openly disdains—and often seeks to target—one entire side of the American political conversation.

THE RISE AND FALL OF MEDIA OBJECTIVITY

From the outset, the American press has been a contentious lot, vying for supremacy and arguing passionately about right and wrong. The notion of a political objectivity in journalism would have seemed bizarre to the Founding Fathers: Thomas Jefferson employed journalist James Callendar to muckrake on behalf of his favored causes and to undermine his enemies.[26] For well over a century, newspapers openly identified with political parties. The era of yellow journalism was markedly free of concerns about objectivity. Only in the aftermath of World War I, with America's intelligentsia falling out of love with democracy itself, did the press begin to conceive of itself as "objective"—as guardian of a unique fact-finding process that could provide audiences with information beyond the realm of political debate.

Leading the charge for "objectivity" was *New Republic* editor Walter Lippmann. Lippmann began life as a progressive activist, a political critic of "the old individualism, with its anarchistic *laissez-faire*," an advocate of Great Leaders "acting through the collective will of the nation." Lippmann disdained "Georgia crackers, poverty-stricken negroes, the homeless and helpless of the great cities," and called for a "governing class." He fretted about the ability of those who disagreed to peddle dissenting ideas—after all, they might be leading the public astray: "Without protection against propaganda, without standards of evidence, without criteria of emphasis, the living substance of all popular decision is exposed to every prejudice and to infinite exploitation." The solution to all of this, Lippmann decided, was to curb free expression in favor of "freedom from error, illusion, and misinterpretation." To this end, Lippmann proposed the notion of journalistic objectivity, explaining that editors were to act as a priestly caste—newspapers were, said Lippmann, "the bible of democracy."[27]

To achieve this objectivity meant shifting the notion of what a journalist *was*. Instead of the sardonic, chain-smoking, flattened-hat-type working the streets, journalists were now transformed into scientific specialists, inculcated in the latest methods, protected from the heresies of the hoi polloi. Many in the press began to see themselves as a class apart; they viewed the freedom of the press guaranteed by the Constitution not as a guarantee that government refrain from infringing on Americans' right to engage in reporting and public debate generally, but as a *specific* protection for a *specific and special group*—people who have the title "reporter" next to their bylines, who work for certain prestigious publications.

Lippmann's idea of regularizing a journalistic process wasn't bad, of course: facts do exist, and we should use rational, scientific methods to suss them out. Where Lippmann went wrong was in assuming that journalists wouldn't use their newfound sense of superiority to re-embrace their bias, while presenting themselves as "objective."

And that's precisely what happened. Establishment institutions declare themselves objective, and thus trustworthy. But in reality, sometimes partisan hacks can print truth, and self-appointed "objective" outlets can print lies; "objective" journalists can lie through omission, favor allies through contextualization, focus on stories most flattering to their own political priors. Bias is simply inseparable from journalism. Some journalists do a better job than others at attempting to remove their own biases from the stories they cover. Virtually all fail—and over the past few years, they have begun to fail more and more dramatically. The establishment media's slavish sycophancy for Barack Obama, followed by their rabidly rancorous coverage of Donald Trump, followed again by their absurd ass kissing for Joe Biden, has ripped the mask away.

Lippmann insisted on at least a façade of nonpartisanship, despite his own elitism: "Emphatically [the journalist] ought not to be serving a cause, no matter how good. In his professional activity it is no business of his to care whose ox is gored. . . . As the observer of the signs of change, his value to society depends upon the prophetic discrimination with which he selects those signs."[28] Our New Ruling Class journalists don't bother. These journalists argue that they are actually better journalists than the forebears who attempted to provide a variety of viewpoints in any controversy. Real journalists, they say, don't engage in "false balance"—meaning, respect for a side other than their own. Real journalists, they say, bring their own experiences to bear. *Real* journalists, they say, are crusaders rather than passive observers.

Real journalists are activists. *Real* objectivity is allegiance to re-fracting facts through the prism of leftism.

The mask is off.

In 2014, *The Washington Post*'s Wesley Lowery found himself un-der arrest in a McDonald's during the Ferguson, Missouri, riots in the aftermath of the shooting of eighteen-year-old Michael Brown by Officer Darren Wilson. He claimed that he had been a victim of police brutality; the police claimed that Lowery had trespassed and refused orders to clear an area from the police.[29] Lowery's perspec-tive on endemic American racism was obvious. Later, he would write about Ferguson that reporting on the details of the shooting itself was irrelevant—instead, the media should have focused on the broader narrative, contextualizing the riots and violence by referring to Amer-ica's history of racial discrimination.[30]

Lowery was an opinionated fellow, and routinely took to Twitter to disparage his critics. In fact, Lowery's Twitter habit eventually ended with *Washington Post* editor Marty Baron threatening to fire him; Lowery had tweeted that the Tea Party was "essentially a hyster-ical grassroots tantrum about the fact that a black guy was president." Baron suggested that Lowery ought to work for an advocacy organi-zation or write an opinion column. Lowery eventually quit, complain-ing, "Should go without saying: reporters of color shouldn't have their jobs threatened for speaking out about mainstream media failures to properly cover and contextualize issues of race. What's the point of bringing diverse experiences and voices into a room only to muzzle them?"[31] Lowery ended up at CBS News.

Lowery is now widely viewed as the future of mainstream journal-ism. In June 2020, Ben Smith of *The New York Times* observed, "Mr. Lowery's view that news organizations' 'core value needs to be the truth, not the perception of objectivity,' as he told me, has been winning in a series of battles, many around how to cover race . . . The shift in mainstream American media—driven by a journalism that is more personal, and reporters more willing to speak what they see as the truth without worrying about alienating conservatives—now feels irreversible." Lowery believes that the "American view-from-nowhere, 'objectivity'-obsessed, both-sides journalism is a failed experiment. We need to rebuild our industry as one that operates from a place of moral clarity."[32]

Of course, moral clarity is generally a matter of opinion. When you maintain that your opinion is fact, and then declare yourself an objective news source *rooted in that opinion*, you are a liar. And our media are, all too often, liars.

THE MEDIA'S WOKE INTERNAL RENORMALIZATION

The religious wokeness that infuses our newsrooms is enforced daily. It turns out that "moral clarity" often looks a lot like the Spanish Inquisition. Nobody expects it. But at this point, everybody should.

The battles in America's newsrooms these days aren't between conservatives and liberals. As we've seen, there *are* no conservatives at most establishment media outlets. The battle is truly between authoritarian leftists and liberals—between people who may largely agree on policy preferences, but who disagree on whether robust discussion should be allowed. The authoritarian Left argues no. The liberals argue yes. Increasingly, the authoritarian leftists are successfully wishing the liberals into the cornfield—or at least intimidating them into dropping any pretense at bipartisanship. The authoritarian Left is only tangentially interested in canceling individual conservatives who occasionally write for liberal outlets. Their true goal is to browbeat liberals into *preemptively* canceling conservatives, thus establishing a total monopoly, assimilating liberals into the woke Borg or extirpating them.

That's what *New York Times* op-ed editor James Bennet found out the hard way when he had the temerity to green-light a column from sitting senator Tom Cotton (R-AR). Cotton's column, written in the midst of the BLM riots, suggested that President Trump invoke the Insurrection Act and use the National Guard to quell violence if state and local officials failed to do so. Not only was this a plausible argument—the argument would later be used by those on the Left to call for more federal presence in Washington, D.C., following the January 6 riots—but at the time, Cotton's comments were considered not merely foolhardy, but *dangerous*. Dangerous, as we know, is one of the predicates used by political opponents to stymie dissent: if your words pose a "danger" to me, they must be banned.

That's precisely what *New York Times* staffers claimed: that because of Cotton's op-ed, they were now under existential threat. This made no sense, given that *Times* staffers presumably weren't engaged in rioting. But the mere idea that law enforcement ought to crack down on violent activity was enough to send these woke staffers into spasms of apoplexy. Staff writers including Jenna Wortham, Taffy Brodesser-Akner, and Kwame Opam tweeted the same message: "Running this puts Black @NYTimes staff in danger." Reporter Astead Herndon messaged out support for coworkers, "particularly the black ones." Columnist Charlie Warzel tweeted, "I feel compelled to say that I disagree with every word in that Tom Cotton op-ed and it does not reflect my values." The company's Slack channel blew up with staffers whining over their discomfort.

Initially, Bennet defended the move. He tweeted that while many opinion writers and the editorial board had defended the protests and "crusaded for years against the underlying, systemic cruelties that led to these protests," the newspaper "owes it to our readers to show them counter-arguments, particularly those made by people in a position to set policy."[33] Within three days, Bennet resigned, with publisher A. G. Sulzberger blaming a "significant breakdown in our editing process," without noting any actual problems with the Cotton piece. Bennet didn't leave without a Maoist struggle session—he apologized to the staff. The newspaper added an editorial note to the Cotton piece suggesting that it carried a "needlessly harsh tone"[34]—a bizarre accusation coming from a newspaper that routinely prints the vile, vitriolic, woke word vomit of columnists ranging from Paul Krugman to Charles Blow to Jamelle Bouie. This was a full authoritarian leftist defenestration: revolutionary aggression against the powers that be; top-down censorship; and a sense of moral superiority.

Bennet's ouster was merely the latest shot in the ongoing war to oust traditional liberals from positions of power—or to cow them into silence. In March 2018, *The Atlantic* hired iconoclastic *National Review* columnist Kevin Williamson. When Jeffrey Goldberg, editor of *The Atlantic*, hired Williamson, he informed Williamson that he'd stand by him—he even defended Williamson publicly by stating that he would not judge people by their "worst tweets, or assertions, in isolation." That stance lasted just a few days. Goldberg backtracked after staffers told Goldberg they felt threatened by Williamson's pro-life viewpoint, expressed in jocular fashion on a podcast. "[T]he language used in the podcast was callous and violent," said Goldberg. "I have come to the conclusion that *The Atlantic* is not the best fit for his talents, and so we are parting ways."[35] Goldberg, the supposed liberal, became yet another tool of the authoritarian Left, unwilling to challenge their dominance, even at the risk of editorial self-castration.

Something similar happened at *Politico* when that publication asked me to guest-host its prestigious *Playbook* in late December 2020. The publication was, an editor explained, having a series of guest editors including MSNBC's Chris Hayes, PBS's Yamiche Alcindor, and CNN's Don Lemon, among others. I thought the project might be fun. But, as always, I warned the editor that the blowback he received would be immense.

My day to write the *Playbook* fell the day after Trump was impeached for the second time in the House of Representatives. I wrote about the generalized Republican unwillingness to vote to impeach, and explained that unwillingness by pointing to the belief by most conservatives that impeachment was merely a way of lumping together Trump supporters more broadly with the Capitol rioters: conservatives correctly saw impeachment as merely the latest club for the Left to wield against an opposing political tribe.

The blowback was, predictably, immense. Within minutes, *Politico* was trending on Twitter. Within hours, *Politico* leadership was hosting a conference call for some 225 staffers enraged over my name sullying the sacred *Playbook*.[36] Some of those participants compared me to Alex Jones and David Duke, adding that to print my words cut against their journalistic mission—which was to shut me up. "I'm spending all this time trying to convince them that we're here for them, and that there's a difference between what Ben Shapiro is doing and what Alex Jones is doing and what Politico is doing," one *Politico* staffer fumed. "I don't even know how to go tell them now not to listen to Ben Shapiro because we published Ben Shapiro."[37] Two weeks later, the staff at *Politico* was still fuming. More than one hundred staffers wrote a letter to the publisher, demanding an explanation for why I had been platformed.[38]

Most of the establishment media agreed: as Erik Wemple of *The Washington Post* sneered, "You know, if you want to hear Shapiro's opinions, there's a place to go for that."[39] Karen Attiah wrote in *The Washington Post* that platforming me in *Politico* granted legitimacy to white supremacy, and called it "willful moral malpractice," adding,

"I am reminded that in this country White people once gathered to watch the public lynching of Black people, and even made souvenir postcards of the events. I am reminded that, in America, White racism against minorities is titillating, not disqualifying—because it is profitable."[40] Less than three months before writing those words, Attiah was joking with me on Twitter about grabbing drinks and finding new common ground.

She couldn't have proved my point better.

Now, this little hubbub had no effect on me. I *do* have an outlet, with extraordinarily high traffic. But the goal of such public shaming rituals is to prevent adventurous editors from even conversing with conservatives. And, as it turns out, that's precisely what happened: I later found out that Guy Benson and Mary Katherine Ham, both mainstream conservatives who had been asked to guest-write the *Playbook* after me, were ghosted by the editors. In effect, they were preemptively canceled.

Liberals are being ousted or cowed into submission across the media.

The same week James Bennet resigned, Stan Wischnowski, top editor of the *Philadelphia Inquirer*, stepped down from his position for the great sin of having published an op-ed titled "Buildings Matter Too," complaining about BLM rioting and looting. The *Inquirer*'s editors issued a groveling apology, mewling, "We're sorry, and regret that we [printed it]. We also know that an apology on its own is not sufficient." That apology followed staff members calling in sick to protest the editorial, and issuing an overwrought letter stating, "We're tired of being told of the progress the company has made and being served platitudes about 'diversity and inclusion' when we raise our concerns. . . . We're tired of being told to show both sides of issues there are no two sides of."[41]

One month later, as the fallout from the BLM purge continued, opinion writer and editor Bari Weiss, a traditional liberal, resigned from *The New York Times*. Her parting letter was a Molotov cocktail tossed in the middle of the *Times* editorial structure. Weiss stated that she had been hired to usher in a variety of viewpoints to the *Times*, but that the newspaper of record had surrendered to the woke. At the *Times*, Weiss wrote, "truth isn't a process of collective discovery, but an orthodoxy already known to an enlightened few whose job is to inform everyone else." Calling Twitter the "ultimate editor" of the paper, she tore into her colleagues—colleagues who had labeled her a Nazi and a racist, and some of whom had publicly smeared her as a bigot. "[I]ntellectual curiosity," Weiss wrote, "is now a liability at *The Times* . . . nowadays, standing up for principle at the paper does not win plaudits. It puts a target on your back." Weiss concluded, "The paper of record is, more and more, the record of those living in a distant galaxy, one whose concerns are profoundly removed from the lives of most people."[42]

The newspaper's lack of defense for Weiss stood in stark contrast to its vociferous defense of woke authoritarian leftist thoughtleader Nikole Hannah-Jones, creator of the *1619 Project*. That effort billed itself as a journalistic attempt to recast American history—to view the country as being founded not in 1776 but in 1619, the year of the first importation of an African slave to North American shores. That idea was in and of itself egregiously flawed: America was founded on the principles of the Declaration of Independence. While chattel slavery was a deep, abiding, and evil feature of America during that time and before—as it was, unfortunately, in a wide variety of countries around the world—it did not provide the core of America's founding philosophy or institutions. But the *1619 Project* not only insisted that slavery lay at the center of America's philosophy and that its legacy inextricably wove its way into every American institution—it lied outright in order to press that falsehood forward. The project compiled a series of essays blaming slavery and endemic white supremacy for everything from traffic patterns to corporate use of Excel spreadsheets to track employee time.

Then there were the blatant errors, ignored or defended by the *Times*. Five historians, including Pulitzer Prize winner James Mc-Pherson and Bancroft Prize winner Sean Wilentz, as well as famed founding-era historian Gordon S. Wood, wrote a letter to the *Times* blasting the accuracy of the project, including its mischaracterizations of the founding, Abraham Lincoln's views of black equality, and the lack of support for black rights among white Americans. The historians asked that the *Times* correct the project before its distribution in schools.[43] Hannah-Jones then derisively referred to McPherson's race in order to dismiss the criticism. Jake Silverstein, editor in chief of the *New York Times Magazine*, then acknowledged that "we are not ourselves historians," but added that Hannah-Jones "was trying to make the point that for the most part, the history of this country has been told by white historians."[44] Similarly, historian Leslie Harris of Northwestern University wrote that she had warned Hannah-Jones that her contention that the American Revolution was fought in large part to preserve slavery was simply false. Hannah-Jones and the *Times* ignored her.[45]

In the end, after the *Times* spent millions of dollars to publicize the *1619 Project*, the Pulitzer Prize committee gave the pseudo-history its highest honor. After all, the narrative had been upheld, and its critics chided. When the *Times* printed a piece from its own columnist Bret Stephens critical of the *1619 Project* in October 2020, the publisher of the newspaper weighed in to call the project a "journalistic triumph that changed the way millions of Americans understand our country, its history and its present," and called the project "one of the proudest accomplishments" of the *Times* generally. *The New York Times* guild actually attacked Stephens personally, stating that "[t]he act, like the article, reeks."[46] Hannah-Jones is currently in a development deal with Oprah Winfrey and LionsGate to develop the *1619 Project* into multiple feature films, TV series, and documentaries.[47]

JOURNALISTS AGAINST FREE SPEECH

Authoritarian leftists often claim that "cancel culture" isn't real—that deplatforming isn't a problem, because conservatives and traditional liberals can simply present their ideas elsewhere. That argument is the height of gaslighting. It also happens to be utterly specious on its face: it is indeed a cancellation to be barred from participation in the most widely read outlets thanks to dissent. But consigning conservatives and traditional liberals to non-establishment outlets has a rather unfortunate side effect for the authoritarian leftists: conservatives and traditional liberals begin consuming nontraditional media at record rates. In the days when the media had a monopoly on the distribution of information—three TV networks, a few national print newspapers—cleansing conservatives would have been the end of the story. But with the rise of the internet, podcasts, and cable news, conservatives have been able to construct media of their own. Websites like the Daily Wire generate enormous traffic *because* the media have silenced conservative voices.

And so the authoritarian leftists must go one step further: they must destroy conservative and traditional liberal voices *outside traditional media*. They first force those they hate into ideological ghettos. Then, when it turns out the ghettos create their own thriving ecosystem, they seek to level them.

To that end, our journalistic New Ruling Class have become full-scale activists. Instead of reporting on the news, they generate it by working with activist groups to motivate advertisers, neutral service

providers, and social media platforms to downgrade or drop dissenting media. They claim that the very presence of conservative ideas
in the public square ratchets up the possibility of violence—and then
they seek to blame advertisers, neutral service providers, and social
media platforms for subsidizing the unwoke or allowing them access
to their services. When that fails, they call for outright government
regulation of free speech. The Founding Fathers would have been as-
tonished to learn that the greatest advocates for curbing free speech in
the United States are now members of the press.

The authoritarian leftist activist journalists pick their targets well.

They begin with advertisers. For nearly two decades, Media Matters, a pathetic hit group started by unstable grifter David Brock and
backed by Hillary Clinton's team, has spent every waking minute
monitoring conservative media for opportunities to push advertiser
boycotts. That generally involves cutting conservatives out of context, then letting media allies know about those out-of-context quotes,
spinning up controversy—and then creating a fake groundswell of
outrage directed at advertisers, who generally wish to be left alone.
The tactic has been sporadically successful when directed at hosts
ranging from Rush Limbaugh to Sean Hannity to Tucker Carlson,
and over time other groups have joined in the game as well. Major
media outlets routinely use Media Matters as a source for coverage;[48]
an ex-employee of Media Matters bragged in February 2012 that the
activist group was "pretty much writing" MSNBC's prime time, and
coordinating with *The Washington Post*'s Greg Sargent, and reporters
from the *Los Angeles Times*, *Huffington Post*, and *Politico*, among others. (Media Matters also reportedly held weekly strategy calls with the
Obama White House communications director, and now Biden chief
spokeswoman, Jen Psaki.)[49]

Members of the media don't merely crib off of Media Matters' out-
of-context clips—they then target advertisers, asking them why they

are continuing to spend their dollars with conservatives. Naturally, such questions aren't designed to elicit a response. They're designed to elicit a cancellation of the advertising dollars. And the media cheer when they start an advertiser cancellation cascade against a conservative. Their glee is fully evident.

Members of establishment media cheer on this tactic. In fact, they go further: they call for anyone who provides services to the unwoke to stop doing so. They call for Comcast to stop carrying Newsmax, One America News, and Fox News. Nicholas Kristof of *The New York Times* recently wrote that in order to dampen the extremism of the Republican Party, "advertisers should stop supporting networks that spread lies and hatred, and cable companies should drop channels that persist in doing so. As a start, don't force people to subsidize Fox News by including it in basic packages." Sure, Kristof acknowledged, this could create a slippery slope. But the slippery slope was a lesser risk than Kristof's opponents being able to make a living.[50] Margaret Sullivan of *The Washington Post* agreed, calling Fox News a "hazard to our democracy," and demanded that "[c]orporations that advertise on Fox News should walk away, and citizens who care about the truth should demand that they do so."[51] Max Boot of *The Washington Post* believes that "large cable companies . . . need to step in and kick Fox News off."[52] CNN's Oliver Darcy joined the chorus, stating that "TV companies that provide platforms to networks" like Fox News ought not escape scrutiny: "it is time TV carriers face questions for lending their platforms to dishonest companies that profit off of disinformation and conspiracy theories." Darcy even called up cable platforms to attempt to pressure them.[53]

This stuff is fully delusional: were conservatives to be deprived of Fox News, they'd seek similar conservative outlets. But that delusion is consistent with the authoritarian Left's true goal: a reestablishment of the media monopoly it had before the death of the Fairness

Doctrine and the rise of Rush Limbaugh. Many on the authoritarian Left celebrated when Limbaugh died, declaring him "polarizing." The reality is that *they* were polarizing, but they had a monopoly . . . and Limbaugh broke that monopoly. Now they want to reestablish it, at all costs.

This is why the media grow particularly vengeful when it comes to distribution of conservative ideas via social media. A shocking number of media members spend their days seeking to pressure social media platforms into curbing free speech standards in order to reinstitute an establishment media monopoly. Now, blaming social media platforms for violence is sort of like blaming free speech for Nazis: yes, bad people can take advantage of neutral platforms to do bad things. That doesn't mean the platforms should be restricted. But for pseudo-journalists like Joe Scarborough of MSNBC, the platforms bear primary responsibility for violence: "Those riots would not have happened but for Twitter, but for Facebook . . . Facebook's algorithms were set up to cause this sort of radicalism to explode."[54]

By citing the danger of free speech, our establishment media can close the pathways of informational dissemination to those outside the New Ruling Class. These media members consider anyone outside their own worldview an enemy worth banning. Mainstream media members simply lump in mainstream conservatives with violent radicals—and *voilà!*—it's time for social media to step in and get rid of them. Kara Swisher of *The New York Times* spends her column space, day after day, attempting to pressure Mark Zuckerberg of Facebook to set restrictive content regulations in violation of free speech principles. "Mr. Zuckerberg," Swisher wrote in June 2020, "has become— unwittingly or not—the digital equivalent of a supercharged enabler because of his enormous power over digital communications that affect billions of people." And, Swisher added, Zuckerberg shouldn't worry about free speech as a value—after all, the First Amendment doesn't mention "Facebook, or any other company. And there's no mention of Mark Zuckerberg, who certainly has the power to rein in speech that violates company rules." Free speech is *the problem*. Corporate censorship is *the solution*.[55]

And what sort of content should be restricted? The tech reporters believe the answer is obvious: anything right of center. That's why, day after day, Kevin Roose of *The New York Times* tweets out organic reach of conservative sites, trying to pressure Facebook into changing its algorithm. It's why *The New York Times* ran a piece by Roose in June 2019 titled "The Making of a YouTube Radical," linking everyone from Jordan Peterson, Joe Rogan, and me to Alex Jones and Jared Taylor. Roose lamented, "YouTube has inadvertently created a dangerous on-ramp to extremism."[56] The goal is obvious: get everybody right of center deplatformed. And threaten the platforms themselves in order to do so.

It won't stop there. Media members have now decided, in the post-Trump age, that it's time to rewrite the First Amendment bargain altogether. Jim VandeHei of *Politico* acknowledges that Blue America hopes desperately to rethink "politics, free speech, the definition of truth and the price of lies."[57] The First Amendment must be rethought. In 2019, Richard Stengel—now the head of Joe Biden's transition team for the US Agency for Global Media—contended that America ought to embrace hate speech laws, since free speech should not "protect hateful speech that can cause violence by one group against another." New York University journalism professor and MSNBC contributor Anand Giridharadas questions, "Should Fox News be allowed to exist?" Steve Coll, dean of Columbia Journalism School, now believes that those in journalism "have to come to terms with the fact that free speech, a principle we hold sacred, is being weaponized against the principles of journalism." Bill Adair, founder of the highly biased news fact-checking source PolitiFact, now believes that the government should use "regulations and new laws" to fight the "problem of misinformation."[58]

Curbing free speech has two particular benefits for the establishment media: first, it boots their competitors; second, it purges the public sphere of views they dislike. It's a win-win. All they require is ideologically authoritarian control.

CONCLUSION

On January 18, 2019, during the March for Life, something frightening happened: a group of high school boys wearing MAGA hats swarmed around an innocent Native American man, taunting him, laughing and dancing. Reports suggested that four black protesters had also been harassed by the cruel white students. The Native American man told the media that he had confronted the students while they shouted, "Build the Wall!" And the journalistic world went to work, journalisming as hard as they could. Kara Swisher tweeted, "[T]hose awful kids and their fetid smirking harassing that elderly man on the Mall: Go f*** yourselves." Joe Scarborough tweeted, "Where are their parents, where are their teachers, where are their pastors?" *The New York Times* headlined, "Boys in 'Make America Great Again' Hats Mob Native Elder at Indigenous People's March." CNN called the incident a "heartbreaking viral video."[59]

There was only one problem.

It wasn't true.

In reality, as Covington Catholic student Nick Sandmann—the kid in the MAGA hat—stated, the white students were accosted by four black members of the Black Hebrew Israelites—a radical group of nut cases who had called them "racists," "bigots," "faggots," and "incest kids." The students were also accosted by the Native American man, who strode into their group and began banging a drum in their faces. Sandmann stood still, smiling awkwardly. As Sandmann related:

> I was not intentionally making faces at the protestor. I did smile at one point because I wanted him to know that I was not going to become angry, intimidated or be provoked into a larger confrontation. I am a faithful Christian and practicing Catholic, and I always try to live up to the ideals my faith teaches me—to remain respectful of others, and to take no action that would lead to conflict or violence.[60]

Sandmann was telling the truth. Nearly every element of the story as reported by the establishment media was false. "[T]he elite media have botched the story so completely that they have lost the authority to report on it," wrote Caitlyn Flanagan of *The Atlantic*. Flanagan went further, slamming *The New York Times*: "You were partly responsible for the election of Trump because you are the most influential newspaper in the country, and you are not fair or impartial. Millions of Americans believe you hate them and that you will casually harm them."[61]

Nothing has changed.

If anything, the problem has grown worse.

The establishment media have declared themselves the heroes of the past four years—the bravest, the most noble, the guardians of our democracy. They weren't, and they aren't. They are willing to attack everyone from commoners to kings to advance their agenda. Doubt them, and they'll cast you out. Compete with them, and they'll work to silence you.

Within days of Joe Biden's ascension to the White House, our Journalisming™ experts reverted from watchdogs to lapdogs. CNN's Dana Bash swooned, "The adults are back in the room."[62] CNN's

White House reporter Jim Acosta tweeted a picture of himself with NBC News' Peter Alexander: "Just a couple of guys covering the White House on the last full day of Trump admin. Think we will finally have time for that drink now @PeterAlexander?"[63] CNN's Brian Stelter, host of the ironically named *Reliable Sources*, wrote a glowing chyron about White House press secretary (and former CNN contributor) Jen Psaki's assurance that she would only speak truth: "Psaki promises to share 'accurate info' (how refreshing)."[64] Margaret Sullivan of *The Washington Post* praised the "Biden White House's return to normalcy," and warned against media members being too *harsh* on the new administration.[65]

It's all fine. Trust them.

This is dangerous stuff. It's dangerous that the guardians of our democracy—the media—aren't guardians but political activists, dedicated to their own brand of propaganda. It's even more dangerous that they now work on an ongoing basis to stymie voices with whom they disagree, and use the power of their platforms to destroy their opponents at every level. A thriving marketplace of ideas requires a basic respect for the marketplace itself. But our ideologically driven, authoritarian leftist media seek to destroy that marketplace in favor of a monopoly.

Every day, they come closer to achieving that goal.

CHAPTER 8

UNFRIENDING AMERICANS

One month before the 2020 election, the *New York Post* released a bombshell report—a report that could have upended the nature of the election. That report centered on Hunter Biden, son of Joe Biden, the Democratic presidential nominee. According to the *Post*'s report, "Hunter Biden introduced his father, then–Vice President Joe Biden, to a top executive at a Ukrainian energy firm less than a year before the elder Biden pressured government officials in Ukraine into firing a prosecutor who was investigating the company, according to emails obtained by the *Post*." A board member of Burisma, the company on whose board Biden sat, sent Hunter Biden a note of appreciation to thank him for the introduction.

The bombshell rebutted Joe Biden's consistent statements that he knew nothing about his son's business activities abroad, and that Hunter's activities had all been aboveboard. The *Post* even reported the provenance of the emails: Hunter Biden's laptop had been dropped off at a computer repair shop in Delaware in 2019, and Hunter had never returned to pick up that computer. The *Post* further reported that "both the computer and hard drive were seized by the FBI in December, after the shop's owner says he alerted the feds to their existence."[1]

It was no surprise to find that Hunter had been trafficking in his father's name—members of Biden's family have been doing that for years. In 2019, *Politico* reported, "Biden's image as a straight-shooting man of the people . . . is clouded by the careers of his son and brother, who have lengthy track records of making, or seeking, deals that cash in on his name."[2] Hunter admitted publicly in October 2019 that he certainly wouldn't have been selected to sit on the board of Burisma were his last name different—he has a long history of self-destructive behavior, zero experience in Ukraine, and zero experience with natural gas and oil. ABC News' Amy Robach asked Hunter, "If your last name wasn't Biden, do you think you would've been asked to be on the board of Burisma?" Hunter responded, "I don't know. I don't know. Probably not, in retrospect. But that's—you know—I don't think that there's a lot of things that would have happened in my life if my last name wasn't Biden. Because my dad was Vice President of the United States. There's literally nothing, as a young man or as a full grown adult that—my father in some way hasn't had influence over."[3] For his part, Joe Biden suggested that it was unthinkable that Hunter shouldn't have taken the position, and absurd to believe that Hunter had been given the position because the company wanted access to Joe.[4]

Hunter's willingness to use his father's name became a front-page issue that same year when Donald Trump, suspicious of corruption in Ukraine, held a controversial phone call with Ukrainian president Volodymyr Zelensky in which he stated, "There's a lot of talk about Biden's son, that Biden stopped the prosecution and a lot of people want to find out about that so whatever you can do with the Attorney General would be great. . . . It sounds horrible to me." Trump's political opponents accused him of blackmailing a foreign power into digging up dirt on Biden by threatening to withhold aid; the phone call resulted in Trump's impeachment in the House of Representatives for the first time.[5]

Now, a year later, the *Post* was reporting that Biden's Ukrainian associates had been promised a meeting with Biden himself. Follow-on stories in the *Post* quoted Hunter Biden's ex–business associate Tony Bobulinski accusing Joe Biden himself of lying about his knowledge of Hunter's activities: "I have heard Joe Biden say he has never discussed his dealings with Hunter. That is false. I have firsthand knowledge about this because I directly dealt with the Biden family, including Joe Biden," Bobulinski alleged.[6]

The Biden campaign and its media allies responded by calling the Hunter Biden story "Russian disinformation."[7]

The story, needless to say, was not Russian disinformation; there was no evidence that it was in the first place. In fact, about a month after the election, media reported that Hunter Biden had been under federal investigation for *years*—CNN reported that the investigation began as early as 2018, and that it had gone covert for fear of affecting the presidential election.[8]

The Hunter Biden story never fully broke through into the mainstream consciousness. According to a poll from McLaughlin & Associates, 38 percent of Democratic supporters weren't aware of the story before the election; by contrast, 83 percent of Republicans were aware of the story.[9]

There was a reason for that: social media companies such as Twitter and Facebook simply shut down the story cold.

When the *Post* tweeted out the story, Twitter itself *suspended* the *Post*'s account. The company went so far as to prohibit users from posting a link to the story itself. Twitter tried to explain that it would not disseminate stories based on hacked materials—even though the *Post*'s story was *not based on hacked materials*. If Twitter had followed the same policies consistently, virtually every major story of the past several decades would have been banned on the platform.

Then, a few days later, Twitter did the same thing with the *Post*'s follow-up story. Those who attempted to post the links were met with the message, "We can't complete this request because this link has been identified by Twitter or our partners as being potentially harmful."

Later, Twitter CEO Jack Dorsey would admit that the "communication around our actions . . . was not great." Spin regarding censorship rarely is.[10]

Meanwhile, Andy Stone, the policy communications director at Facebook—and an alumnus of the Democratic House Majority PAC, former press secretary for Senator Barbara Boxer (D-CA), and former press secretary of the Democratic Congressional Campaign Committee[11]—tweeted, "While I will intentionally not link to the New York Post, I want to be clear that this story is eligible to be fact checked by Facebook's third-party fact checking partners. In the meantime, we are reducing its distribution on our platform."[12] He added, "This is part of our standard process to reduce the spread of misinformation. We temporarily reduce distribution pending fact-checker review."[13] In other words, Facebook *admitted* to curbing the reach of the *Post* story *before it had been fact-checked at all*. It had no evidence the story was false—as it turns out, the *Post* story was true. But Facebook restricted the reach of the *Post* piece anyway.

Facebook actually had moderators *manually intervene* in order to shut down the *Post* story, as the company admitted: "[W]e have been on heightened alert because of FBI intelligence about the potential for hack and leak operations meant to spread misinformation. Based on that risk, and in line with our existing policies and procedures, we made the decision to temporarily limit the content's distribution while our factcheckers had a chance to review it. When that didn't happen, we lifted the demotion."[14]

Just in time for Joe Biden to cruise to the presidency.

FROM OPEN AND FREE TO THE NEW GATEKEEPERS

The *real* story of the Hunter Biden saga, as it turned out, was not about Hunter Biden per se: it was about the power and willingness of an oligopoly to restrict access to information in unprecedented ways. Social media companies were founded on the promise of broader access to speech and information; they were meant to be a marketplace of ideas, a place for coordination and exchange. They were, in other words, the new town square.

Now social media are quickly becoming less like open meeting places and more like the town squares in Puritan New England circa 1720: less free exchange of ideas, more mobs and stocks.

The saga of the social media platforms begins with the implementation of the much-maligned and misunderstood Section 230 of the Communications Decency Act in 1996. The section was designed to distinguish between material for which online platforms could be held responsible and material for which they could not. The most essential part of the law reads, "No provider or user of an interactive computer service shall be treated as the publisher or speaker of any information provided by another information content provider." *The New York Times*, for example, can be held liable as a publisher for information appearing in its pages. *The New York Times'* comments section, however, does not create liability—if a user posts defamatory material in the comments, the *Times* does not suddenly become responsible.

The purpose of Section 230, then, was to open up conversation by shielding online platforms from legal liability for third parties posting content. Section 230 itself states as much: the goal of the section is to strengthen the internet as "a forum for a true diversity of political discourse, unique opportunities for cultural development, and myriad avenues for intellectual activity."[15] As the Electronic Freedom Foundation describes, "This legal and policy framework has allowed for YouTube and Vimeo users to upload their own videos, Amazon and Yelp to offer countless user reviews, craigslist to host classified ads, and Facebook and Twitter to offer social networking to hundreds of millions of Internet users."[16]

There is one problem, however: the stark divide between platforms for third-party content and publishers who select their content begins to erode when platforms restrict the content third parties can post. Thus, for example, a New York court found in 1995 that Prodigy, a web services company with a public bulletin board, became a publisher when it moderated that board for "offensiveness and 'bad taste.'"[17] In reaction, Section 230 created an extremely broad carve-out for platforms to remove offending content; bipartisan legislators wanted to protect platforms from liability just for curating content in order to avoid seamy or ugly content. Thus Section 230 provides that no platform shall incur liability based on "any action voluntarily taken in good faith to restrict access to or availability of material that the provider or user considers to be obscene, lewd, lascivious, filthy, excessively violent, harassing, or otherwise objectionable, whether or not such material is constitutionally protected."[18]

At the beginning, our major social media companies understood full well the intent behind Section 230. In fact, they celebrated it. Facebook's mission statement for its first decade was "to make the world more open and connected."[19] Twitter said that its goal was "to give everyone the power to create and share ideas and information instantly, without barriers."[20] Google's working motto was simple: "Don't be evil."

For a while, it worked.

The social media giants were essentially open platforms, with a light hand in terms of censorship. Then the 2016 election happened.

The shock that greeted Trump's victory in 2016 fundamentally altered the orientation of the social media platforms. That's because, up until that moment, the personal political preferences of executives and staffers—overwhelmingly liberal—had meshed with their preferred political outcomes. But with Trump's win, that math changed dramatically. Members of the media and the Democratic Party began looking for a scapegoat. They found one in social media. If, the logic went, Americans had been restricted to viewing news the New Ruling Class wanted them to view, Hillary Clinton would have been installed as president rather than Trump. The dissemination of information was the problem.

Media elites and Democratic Party members couldn't make that argument explicitly—it was simply too authoritarian. So instead, they designed the concept of "fake news"—false news that Americans had apparently been bamboozled by. Post-election, the term gained ground in rapid fashion, with left-wing sites like PolitiFact explaining, "In 2016, the prevalence of political fact abuse—promulgated by the words of two polarizing presidential candidates and their passionate supporters—gave rise to a spreading of fake news with unprecedented impunity." Predictably, PolitiFact blamed Facebook and Google.[21] After the election, President Barack Obama—a man who certainly was no stranger to dissemination of false information, often with the compliance of a sycophantic press—complained about the "capacity to disseminate misinformation, wild conspiracy theories, to paint the opposition in wildly negative light without any rebuttal—that has accelerated in ways that much more sharply polarize the electorate and make it very difficult to have a common conversation."[22] In November 2017, Senator Dianne Feinstein (D-CA) openly threatened the social media companies, growling, "You created these platforms . . . and now they're being misused. And you have to be the ones who do something about it—or we will. . . . We are not going to go away, gentlemen. . . . Because you bear this responsibility."[23]

Initially, Facebook rejected the idea that as a platform it had somehow shifted the election to Trump—or that it bore responsibility for the material on its platform. That, of course, was the basic supposition of Section 230: that platforms *do not bear responsibility for material placed there by third parties*. Zuckerberg correctly countered the criticisms: "I do think that there is a certain profound lack of empathy in asserting that the only reason why someone could have voted the way that they did was because they saw some fake news. I think if you believe that, then I don't think you have internalized the message that Trump supporters are trying to send in this election."[24]

But the tsunami of rage at social media continued.

And, faced with the combined power of staff unrest, media manipulation, and Democratic Party threats, the social media companies shifted. They began to jettison their roles as the guardians of open and free discourse and began to embrace their new roles as informational gatekeepers.

In February 2017—just weeks after the inauguration of President Trump—Zuckerberg redefined Facebook's mission. Now, he said, the goal of the company was to "develop the social infrastructure to give people the power to build a global community that works for all of us." This was a far more collectivist vision than the original vision. And it called for new content standards to help reach this utopian goal, designed to "mitigat[e] areas where technology and social media can contribute to divisiveness and isolation."[25]

Facebook would no longer stay on the sidelines. Facebook would get involved. In a congressional hearing in April 2018, Zuckerberg went so far as to state that "we are responsible for the content" on the platform—a direct contravention of Section 230.

On a personal level, Zuckerberg continued to maintain his allegiance to free speech principles. In that April 2018 hearing, Zucker-berg stated, "I am very committed to making sure that Facebook is a platform for all ideas. . . . We're proud of the discourse and the differ-ent ideas that people can share on the service, and that is something that, as long as I'm running the company, I'm going to be committed to making sure is the case."[26] Speaking at Georgetown University in 2019, Zuckerberg maintained, "People no longer have to rely on tra-ditional gatekeepers in politics or media to make their voices heard, and that has important consequences. I understand the concerns about how tech platforms have centralized power, but I actually believe the much bigger story is how much these platforms have decentralized power by putting it directly into people's hands." He then correctly noted, "We can continue to stand for free expression, understand-ing its messiness, but believing that the long journey toward greater progress requires confronting ideas that challenge us. Or we can de-cide the cost is simply too great. I'm here today because I believe we must continue to stand for free expression."[27]

That allegiance to free speech principles—principles commonly held by the tech bros at the launch of their companies—didn't extend to other tech leaders. These tech leaders suggested that the very ba-sis for their companies—free access to speech platforms—had to be reversed. Their companies would no longer be about free speech, but about free speech for the approved members of the New Ruling Class. Jack Dorsey, the new darling of the media establishment, slammed Zuckerberg for pledging himself to traditional liberalism: "We talk a lot about speech and expression and we don't talk about reach enough, and we don't talk about amplification," said Dorsey. The tech com-panies, Dorsey suggested, should decide which posts deserved am-plification.[28] (Dorsey, it should be noted, is no critic of authoritarian wokeness—in fact, he's one of its biggest proponents. In 2020, Dorsey cut a $10 million donation to Ibram X. Kendi's "Center for Antiracism

Research,"[29] which has to date presented no actual research. Kendi's website explains, "Our work, like our center, is in the process of being developed.")

This angle—free speech is not free reach—has become the new standard in establishment media, of course: Kara Swisher, the activist masquerading as a tech reporter for *The New York Times*, says, "Congress shall make no law. There's no mention of Facebook, or any other company."[30] That's easy for her to say, considering she's paid to write repetitive, censorious garbage by an establishment media company given favorable treatment by the social media companies.

This perspective, not coincidentally, mirrored the prevailing view in the Democratic Party: the tech companies should simply censor the views of political opponents. Representative Alexandria Ocasio-Cortez (D-NY) browbeat Zuckerberg about even meeting with conservative figures, labeling them "far-right" and calling the Daily Caller "white supremacist." Representative Maxine Waters (D-CA) lambasted Zuckerberg's commitment to open discourse, stating that he was "willing to step on or over anyone, including your competitors, women, people of color, your own users, and even our democracy to get what you want."[31] In January 2020, Joe Biden personally ripped Zuckerberg, stating, "I've never been a big Zuckerberg fan. I think he's a real problem." In June 2020, the Biden campaign circulated a petition and open letter to Mark Zuckerberg, calling for "real changes to Facebook's policies for their platform and how they enforce them" in order to "protect against a repeat of the role that disinformation played in the 2016 election and that continues to threaten our democracy today."[32]

The social media companies have increasingly taken heed.

And they've moved right along with the clever switch made over the course of the past several years from "fighting disinformation" to "fighting misinformation." After 2016, the argument went, Russian "disinformation" had spammed social media, actively undermining truth in favor of a narrative detrimental to Democratic candidate Hillary Clinton.

There was some evidence of this—although the amount of actual Russian disinformation on Facebook, for example, wasn't overwhelming in the grand scheme of things. According to a Senate report in 2018, for example, the last month of the 2016 campaign generated 1.1 billion likes, posts, comments, and shares related to Donald Trump, and another 934 million related to Hillary Clinton.[33] In total, according to a report from New Knowledge, of Russian-created posts from 2015 to 2017, 61,500 posts from the Russian influence operation garnered a grand total of 76.5 million engagements. Total. Over two years. That's an average of 1,243 engagements per post—an extremely low total.[34]

But put aside the relative success or unsuccess of the Russian manipulation. We can all agree that Russian disinformation—typically meaning overtly false information put out by a foreign source, designed to mislead domestic audiences—is worth censoring. Democrats and media, however, shifted their objection from Russian disinformation to "misinformation"—a term of art that encompasses everything from actual, outright falsehood to narratives you dislike. To declare something "misinformation" should require showing its falsity, at the least.

No longer.

In December 2019, according to *Time*, Zuckerberg met with nine civil rights leaders at his home to discuss how to combat "misinformation." Vanita Gupta, CEO of the Leadership Conference on Civil and Human Rights—and now associate attorney general of the United States for Joe Biden—later bragged that she had cudgeled Facebook into changing informational standards. "It took pushing, urging, conversations, brainstorming, all of that to get to a place where we ended up with more rigorous rules and enforcement," she later told *Time*.[35]

The result: our social media now do precisely what government could not—act in contravention of free speech, with members of the Democratic Party and the media cheering them on. They follow no consistent policy, but react with precipitous and collusive haste in group-banning those who fall afoul of the ever-shifting standards of appropriate speech. That's what happened with the domino effect of banning the Hunter Biden story, for example.

Section 230, designed to protect open discourse by allowing platforms to prune the hedges without killing the free speech tree, has been completely turned upside down: a government privilege granted to social media has now become a mandate from the government and its media allies to take an ax to the tree. The iron triangle of informational restriction has slammed into place: a media, desperate to maintain its monopoly, uses its power to cudgel social media into doing its bidding; the Democratic Party, desperate to uphold its allied media as the sole informational source for Americans, uses threats to cudgel social media into doing its bidding; and social media companies, generally headed by leaders who align politically with members of the media and the Democratic Party, acquiesce.

COVERING FOR CENSORSHIP

So, how is material removed from these platforms—the platforms that were originally designed to foster free exchange of ideas? In the main, algorithms are designed to spot particular types of content. Some of the content to be removed is uncontroversially bad, and should come down—material that explicitly calls for violence, or pornographic material, or, say, actual Russian disinformation. But more and more, social media companies have decided that their job is not merely to police the boundaries of free speech while leaving the core untouched—more and more, they have decided that their job is to foster "positive conversation," to encourage people to click on videos they wouldn't normally click on, to quiet "misinformation."

In the first instance, this can be done via algorithmic changes.

Those changes are largely designed to reestablish a monopoly on informational distribution by establishment media. The internet broke the establishment media's model; just as cable wrecked network television, the internet wrecked cable and print news. Originally, consumers went directly to websites in order to view the news—they'd bookmark Drudge Report or FoxNews.com, and go straight there. But then, as social media began to aggregate billions of eyeballs, people began to use social media as their gateway to those news sources. By 2019, according to the Pew Research Center, 55 percent of adults got their news from social media either "sometimes" or "often," including a plurality of young people.[36]

Establishment media saw an opportunity. By targeting the means of distribution—by going after the social media companies and getting them to down-rank alternative media—they could reestablish the monopoly they had lost.

And so the establishment media went to work. As we've already discussed, it's rare to find a voice in the establishment media dedicated to the proposition that dissemination of information on social media ought to be *more* open.

Social media companies have complied. So, for example, in 2019, in response to media reports blaming YouTube for violent acts supposedly inspired by viral videos—the media actually went further, blaming nonviolent, non-extremist videos for creating a "pipeline" to more violent and extremist content, all based on the flimsiest of conjecture[37]—YouTube changed its algorithm. As CBS News reported, "YouTube started re-programming its algorithms in the U.S. to recommend questionable videos much less and point users who search for that kind of material to authoritative sources, like news clips."[38] Facebook infamously did the same, demoting "borderline content" that supposedly trafficked in "sensationalist and provocative content." The goal was to manipulate what people could click on by deliberately making it more *difficult* to click on clickable stories.[39] The month after the 2020 election, in an attempt to tamp down speculation about voter fraud and irregularity, Facebook gave more algorithmic weight to sources that had higher "news ecosystem quality" scores.

Who were these mystical "authoritative sources" that ranked highly in terms of "news ecosystem quality"? Why, establishment media sources, of course—the same exact outlets attempting to browbeat social media platforms into censoring their competitors. As *The New York Times* reported, "The change was part of the 'break glass' plans Facebook had spent months developing for the aftermath of a contested election. It resulted in a spike in visibility for big, mainstream publishers like CNN, *The New York Times* and NPR, while posts from highly engaged hyperpartisan pages . . . became less visible." And, added the Very Authoritative *New York Times*, all this was a "vision of what a calmer, less divisive Facebook might look like." The *Times* also reported that Facebook's "idealist" employees wanted Facebook to maintain the system; only its presumably corrupt, greedy "pragmatists" wanted to maintain an open standard in terms of informational dissemination. And, lamented the *Times*, if the pragmatists continued to win, "morale" within the company would continue to drop.[40]

In establishing which sources ought to be "trusted," social media have outsourced their judgment to left-wing pseudo-fact-checkers. In December 2016, Facebook announced that it would partner with a slate of fact-checkers to determine which sources were most trustworthy. According to BuzzFeed, Facebook would verify "participating partners"; those participating partners would then have access to a "special online queue that will show links Facebook determined may be suitable for a fact-check." How do links end up in the queue? Users report them as false, or the link goes viral. It's easy to see how such a system can be gamed: just put together an action response team, email them to spam Facebook's system, and then refer conservative links to fact-checks by left-wing organizations.

And that's precisely how the fact-checking business works. Facebook's original "participating partners": the Associated Press, Politi-Fact, FactCheck.org, Snopes, *The Washington Post*, and ABC News. That would be three mainstream media outlets, and three left-wing fact-checking organizations. These pseudo-fact-checkers spent most of their time checking "misinformation"—which means, in many cases, declaring claims false based on "lack of context," even if the claims are overtly true. PolitiFact, for example, rated President Obama's lies about keeping your health-care plan if you like your health-care plan "half-true" *twice* before labeling it their "lie of the year."[41] Snopes.com recently rated "Mostly False" the claim that Representative Alexandria Ocasio-Cortez (D-NY) exaggerated "the danger she was in during the January 6, 2021, Capitol Riot, in that she 'wasn't even in the Capitol building' when the rioting occurred." That fact-check included the as-tonishing acknowledgment that it was true that Ocasio-Cortez "wasn't in the main Capitol building." Which, as it turns out, was the basis for the statement they were also calling "mostly false."[42]

The fact-checkers are certainly not unbiased. "When it comes to partisan fact-checking about complex issues—which describes much of the fact-checking that takes place in the context of political news—the truth as stated is often the subjective opinion of people with shared political views," says Professor Stephen Ceci of Cornell University.[43] And social media companies know that. They just happen to agree with the political leanings of the fact-checkers to whom they out-source their responsibilities.

Algorithmic censorship doesn't stop there. According to *The*

Washington Post in December, Facebook made the decision to begin policing anti-black hate differently than anti-white hate. Race-blind practices would now be discarded, and instead, the algorithm would allow hate speech directed against white users to remain. Only the "worst of the worst" content would be automatically deleted—"Slurs directed at Blacks, Muslims, people of more than one race, the LGBTQ community and Jews, according to the documents." Slurs directed at whites, men, and Americans would be "deprioritized." The goal: to allow people to "combat systemic racism" by using vicious language.

Facebook would now apply its algorithmic standards differently "based on their perceived harm." Thus, woke standards of intersectional victimhood would be utilized, rather than an objective standard rooted in the nature of the language used. "We know that hate speech targeted toward underrepresented groups can be the most harmful," explained Facebook spokeswoman Sally Aldous, "which is why we have focused our technology on finding the hate speech that users and experts tell us is the most serious."[44] All hate speech is bad, except for the hate speech the experts say is nondamaging.

The so-called community standards put forward by the tech companies follow the same pattern: originally designed to protect more speech, they have been gradually ratcheted tighter and tighter in order to allow broader discretion to companies to ban dissenting material. As Susan Wojcicki, the head of YouTube, explained in June 2019, "We keep tightening and tightening the policies."[45] The ratchet only works one way.

These policies are often vague and contradictory. Facebook's "hate speech" policy, for example, bans any "direct attack" against people on the "basis of race, ethnicity, national origin, disability, religious affiliation, caste, sexual orientation, sex, gender identity and serious disease." What, exactly, constitutes an "attack"? Any "expression of . . . dismissal," or any "harmful stereotypes," for example.[46] So, would

Facebook ban members for the factually true statement that biological men are men? How about the factually true statement that women generally do not throw baseballs as hard as men? Are these "stereotypes" or biological truths? What about jokes, which often traffic in stereotypes? How about quoting the Bible, which is not silent on matters of religion or sexuality? Facebook is silent on such questions.

And that's the point. The purpose of these standards *isn't* to provide clarity, so much as to grant cover when banning someone for *not* violating the rules. That's why it's so unbelievably easy for big tech's critics to point to inconsistencies in application of the "community standards"—Alex Jones gets banned, while Louis Farrakhan is welcomed; President Trump gets banned, while Ayatollah Khamenei is welcome.

When President Trump was banned from Twitter, Facebook, Instagram, and YouTube in the aftermath of January 6, none of the companies could explain precisely what policy Trump had breached to trigger his excision. Zuckerberg simply stated, "We believe the risks of allowing the President to continue to use our service during this period are simply too great."[47] Twitter explained that it had banned Trump "due to the risk of further incitement of violence." The tweets that supposedly created additional danger: "The 75,000,000 great American Patriots who voted for me, AMERICA FIRST, and MAKE AMERICA GREAT AGAIN, will have a GIANT VOICE long into the future. They will not be disrespected or treated unfairly in any way, shape or form!!!" and "To all of those who have asked, I will not be going to the Inauguration on January 20th." Twitter did provide a strained explanation of how those two rather benign tweets would incite further violence. It remains unconvincing.[48]

For the authoritarian Left, none of this goes far enough. The goal is to remake the constituency of companies themselves, so that the authoritarians can completely remake the algorithms in their own image. When Turing Award winner and Facebook chief AI scientist Yann LeCun pointed out that machine learning systems are racially biased only if their inputs are biased, and suggested that inputs could be corrected to present an opposite racial bias, the authoritarian woke critics attacked: Timnit Gebru, technical co-lead of the Ethical Artificial Intelligence Team at Google, accused LeCun of "marginalization" and called for solving "social and structural problems." The answer, said Gebru, was to hire members of marginalized groups, not to change the data set used by machine learning.[49]

CROWDSOURCING THE REVOLUTION

For most Americans, the true dangers of social media don't even lie in the censorship of news itself: the largest danger lies in the roving mobs social media represent. The sad truth is that the media, in their ever-present quest for authoritarian rule, use social media as both their tip line and their action arm. They dig through the social media histories of those they despise, or receive tips from bad actors about "bad old tweets," and proceed to whip the mob into a frenzy. Then they cover the frenzy. The same media that declaim their hatred for misinformation and bullying engage in them regularly when it comes to mobbing random citizens with the help of social media.

In December 2020, a recent high school graduate, Mimi Groves, found herself the subject of an interminable hit piece from *The New York Times*. Groves had, back in 2016, just received her learner's permit to drive. She took a video of herself on Snapchat, jocularly exclaiming, "I can drive, n***ah." As the *Times* reported, the video "later circulated among some students at Heritage High School," but it didn't raise any hackles—after all, she was a fifteen-year-old girl mimicking the tropes of rap.

But one student—an utterly despicable douche bag named Jimmy Galligan—held on to the video. Galligan, who is black, decided to post the video "publicly when the time was right." That time came in 2020, by which time Groves was a senior, headed to the University of Tennessee, Knoxville, to be part of the cheer team. During the Black Lives Matter protests, Groves made the critical error of *supporting* BLM; she posted to Instagram urging comrades to "protest, donate, sign a petition, rally, do something."

And so Galligan struck. He posted the old video to Snapchat, Tik-Tok, and Twitter. Groves was booted from the University of Tennessee cheer team, then withdrew from UT altogether thanks to the social media frenzy. An admissions officer said that the university had received "hundreds of emails and phone calls from outraged alumni, students and the public."

The *Times* reported this story, not as a horrific attempt by a vicious grandstander to destroy a girl's life, but as a referendum on the "power of social media to hold people of all ages accountable." Galligan is portrayed as a hero, standing up to the threat of endemic white supremacy.[50]

This story should raise two questions, one about social media, and one about the media. First, why has social media become such a flaming dumpster fire of visceral hatred? Second, why have the media degraded themselves to the point where nonstories about individual *high school students* are worthy of national coverage?

For social media, the answer lies in virality. Social media companies *encourage* such activities, treating them as a source of traffic and news. Twitter's trending topics are a perfect example of how minor issues can quickly snowball; Twitter highlights the most controversial stories and elevates them, encouraging minor incidents to become national stories; velocity of attention matters more than sheer scope of attention. Thus, for example, topics that garner tons of tweets day after day don't trend; topics that spike in attention from a low baseline do. So if there's a random woman in a city park who says something racially insensitive and garners two thousand tweets for it, she's more likely to trend than President Biden on any given day. And it's not difficult for two thousand tweets to become 20,000, once a topic starts to trend: social media rewards speaking out, and devalues silence. On social media, refusal to weigh in on a trending topic is generally taken as an indicator of apathy or even approval.

It doesn't take much to form a mob, either. Social media mobs form daily, with the speed of an aggressive autoimmune disorder. Where in the past, people had to find commonality in order to mobilize a mob, now social media provides a mob milling around, waiting to be mobilized. The cause need not be just. All it must do is provide an evening's entertainment for several thousand people, and a story for the media to print. Justine Sacco, a thirty-year-old senior director of corporate communications at IAC, watched her life crumble after sending a tweet joking about AIDS in Africa to her 170 followers. The tweet read, "Going to Africa. Hope I don't get AIDS. Just kidding. I'm white!" The tweet was apparently supposed to be a joke about the insufficiency of Western aid to Africa. Nonetheless, when she got off her eleven-hour flight, she had been targeted with "tens of thousands of tweets." She lost her job. She experienced PTSD, depression, and insomnia.

Which brings us to the second question: why do the media cover this stuff?

The answer: they are, in large measure, social authoritarians who use social media as a cheap and easy way of both creating traffic and finding stories.

Sacco's tweet only became a worldwide trend because a tipster sent it to Sam Biddle, a writer for Gawker Media. He promptly retweeted it. Biddle later explained, "It's satisfying to be able to say, 'OK, let's make a racist tweet by a senior IAC employee count this time.'"[51] Too many in the media have the same perspective. Twitter has enabled our journalistic establishment to play at both crusader and reporter with a single retweet. That's why whatever the latest Twitter trend, it's likely a media member will have the top tweet.

Singular events that chart on social media also allow members of the media to manipulate the narrative. The media overwhelmingly believe the woke tale that America is systemically racist—but the data for such contentions are vanishingly hard to find. In America, the demand for racism from authoritarians seeking social control wildly outstrips the supply of actual racism. To that end, media members seek out individual, non-national stories and then suggest they are indicative of broader trends, citing social media attention as the rationale for the story in the first place.

In the real world, Twitter trends rarely used to matter. But as social media becomes our new shared space, and as our media treat the happenings on social media platforms as the equivalent of real life, social media mobs become real mobs with frightening momentum.

THE NEW INFORMATIONAL OLIGOPOLY

Our social media oligopoly—cudgeled, wheedled, and massaged into compliance by a rabid media and a censorious Democratic Party— threatens true social authoritarianism at this point. In a free market system, the solution would be to create alternatives.

Parler attempted to do just that.

Angered at the capricious nature of Twitter's management, Parler began as an alternative. In 2020, as big tech began to unleash its power in the election, Parler steadily gained adherents: in late July, Parler saw over a million people join in one week. After the 2020 election, as big tech moved to stymie alternative media, conservatives jumped to Parler: Parler hit the top spot in Apple's App Store, and jumped by more than 4.5 million members in one week. Parler's chief selling point: it would not ban people based on political viewpoint. Parler's CEO, John Matze, said, "We're a community town square, an open town square, with no censorship. If you can say it on the street of New York, you can say it on Parler."[52]

Until you couldn't.

After the January 6 riots, based on vaguely sourced reports that Parler had been an organizing place for the rioters, Apple, Amazon, and Google all barred Parler. Apple's App Store barred Parler on the basis that Parler's processes were "insufficient" to "prevent the spread of dangerous and illegal content." Amazon Web Services used its power to kick Parler off the internet entirely, denying it access to its cloud hosting service. Amazon's excuse: Parler had allowed "posts that clearly encourage and incite violence," and that it had no "effective process to comply with the AWS terms of service."[53]

None of the big tech companies could explain what, precisely, a minimum standard would have looked like. And none of them could explain why Parler was supposedly more dangerous than the far larger platforms Facebook and Twitter—especially since, as Jason King has reported, nearly one hundred people involved in the January 6 riot used Facebook or Instagram, twenty-eight used YouTube, and only eight used Parler.[54]

The informational monopoly is being reestablished in real time. And alternatives are being actively foreclosed by social media companies determined to invoke their standard as the singular standard, a media that knows it can co-opt those standards, and Democrats who benefit from those standards. After having killed Parler, members of the media have turned their attention to Telegram and Signal, encrypted messaging services. All streams of dissent—or uncontrolled informational streams—must be crushed.[55]

Perhaps the only good news is that most Americans know they're being manipulated by the gatekeepers in social media. Fully 82 percent of adults told Pew Research that social media "treat some news organizations differently than others," 53 percent said that one-sided news was a "very big problem" on social media, and 35 percent worried about "censorship of the news." Some 64 percent of Republicans said that the news they saw on social media leaned to the Left; 37 percent of Democrats agreed. Just 21 percent of Democrats said that the news they saw via social media leaned to the Right.[56]

The bad news is that social media will remain the biggest players on the stage so long as they have the most eyeballs—and with alternatives increasingly foreclosed, that means for the foreseeable future. Facebook has 2.8 billion monthly active users;[57] more than 90 percent of all web searches happen via either Google or its subsidiary YouTube;[58] fully 70 percent of digital ad spending goes to Google, Facebook, and Amazon.[59] Building competition in the face of that oligopoly won't be easy.

What's more, our government actors have an interest in upholding the oligopoly: it's easy to control a market with just a few key players. And our media have an interest in upholding the oligopoly, too: these companies are run by like-minded allies, all of whom are either committed to or can be pushed into support for woke authoritarianism.

And these companies, as it turns out, aren't the only ones.

THE CHOICE BEFORE US

In early February 2021, actress Gina Carano made a fateful decision. She posted a meme on Instagram.

Carano, who played popular character Cara Dune on Disney+'s hit series *The Mandalorian*, had been verging on the edge of cancellation for months. That's because Carano is conservative. She'd jokingly posted that her pronouns were beep/boop/bop in order to mock woke authoritarians pressuring strangers to list their gender pronouns. In the aftermath of the 2020 election, she'd posted on Twitter, "We need to clean up the election process so we are not left feeling the way we do today." She'd posted a meme challenging the elite consensus on Covid by suggesting that Americans were putting masks over their eyes.[1]

All of this had already made Carano persona non grata with Disney+ and Lucasfilm. According to *The Hollywood Reporter*, citing a person inside the companies, the bosses had been looking to can Carano for two months; Disney+ and Lucasfilm had scrapped plans for Carano to star in her own spin-off inside the *Star Wars* universe in December.[2]

Carano's fatal error came in posting a meme citing the Holocaust.

The picture showed a Jewish woman running away from a crowd of Germans, and carried this caption: "Jews were beaten in the streets, not by Nazi soldiers but by their neighbors. . . . even by children. Because history is edited, most people today don't realize that to get to the point where Nazi soldiers could easily round up thousands of Jews, the government first made their own neighbors hate them simply for being Jews. How is that any different from hating someone for their political views?"[3]

Now, comparisons to the Holocaust are generally overwrought. But Carano's post certainly was *not* anti-Semitic (as a recipient of more anti-Semitic memery than perhaps any person alive, I can spot anti-Semitism a mile off). The post was making the point that oppression of others doesn't start with violence. It starts with dehumanization of the other. That's a fairly generic and true point, even though Carano—as she herself acknowledged—shouldn't have invoked the Holocaust.

The blowback was immediate and final.

Disney+ and Lucasfilm fired her outright. They stated, wrongly, that she had "denigrat[ed] people based on their cultural and religious identities."[4] They could not explain precisely how she had denigrated anyone, particularly Jews. But authoritarian leftism requires only an excuse for cancellation, not a real justification.

One might think that Disney was merely setting a standard that overwrought Holocaust comparisons were forbidden on social media. Not so. Pedro Pascal, star of *The Mandalorian*, tweeted in 2018 comparing the Trump border policy with regard to children to Nazi concentration camps. To the sound of crickets.[5]

Normally, in our authoritarian culture, this is where the story would end.

But that's not where the story ended.

As soon as I heard what had happened to Carano—we'd never met before—I reached out to her personally; my business partner reached out to her business manager. And we offered Gina a job. To push back against Hollywood's absurd cancel culture, we would partner with her in producing a film, to star her. Gina's statement tells the tale:

> The Daily Wire is helping make one of my dreams—to develop and produce my own film—come true. I cried out and my prayer was answered. I am sending out a direct message of hope to everyone living in fear of cancellation by the totalitarian mob. I have only just begun using my voice which is now freer than ever before, and I hope it inspires others to do the same. They can't cancel us if we don't let them.[6]

They can't cancel us if we don't let them.

This should be our rallying cry. Because if we say it together—liberals, centrists, conservatives—the authoritarian Left loses.

Our institutions have been remade in the mold of authoritarian leftism by elites who deem themselves worthy of holding the reins of power. But we don't have to acquiesce in that power grab.

We can say "no."

After announcing our partnership with Gina, tens of thousands of Americans joined Daily Wire as members. I personally received hundreds of emails from people asking how they could help—and hundreds more from people in Hollywood asking if they could escape the system. Americans recognized not just that we were attempting to challenge Hollywood on its own terms, but that we must all act in solidarity—that while we are individualists by ideology, cohesive action is necessary if we wish to make a consolidated counterattack on the authoritarians.

So, how exactly do we go about wresting control of our institutions away from an authoritarian Left hell-bent on American renormalization? We begin with an educational mission. And then we get practical.

EDUCATING AMERICA, REDUX

The authoritarian Left has successfully pursued an educational project: inculcating Americans into embarrassment at America's founding philosophy, her institutions, and her people. Their argument—that America is systemically racist, that her institutions fundamentally broken—has won the day on an emotional level. To even challenge this argument is deemed vicious. But the argument is fundamentally wrong.

America is not systemically racist. Racism does exist; slavery was one of history's greatest evils; history does have consequences. It's terrible and sad that gaps between white and black success remain a feature of American life. All of those things are undeniably true. And the solution to all of those evils is *not* the overthrow of all existing American systems. In fact, the "anti-racist" policies the authoritarian Left loves so much have been tried—and they have failed miserably. That won't stop the authoritarian Left from calling you a racist for pointing that out.

The solution is the same as it was in 1776: a government instituted to protect the preexisting rights of its citizens, and a commitment to both virtue and reason. America was not founded in 1619; it was founded in 1776. The principles of American liberty are eternal and true. The fact that America has not always lived up to those principles isn't a referendum on the principles themselves. And the greatness of America—the greatness of her individual freedom, of her powerful economy, of her moral people—represents the unique outgrowth of those principles.

The sins of 1619—the sins of brutality, of bigotry, of violence, of greed, of lust, of radical dehumanization—are sins that adhere to nearly all of humanity over the course of time. Human beings are sinful and weak. But we are capable of more. It is not a coincidence that America has been history's leading force in favor of human freedom and prosperity. The great lie of our time—perhaps of all time—is that such freedom and prosperity are the natural state of things, and that America's systems stop us from fulfilling their promise. Precisely the opposite is true.

So, how do we—the new resistance—fight back against an authoritarian Left that has embedded itself at the top of our major institutions? How do we stop an authoritarian Left dedicated to revolutionary aggression, top-down censorship, and anti-conventionalism?

We reverse the process begun by the authoritarian Left so long ago: we refuse to allow the authoritarian Left to silence us; we end the renormalization of our institutions and return them back to actual normalcy; and we pry open the doors they have welded shut.

OUR REFUSAL IS A WEAPON

The first step in unraveling authoritarian leftist dominance of our institutions is our refusal to abide by their rules. The authoritarian Left engaged in a three-step process directed toward cudgeling Americans into supporting their agenda. First, they relied on the Cordiality Principle—the principle that Americans ought to be cordial, and thus inoffensive—to make Americans uncomfortable about dissenting from prevailing social views of the New Ruling Class. Next, they made the argument that to speak up against the New Ruling Class amounted to a form of violence. Finally, they argued that failure to *echo* the New Ruling Class was itself a form of harm—"Silence is violence."

We must reject each one of these steps, in reverse order.

First, we must reject the imbecilic notion that "silence is violence." It isn't. All too often, it's sanity. When it comes to children—whom radical authoritarian leftists all too often resemble—bad behavior should be met with a simple response: ignoring them. This is a tough principle for parents to learn (I know, I've had to practice it routinely): the natural tendency when faced with radical behavior is to *engage*. But it's precisely our attention that often gives radicals their power. Imagine if, instead of rushing to respond to the pseudo-urgent needs of the latest establishment media–driven mob, we simply shrugged. Imagine if, next time someone declared that they had been harmed by mere dissent, we chuckled at them and moved on. Their power would be gone. We don't have to engage. And we certainly don't have to echo.

Second, we must firmly reject the notion that speech is violence. Dissent isn't violence; disagreement isn't harm. That's because politics *isn't an identity*; it isn't a denial of someone's identity to disagree with them. We know this in our everyday personal relationships—we disagree with those we love most of all, on a regular basis. They don't feel that we're "denying their humanity" or "doing them violence." They understand that if they wish to be treated as adults, they ought to subject their views to the scrutiny of others. Anyone who utters the phrase "speech is violence" should be immediately discounted as a serious human being.

Finally—and most carefully—we must deny the conflation of cordiality and inoffensiveness implicit in the Cordiality Principle. To be cordial does not mean to be inoffensive. As I'm fond of saying, facts don't care about our feelings. That doesn't mean that we should be deliberately rude. It does mean, however, that we shouldn't allow others' subjective interpretations of our viewpoints to rule our minds. We cannot grant others an emotional veto over our perspectives. To oppose same-sex marriage, for example, should not be considered prima facie offensive—one can make a perfectly plausible argument for the superior societal importance of traditional marriage over same-sex marriage without insulting those who are homosexual. To go silent in the face of important societal issues out of fear that you might offend is to grant unending power to those who are quickest to rise to offense. And that's a recipe for emotional blackmail.

In rejecting the Cordiality Principle, we need not give cover to those who deliberately offend. To be politically incorrect means to say that which requires saying, not to be a generic, run-of-the-mill jackass. There is a difference between making an argument against same-sex marriage and calling someone an ugly name. In fact, conflating the two grants the authoritarian Left enormous power: it allows them to argue that nonliberal points of view ought to be quashed in order to prevent terrible behavior. Fighting political correctness requires a willingness to speak truth and the brains to speak the truth in cogent, clear, and objectively decent language.

When we fight back in this way, we win. We win because bravery draws followers; we win because honesty without vile behavior draws admirers. Once again, this isn't an issue of Left versus Right. It's an issue of upholding values dear to a pluralistic democracy—values that should be held in common across the political spectrum, and in direct opposition to the authoritarian Left.

RENORMALIZING OUR INSTITUTIONS

As I've argued throughout this book, our institutions have been steadily renormalized by an intransigent minority, making common cause with other "marginalized" populations in opposition to the majority. But this process can be *reversed*. It's time to renormalize—return normalcy—our institutions.

To do this requires the creation of an intransigent minority. Because too many Americans have allowed the authoritarian Left to cudgel them into silence or agreement, the key here is *courage*. Americans must be willing to stand up, speak out, and *refuse to acquiesce to the power hierarchy*.

Take, for example, the case of Donald McNeil Jr., a science reporter for *The New York Times*. In February 2021, McNeil was forced out of his job. It turns out that two years before, in 2019, McNeil acted as an expert guide on a *Times* student trip in Peru. During that trip, a student asked McNeil whether he thought a twelve-year-old ought to be canceled for using the n-word. In the process of explaining contextual differences in using the n-word, McNeil uttered the infamous slur. Some of the students complained. And some woke staffers at the *Times* demanded action; they sent yet another in their endless stream of whining letters to the editors, demanding action. The editors quickly acquiesced, thanking the authoritarian leftist brute squad for their input. So McNeil lost his job.[7] Executive editor Dean Baquet went so far as to state, "We do not tolerate racist language regardless of intent"—a standard so insanely authoritarian that Baquet later had to walk it back.[8]

But here's the thing: a *lot* of *New York Times* staffers thought McNeil should have retained his job. McNeil was a member of the NewsGuild, a union of 1,200 *Times* employees. As *Vanity Fair* reported, "McNeil is not without sympathy or support, both inside the *Times* and out. Some people feel that he was the latest victim of cancel culture run amok, forced out of his job by a public pressure campaign."[9]

So, here's the question: *where were they?*

What would have happened if the *Times* staffers, instead of allowing intellectual authoritarians like Nikole Hannah-Jones to rule the roost, stood up in favor of McNeil? There are 1,200 employees at the *Times*. Just 150 staffers signed the letter to the editors. What if 400 employees had signed a letter *the other way*? What if instead of caving to an intransigent minority, the *Times* employees who backed McNeil had formed their own intransigent minority—or even an intransigent majority? What if those staffers had forced the editors into a binary choice: side with free speech and non-authoritarianism or side with a relatively small group of malcontents?

The same logic holds throughout American life. What if employees banded together and simply refused to go along with the latest cancellations, or the latest demand for "diversity training," or the latest Maoist struggle session? What if religious Americans, who comprise a plurality of Americans in nearly every organization, said that they would not go along with attempts to force them into silence?

The answer has been shown time and time again: authoritarian leftists back down when faced with an intransigent majority. That's why they are authoritarians in the first place: if they could convince others of their arguments, they wouldn't need to create social stigma around their opponents, or militarize weapons of power against them.

In December 2020, Pedro Domingos, professor emeritus of computer science and engineering at the University of Washington, wrote publicly about the standards for scientific research at the Conference on Neural Information Processing Systems (NeurIPS). NeurIPS now suggests that "[r]egardless of scientific quality or contribution, a submission may be rejected for ethical considerations, including methods, applications, or data that create or reinforce unfair bias." This means that good research cannot be conducted under the NeurIPS auspices so long as such research challenges prevailing leftist politics.

Domingos wrote that this was a terrible idea. This prompted a backlash, naturally, with authoritarian leftists labeling Domingos a racist; as Domingos wrote, his own department distanced itself from him. Other professors suggested that anyone who cited Domingos's work was, by definition, a bigot.

But once again, that wasn't the end of the story. Domingos writes: "as the days passed, and it became clear who the real radicals were, something interesting happened. Many of the usually reticent moderates in our community began to speak up, and denounce the unhinged and ruthless tactics applied against me and my supporters. In the end, I suffered no professional consequences (at least not in any formal way). And the cancel crowd's ringleader even issued a public apology and promised to mend her ways."

So what happened? According to Domingos, solidarity kicked in: a network of like-minded people willing to speak up actually spoke up. Activate when you're on solid ground—and try to pick fights in which you can knock off the authoritarian Goliath. Never apologize. And direct your resistance not merely at authoritarian leftists, but at those *in charge of the institutions*. As Domingos writes, "Even companies that posture heavily in the area of social justice don't actually want to be stained by the disgraceful behavior of mob leaders."

If an intransigent minority can be activated, then renormalization can occur. Those in the middle rarely like the authoritarian Left. They're just afraid to speak out against them. So form a core group of intransigent people who share your values. And then build.[10]

PRYING OPEN THE INSTITUTIONS

All of this may work for institutions that are still up for grabs. But what do you do if the heads of these institutions aren't merely going along to get along, or blowing with the wind—what if the heads of these institutions are dedicated authoritarian leftists themselves, invulnerable to intransigent minorities, fully willing to utilize every power they have to silence dissent?

At this point, Americans are left with three options. And they should exercise all three.

First, the legal options. The authoritarian Left is extraordinarily litigious. When they can't win victories in the court of public opinion, they seek victory in the courts themselves. In fact, authoritarian leftists frequently use the mere threat of lawsuit to force compliance from those in power. Other Americans are generally reluctant to invoke the use of courts to force their employers to do their bidding.

That's usually the right instinct. But it's precisely the wrong instinct when it comes to fighting the authoritarian Left.

When it comes to the authoritarian Left's desire to cram down "diversity training" that discriminates based on race, for example, lawsuits are fully merited. If companies force employees to attend training sessions segregated by race, or in which white employees are taught of their inherent privilege, white employees ought to seek legal redress. So-called anti-racism training often violates the provisions of the Civil Rights Act of 1965 by explicitly discriminating on the basis of race. Make your employer pay the price for doing so—or threaten to do so if the company doesn't stop its legal violations.

Another option is available politically for those who wish to fight the authoritarian Left: the formal expansion of anti-discrimination law to include matters of politics. Many states bar discrimination on the basis of sex, sexual orientation, gender identity, race, religion, age, and disability, among other standards. Yet you can still be discriminated against based on your politics. If we wish to hold the authoritarian Left to its own standards—if we wish to use the bulwark of the law to prevent "discrimination" by limiting free association—then why give the authoritarian Left a monopoly on anti-discrimination law? Why not *force* the authoritarian Left to back down by using the same legal tools they have utilized themselves to silence dissent? If you're a traditionally conservative baker who doesn't want to violate his political precepts by catering a same-sex wedding, you'll find yourself on the wrong end of a lawsuit. If you're a leftist caterer who doesn't want to violate his political precepts by serving a Republican dinner meeting, you're off the hook. Perhaps that should change.

This is an ugly option, particularly for those of us who still believe in core freedoms like freedom of association. I happen to believe that people should be able to hire and fire whomever they want to. But the authoritarian Left disagrees. And not only do they disagree, they've captured the legal system to the extent that you can *only* be targeted for having the wrong politics today.

All of this raises a broader strategic possibility: the possibility of mutually assured destruction. Before I founded the Daily Wire, I ran an organization called Truth Revolt. The goal of the organization was to act as a sort of reverse Media Matters: to use a team of activists to encourage advertisers *not* to spend their money with left-wing outlets. In launching Truth Revolt, we openly acknowledged that we didn't like our own tactics. In fact, as my business partner Jeremy Boreing stated at our founding, we'd happily dissolve our organization if Media Matters did the same. But if the authoritarian Left was going to utilize nasty tactics in order to force institutions to cave to them, we'd have to make clear that the Right could do the same. Either organizations would begin to ignore both sides—a preferable outcome—or they would simply stop engaging with the political universe generally. In our view, there was only one strategy worse than arming up against the authoritarian Left: unilateral disarmament.

Americans can engage in the same tactics as the Left when it comes to our most powerful institutions. We can withhold our money from

Hollywood, refuse to shop at the wokest corporations, remove our endowments from authoritarian-run universities. We can stop subscribing to media outlets, and we can pressure advertisers to stop spending their money there. Either these institutions will learn to tune out all the insanity—which they should—or they can remove themselves from the business of politics.

Then there's the final option: building alternative institutions.

At the Daily Wire, we call ourselves alternative media, because that's what we want to be: a place for people who have been ignored by institutional media to access information they want to see. We're building up an entertainment wing to serve the needs of Americans who are tired of being lectured about the evils of their non-woke politics. This is necessary, because the authoritarian Left hasn't just captured most of our major institutions, they've closed the doors behind them. It would be nice if real conservatives wrote regularly at *The New York Times* or *The Atlantic*, but that seems like a pipe dream. Exclusion is the order of the day.

In shutting the doors of our most powerful institutions, the authoritarian Left has left those of us outside with one option: build it ourselves.

The outcome, unfortunately, will be a completely divided America. We might patronize different coffee brands, wear different shoes, subscribe to different streaming services. Our points of commonality might disappear.

That's not our preferred outcome. But it may be the most realistic outcome: two separate Americas, divided by politics.

None of these options are mutually exclusive. In fact, all of them should be pursued simultaneously. Our institutions must be opened up again. If they aren't, the social fabric of the country will continue to disintegrate.

FOR OUR CHILDREN

These days, I find myself worried for America on a bone-deep level.

I grew up in an America that made room for different points of view, an America that could tolerate political differences. I grew up in an America where we could attend ball games together without worrying about who voted for whom, where we could attend different schools and recognize our differences without trying to beat each other into submission. I grew up in an America where we could make the occasional offensive joke—and then apologize for it—and not have to worry about our livelihoods being stolen, because we all understood that we were human. Most of all, I grew up in an America where we could all participate in a search for truth, without fear that the mere searching would end in our societal excommunication.

That America is simply disappearing.

And that scares me for my kids.

I'm afraid that by the time they become adults, they'll take their lack of freedom for granted. I'm afraid that they'll already know not to speak out, because they'll have seen too many others lose their heads for doing so. I'm afraid that they won't explore interesting and diverse ideas, because to do so might mean social ostracizing or career suicide.

It's my job to protect my kids from this authoritarian culture. But as the institutions of America mobilize against families like yours and mine, we lose options.

What happens if my kids are *required* to reject my values—to dishonor their father and mother, the tradition they've been taught—as a ticket into approved society?

What happens if my kids are told they can't speak truth about the nature of the world—and what happens if I fight back against the un-truth?

What happens if I lose my job tomorrow because the authoritarian mob puts a target on my back?

Millions of Americans are asking these questions. Tens of millions. *Most of us.*

That's the problem. But that's also the solution.

The authoritarian moment relies on the acquiescence of a silent majority.

We must no longer be silent.

When we stand up to the institutional dominance of an intransigent minority of Americans; when we announce that our values matter, that our ideas matter; when we speak out together, recognizing the diversity of our politics but cherishing our common belief in the power of liberty—the authoritarian moment finally ends.

And a new birth of freedom begins.

ACKNOWLEDGMENTS

Every book is the work of dozens, not merely the author. That's certainly true of this book, too. To that end, thank you to Eric Nelson, my intrepid editor at HarperCollins, whose good humor, bravery, and nuanced thinking help me hone my own thinking and writing.

Thanks to my business partners, Jeremy Boreing and Caleb Robinson—both of them brilliant businessmen, true friends, and the guys with whom you'd want to walk into battle. Thanks to the entire staff at the Daily Wire, without whom our movement would be utterly debilitated, whose hard work makes my own possible, and whose constant sense of mischief enlivens every day and reminds me that the culture war is supposed to be fun. Thanks to our partners at Westwood One, who don't just help us keep the lights on but stand with us when the going gets tough. Thanks to my longtime syndicators at Creators Syndicate, who discovered me two decades ago and have stood by that odd and incredible decision ever since.

Thanks to my parents, who are bulwarks for our family and for me personally, whose first response is always "How can we help?," and who instilled in me the values I hope to pass on to my children.

Speaking of which, thanks to my kids: my inspiration, my joy, and the source of my lack of sleep. Their hilarity, inventiveness, and imagination never fail to amaze.

Finally, thanks to my wife, who isn't just the world's greatest mom but the only person in the world with whom I'd want to forge forth on this adventure of a lifetime. I'm so glad I asked. And I'm more ecstatic every single day you said yes.

NOTES

INTRODUCTION

1. Jonathan Chait, "Trump Authoritarianism Denial Is Over Now," NYMag.com, January 12, 2021, https://nymag.com/intelligencer/article/trump-authoritarianism -capitol-insurrection-mob-coup.html.

2. Paul Krugman, "This Putsch Was Decades in the Making," NYTimes.com, January 11, 2021, https://www.nytimes.com/2021/01/11/opinion/republicans -democracy.html.

3. Greg Sargent, "Trump's GOP has an ugly authoritarian core. A new poll exposes it," WashingtonPost.com, January 15, 2021, https://www.washingtonpost.com /opinions/2021/01/15/new-poll-trump-gop-approval-authoritarian/.

4. Lisa McGirr, "Trump Is the Republican Party's Past and Its Future," NYTimes .com, January 13, 2021, https://www.nytimes.com/2021/01/13/opinion/gop-trump .html.

5. CNN, January 14, 2021, https://twitter.com/tomselliott/status/13496726444 55575554.

6. Charles M. Blow, "Trump's Lackeys Must Also Be Punished," NYTimes .com, January 10, 2021, https://www.nytimes.com/2021/01/10/opinion/trump -republicans.html.

7. Joseph Wulfsohn, "MSNBC's Joy Reid suggests GOP needs a 'de-Baathification' to rid support for Trump," FoxNews.com, January 15, 2021, https://www.foxnews .com/media/msnbcs-joy-reid-suggests-gop-needs-a-de-baathification-to-rid -support-for-trump.

8. 1 Samuel 8:7–20.

9. James Madison, *Federalist No. 10* (November 22, 1787).

10. John Adams, *The Political Writings of John Adams* (Washington, DC: Regnery, 2000), 13.

11. Theodor Adorno, Else Frenkel-Brenswik, Daniel J. Levinson, and R. Nevitt Sanford, *The Authoritarian Personality* (London: Verso, 2019).

12. Bob Altemeyer, *The Authoritarian Specter* (Cambridge, MA: Harvard University Press, 1996), 13–15.

13. Ibid., 216.

14. Ibid., 220–21.

15. Ronald Bailey, "Tracking Down the Elusive Left-Wing Authoritarian," Reason.com, March 8, 2018, https://reason.com/2018/03/08/tracking-down-the-elusive-leftwing-autho/.

16. Thomas H. Costello, Shauna M. Bowes, Sean T. Stevens, Irwin D. Waldman, Arber Tasimi, and Scott O. Lilienfeld, "Clarifying the Structure and Nature of Left-Wing Authoritarianism," ResearchGate, May 11, 2020, https://www.researchgate.net/publication/341306723_Clarifying_the_Structure_and_Nature_of_Left-Wing_Authoritarianism.

17. Herbert Marcuse, "Repressive Tolerance" (1965), https://www.marcuse.org/herbert/pubs/60spubs/65repressivetolerance.htm.

18. Theodor Adorno and Herbert Marcuse, *Correspondence on the German Student Movement*, February 14, 1969, to August 6, 1969, https://hutnyk.files.wordpress.com/2013/06/adornomarcuse_germannewleft.pdf.

19. https://twitter.com/Mike_Pence/status/1346879811151605762.

20. Elliott C. McLaughlin, "Violence at Capitol and beyond reignites a debate over America's long-held defense of extremist speech," CNN.com, January 19, 2021, https://www.cnn.com/2021/01/19/us/capitol-riots-speech-hate-extremist-first-amendment/index.html?utm_content=2021-01-19T14%3A35%3A03&utm_source=twCNN&utm_term=link&utm_medium=social.

21. https://twitter.com/nhannahjones/status/1348382948005982208.

22. Max Boot, "Trump couldn't have incited sedition without the help of Fox News," WashingtonPost.com, January 18, 2021, https://www.washingtonpost.com/opinions/2021/01/18/trump-couldnt-have-incited-sedition-without-help-fox-news/.

23. Judd Legum and Tesnim Zekeria, "Major corporations say they will stop donating to members of Congress who tried to overturn the election," Popular.info, January 10, 2021, https://popular.info/p/three-major-corporations-say-they.

24. Elizabeth A. Harris and Alexandra Alter, "Simon & Schuster Cancels Plans for Senator Hawley's Book," NYTimes.com, January 7, 2021, https://www.nytimes.com/2021/01/07/books/simon-schuster-josh-hawley-book.html.

25. Jazz Shaw, "The Cancel Culture Comes for Elise Stefanik," HotAir.com, January 13, 2021, https://hotair.com/archives/jazz-shaw/2021/01/13/cancel-culture-comes-elise-stefanik/.

26. Jordan Davidson, "The Biggest Gun Forum on the Planet Was Just Kicked Off the Internet Without Explanation," TheFederalist.com, January 12, 2021, https://thefederalist.com/2021/01/12/the-biggest-gun-forum-on-the-planet-was-just-kicked-off-the-internet-without-explanation/.

27. Brian Fung, "Parler has now been booted by Amazon, Apple and Google," CNN .com, January 11, 2021, https://www.cnn.com/2021/01/09/tech/parler-suspended -apple-app-store/index.html.

28. https://twitter.com/tomselliott/status/1351140855478947844.

29. Robby Soave, "No, AOC, It's Not the Government's Job to 'Rein in Our Media,'" Reason.com, January 14, 2021, https://reason.com/2021/01/14/aoc-rein-in-our -media-literacy-trump-capitol-rots/.

30. https://twitter.com/coribush/status/1346985140912844805.

31. Senator Ron Wyden, "The Capitol riots prove we need to strengthen our democracy. That begins with voting rights," NBCNews.com, January 11, 2021, https:// www.nbcnews.com/think/opinion/capitol-riots-prove-we-need-strengthen-our -democracy-begins-voting-ncna1253642.

32. Eric Lutz, "Clyburn compares GOP bowing to Trump to Nazi Germany," Vanity Fair.com, March 13, 2020, https://www.vanityfair.com/news/2020/03/clyburn -compares-gop-bowing-to-trump-to-nazi-nazi-germany.

33. "Representative Clyburn: Biden Should Use Executive Authority if the Other Side Refuses to Cooperate," Grabien.com, January 18, 2021, https://grabien.com/story .php?id=321515.

34. Emily Ekins, "Poll: 62% of Americans Say They Have Political Views They're Afraid to Share," CATO.org, July 22, 2020, https://www.cato.org/publications /survey-reports/poll-62-americans-say-they-have-political-views-theyre-afraid -share.

35. https://twitter.com/MarkDuplass/status/1019946917176881152?ref_src=twsrc %5Etfw%7Ctwcamp%5Etweetembed%7Ctwterm%5E1019946917176881152%7Ctwgr %5E%7Ctwcon%5Es1_&ref_url=https%3A%2F%2Fwww.vox.com%2Fpolicy-and -politics%2F2018%2F7%2F19%2F17593174%2Fmark-duplass-ben-shapiro-apology.

36. Zack Beauchamp, "Actor Mark Duplass apologizes for praising conservative pundit Ben Shapiro," Vox.com, July 19, 2018, https://www.vox.com/policy-and -politics/2018/7/19/17593174/mark-duplass-ben-shapiro-apology.

37. Alexis de Tocqueville, *Democracy in America* (Chicago: University of Chicago Press, 2000), 244–45, trans. Harvey C. Mansfield and Delba Winthrop.

38. Jim VandeHei, "Our new reality: Three Americas," Axios.com, January 10, 2021, https://www.axios.com/capitol-siege-misinformation-trump-d9c9738b-0852-408d -a24f-81c95938b41b.html?stream=top.

CHAPTER 1: HOW TO SILENCE A MAJORITY

1. Eric Kaufman, "Who are the real Shy Trumpers?," Unherd.com, November 6, 2020, https://unherd.com/2020/11/meet-the-shy-trumpers/.

2. Thomas Piketty, "Thomas Piketty on Trump: 'The main lesson for Europe and the world is clear,'" BusinessInsider.com, November 16, 2016, https://www.business insider.com/thomas-piketty-on-trump-the-main-lesson-for-europe-and-the-world -is-clear-2016-11.

3. Nate Cohn, "The Election's Big Twist: The Racial Gap Is Shrinking," NYTimes

.com, October 28, 2020, https://www.nytimes.com/2020/10/28/upshot/election
-polling-racial-gap.html.

4. Russell Kirk, "Ten Conservative Principles," KirkCenter.org, https://kirkcenter
.org/conservatism/ten-conservative-principles/.

5. Leviticus 19:17.

6. Roger Scruton, *The West and the Rest: Globalization and the Terrorist Threat* (New-
buryport, MA: Intercollegiate Studies Institute, 2014).

7. Joel Feinberg, *Offense to Others: The Moral Limits of the Criminal Law* (New York:
Oxford University Press, 1985).

8. https://twitter.com/marcatracy/status/1357804321421881348.

9. Nassem Nicholas Taleb, *Skin in the Game: Hidden Asymmetries in Daily Life* (New
York: Random House, 2018), 75–77.

10. Rachel Brazil, "The physics of public opinion," Physicsworld.com, January 14,
2020, https://physicsworld.com/a/the-physics-of-public-opinion/.

11. Christina Zhao, "Coca-Cola, Facing Backlash, Says 'Be Less White' Learning
Plan Was About Workplace Inclusion," Newsweek.com, February 21, 2021, https://
www.newsweek.com/coca-cola-facing-backlash-says-less-white-learning-plan
-was-about-workplace-inclusion-1570875.

12. "ACLU Case Selection Guidelines: Conflicts Between Competing Values or Priorities," WSJ.com, June 21, 2018, http://online.wsj.com/public/resources/documents
/20180621ACLU.pdf?mod=article_inline.

13. "A Letter on Justice and Open Debate," *Harper's Weekly*, July 7, 2020, https://
harpers.org/a-letter-on-justice-and-open-debate/.

14. Conor Friedersdorf, "Why Matthew Yglesias Left Vox," TheAtlantic.com, November 13, 2020, https://www.theatlantic.com/ideas/archive/2020/11/substack
-and-medias-groupthink-problem/617102/.

15. "Read Joe Biden's President-Elect Acceptance Speech: Full Transcript," NY
Times.com, November 9, 2020, https://www.nytimes.com/article/biden-speech
-transcript.html.

16. Ryan Saavedra, "Michelle Obama Demonizes 70 Million Americans Who Voted
for Trump: Support 'Hate, Chaos, Division,'" DailyWire.com, November 7, 2020,
https://www.dailywire.com/news/michelle-obama-demonizes-70-million-americans
-who-voted-for-trump-support-hate-chaos-division.

17. Editorial Board, "Canceling Trump Alumni," WSJ.com, November 9, 2020,
https://www.wsj.com/articles/canceling-trump-alumni-11604962923.

18. Harriet Alexander, "Lincoln Project urges 2.7m followers to bombard law first
trying to overturn Pennsylvania election result," Independent.co.uk, November 10,
2020, https://www.independent.co.uk/news/world/americas/us-election-2020
/lincoln-project-election-pennsylvania-law-firm-linkedin-b1720710.html.

19. Laura Barron-Lopez and Holly Otterbein, "Tlaib lashes out at centrist Dems over
election debacle: 'I can't be silent,'" Politico.com, November 10, 2020, https://www
.politico.com/news/2020/11/11/rashida-tlaib-progressives-election-435877.

20. Memo from New Deal Srategies, Justice Democrats, Sunrise Movement, Data for

Progress re: What Went Wrong for Congressional Democrats in 2020, November 10, 2020, https://www.politico.com/f/?id=00000175-b4b4-dc7f-a3fd-bdf660490000.

CHAPTER 2: HOW THE AUTHORITARIAN LEFT RENORMALIZED AMERICA

1. Josh Bivens, "Inadequate GDP growth continues in the third quarter," Economic Policy Institute, October 26, 2012, https://www.epi.org/publication/gdp-growth-picture-october-2012/.

2. "President Exit Polls," *New York Times*, https://www.nytimes.com/elections/2012/results/president/exit-polls.html.

3. Barack Obama, *The Audacity of Hope* (New York: Crown, 2006), 11.

4. Ronald J. Pestritto, ed., *Woodrow Wilson: The Essential Political Writings* (Lanham, MD: Rowman & Littlefield, 2005), 77–78.

5. John R. Shook and James A. Good, *John Dewey's Philosophy of Spirit, with the 1897 Lecture on Hegel* (New York: Fordham University Press, 2010), 29.

6. Erick Trickey, "When America's Most Prominent Socialist Was Jailed for Speaking Out Against World War I," Smithsonianmag.com, June 15, 2018, https://www.smithsonianmag.com/history/fiery-socialist-challenged-nations-role-wwi-180969386/.

7. *Buck v. Bell* (1927), 274 US 200.

8. Margaret Sanger, "My Way to Peace," January 17, 1932, https://www.nyu.edu/projects/sanger/webedition/app/documents/show.php?sangerDoc=12 9037.xml.

9. Calvin Coolidge, "Speech on the 150th Anniversary of the Declaration of Independence," July 5, 1926, https://teachingamericanhistory.org/library/document/speech-on-the-occasion-of-the-one-hundred-and-fiftieth-anniversary-of-the-declaration-of-independence/.

10. Franklin D. Roosevelt, "Campaign Address," October 14, 1936, https://teachingamericanhistory.org/library/document/campaign-address/.

11. Franklin D. Roosevelt, "State of the Union Message to Congress," January 11, 1944, http://www.fdrlibrary.marist.edu/archives/address_text.html.

12. Jonah Goldberg, *Liberal Fascism: The Secret History of the American Left, from Mussolini to the Politics of Change* (New York: Broadway Books, 2007), 158–59.

13. Samuel Staley, "FDR Policies Doubled the Length of the Great Depression," Reason.org, November 21, 2008, https://reason.org/commentary/fdr-policies-doubled-the-lengt/.

14. Amity Shlaes, *Great Society: A New History* (New York: Harper Perennial, 2019).

15. Alan Greenspan and Adrian Woolridge, *Capitalism in America: A History* (New York: Penguin, 2018), 306.

16. Alex J. Pollock, "Seven decades of inflation-adjusted Dow Jones industrial average," RStreet.org, April 18, 2018, https://www.rstreet.org/2018/04/18/seven-decades-of-the-inflation-adjusted-dow-jones-industrial-average/.

17. Jimmy Carter, "Energy and the National Goals," July 15, 1979, https://www.americanrhetoric.com/speeches/jimmycartercrisisofconfidence.htm.

18. First Inaugural Address of Ronald Reagan, January 20, 1981, https://avalon.law.yale.edu/20th_century/reagan1.asp.

19. President William Jefferson Clinton, State of the Union Address, January 23, 1996, https://clintonwhitehouse4.archives.gov/WH/New/other/sotu.html.

20. George W. Bush, "Full Text of Bush's Acceptance Speech," NYTimes.com, August 4, 2000, https://movies2.nytimes.com/library/politics/camp/080400wh-bush-speech.html.

21. "Barack Obama's Remarks to the Democratic National Convention," July 24, 2004, https://www.nytimes.com/2004/07/27/politics/campaign/barack-obamas-remarks-to-the-democratic-national.html.

22. Rolf Wiggershaus, *The Frankfurt School: Its History, Theories, and Political Significance* (Cambridge, MA: MIT Press, 1995), 135.

23. Erich Fromm, *Escape from Freedom* (New York: Henry Holt, 1941), 240.

24. Herbert Marcuse, "Repressive Tolerance" (1965), https://www.marcuse.org/herbert/pubs/60spubs/65repressivetolerance.htm.

25. Stokely Carmichael, "Toward Black Liberation," *Massachusetts Review*, Autumn 1966, http://nationalhumanitiescenter.org/pds/maai3/segregation/text8/carmichael.pdf.

26. Richard Delgado and Jean Stefancic, *Critical Race Theory: An Introduction* (New York: New York University Press, 2012), 7–8.

27. Derrick A. Bell Jr., "Racial Realism," in George Wright and Maria Stalzer Wyant Cuzzo, eds., *The Legal Studies Reader* (New York: Peter Lang, 2004), 247.

28. Fred A. Bernstein, "Derrick Bell, Law Professor and Rights Advocate, Dies at 80," *New York Times*, October 6, 2011, https://www.nytimes.com/2011/10/06/us/derrick-bell-pioneering-harvard-law-professor-dies-at-80.html.

29. Christopher Caldwell, *The Age of Entitlement* (New York: Simon & Schuster, 2020), 6–7.

30. Ibid., 10.

31. Ibid., 34.

32. David Mills, "Sister Souljah's Call to Arms: The rapper says the riots were payback. Are you paying attention?," *Washington Post*, May 13, 1992, https://www.washingtonpost.com/wp-dyn/content/article/2010/03/31/AR2010033101709.html.

33. Thomas B. Edsall, "Clinton Stuns Rainbow Coalition," *Washington Post*, July 14, 1992, https://www.washingtonpost.com/archive/politics/1992/06/14/clinton-stuns-rainbow-coalition/02d7564f-5472-4081-b6b2-2fe5b849fa60/.

34. Rashawn Ray and William A. Galston, "Did the 1994 crime bill cause mass incarceration?," Brookings Institution, August 28, 2020, https://www.brookings.edu/blog/fixgov/2020/08/28/did-the-1994-crime-bill-cause-mass-incarceration/.

35. "Barack Obama's Remarks to the Democratic National Convention," July 24, 2004, https://www.nytimes.com/2004/07/27/politics/campaign/barack-obamas-remarks-to-the-democratic-national.html.

36. Jonathan V. Last, "Michelle's America," *Weekly Standard*, February 18, 2008, https://www.washingtonexaminer.com/weekly-standard/michelles-america.

37. Victor Davis Hanson, "Obama: Transforming America," RealClearPolitics.com,

October 1, 2013, https://www.realclearpolitics.com/articles/2013/10/01/obama _transforming_america_120170.html.

38. Ed Pilkington, "Obama angers midwest voters with guns and religion remark," TheGuardian.com, April 14, 2008, https://www.theguardian.com/world/2008/apr /14/barackobama.uselections2008.

39. Mark Preston and Dana Bash, "McCain defends charge that Obama playing race card," CNN.com, July 31, 2008, https://www.cnn.com/2008/POLITICS/07/31 /campaign.wrap/index.html.

40. Dan Merica, Kevin Liptak, Jeff Zeleny, David Wright, and Rebecca Buck, "Obama memoir confronts role his presidency played in Republican obstructionism and Trump's rise," CNN.com, November 15, 2020, https://www.cnn.com/2020/11/12 /politics/obama-memoir-promised-land/index.html.

41. Saul D. Alinsky, *Rules for Radicals: A Practical Primer for Revolution* (New York: Vintage Books, 1989), 184–86.

42. Kimberle Crenshaw, "Why intersectionality can't wait," *Washington Post*, September 24, 2015, https://www.washingtonpost.com/news/in-theory/wp/2015/09/24 /why- intersectionality-cant-wait/?noredirect=on&utm_term=.179ecf062277.

43. Josh Earnest, "President Obama Supports Same-Sex Marriage," ObamaWhite House.Archives.gov, May 10, 2012, https://obamawhitehouse.archives.gov/blog/2012 /05/10/obama-supports-same-sex-marriage.

44. Julia Preston and John H. Cushman Jr., "Obama to Permit Young Migrants to Remain in US," NYTimes.com, June 15, 2012, https://www.nytimes.com/2012/06/16 /us/us-to-stop-deporting-some-illegal-immigrants.html.

45. Shannon Travis, "Is Obama taking black vote for granted?," CNN.com, July 13, 2012, https://www.cnn.com/2012/07/12/politics/obama-black-voters/index .html.

46. Rodney Hawkins, "Biden tells African-American audience GOP ticket would put them 'back in chains,'" CBSNews.com, August 14, 2012, https://www.cbsnews .com/news/biden-tells-african-american-audience-gop-ticket-would-put-them -back-in-chains/.

47. Ewen MacAskill, "Obama steps up criticism of Romney in battle for women voters," TheGuardian.com, October 17, 2012, https://www.cbsnews.com/news/biden -tells-african-american-audience-gop-ticket-would-put-them-back-in-chains/.

48. Dan Balz, "Obama's coalition, campaign deliver a second term," WashingtonPost .com, November 7, 2012, https://www.washingtonpost.com/politics/decision2012 /obamas-coalition-campaign-deliver-a-second-term/2012/11/07/fb156970-2926 -11e2-96b6-8e6a7524553f_story.html.

49. Ruy Texiera and John Hapin, "The Return of the Obama Coalition," Center for American Progress, November 8, 2012, https://www.americanprogress.org/issues /democracy/news/2012/11/08/44348/the-return-of-the-obama-coalition/.

50. Yoni Appelbaum, "How America Ends," *Atlantic*, December 2019, https://www .theatlantic.com/magazine/archive/2019/12/how-america-ends/600757/.

51. Domenico Montanaro, "How the Browning of America Is Upending Both Political

Parties," NPR.org, October 12, 2016, https://www.npr.org/2016/10/12/497529936
/how-the-browning-of-america-is-upending-both-political-parties.

52. David Siders, Christopher Cadelago, and Laura Barron-Lopez, "To defeat
Trump, Dems rethink the Obama coalition formula," Politico.com, November 26,
2019, https://www.politico.com/news/2019/11/25/race-identity-democrats-2020
-electability-072959.

53. Matt Stevens, "Read Joe Biden's President-Elect Acceptance Speech: Full Text,"
NYTimes.com, November 9, 2020, https://www.nytimes.com/article/biden-speech
-transcript.html.

54. Byron York, July 15, 2020, https://twitter.com/ByronYork/status/1283372
233730203651?ref_src=twsrc%5Etfw%7Ctwcamp%5Etweetembed%7Ctwterm%5E1
283372233730203651%7Ctwgr%5E%7Ctwcon%5Es1_&ref_url=https%3A%2F%2F
www.foxnews.com%2Fus%2Fdc-museum-graphic-whiteness-race.

55. Ben Weingarten, "Would a President Joe Biden Institute Systemic Racism in
Our Legal System?," TheFederalist.com, October 22, 2020, https://thefederalist
.com/2020/10/22/would-a-president-joe-biden-institute-systemic-racism-in-our
-legal-system/.

56. Russell Vought, "Memorandum for the Heads of Executive Departments and
Agencies," September 4, 2020, https://www.whitehouse.gov/wp-content/uploads
/2020/09/M-20-34.pdf.

57. Ibram X. Kendi, "Pass an Anti-Racist Constitutional Amendment," Politico.com,
2019, https://www.politico.com/interactives/2019/how-to-fix-politics-in-america
/inequality/pass-an-anti-racist-constitutional-amendment/.

58. Sheryll Cashin, "A Blueprint for Racial Healing in the Biden Era," *Politico Magazine*, November 21, 2020, https://www.politico.com/news/magazine/2020/11/21
/biden-era-racial-healing-blueprint-438900.

59. Associated Press, "Spanberger to House Dems: Never 'use the word "socialist"
or "socialism" again,'" November 6, 2020, https://wjla.com/news/local/house
-democrats-blame-losses-on-polls-message-even-trump-11-06-2020.

60. Open Letter from New Deal Strategies, Justice Democrats, Sunrise Movement,
Data for Progress, November 10, 2020, https://www.politico.com/f/?id=00000175
-b4b4-dc7f-a3fd-bdf660490000.

CHAPTER 3: THE CREATION OF A NEW RULING CLASS

1. Graham Kates, "Lori Loughlin and Felicity Huffman among dozens charged in
college bribery scheme," CBSNews.com, March 12, 2019, https://www.cbsnews
.com/news/college-admissions-scandal-bribery-cheating-today-felicity-huffman
-arrested-fbi-2019-03-12/.

2. Kate Taylor, "By Turns Tearful and Stoic, Felicity Huffman Gets 14-Day Prison
Sentence," NYTimes.com, September 13, 2019, https://www.nytimes.com/2019
/09/13/us/felicity-huffman-sentencing.html.

3. Graham Kates, "Lori Loughlin and Felicity Huffman among dozens charged in
college bribery scheme," CBSNews.com, March 12, 2019, https://www.cbsnews

.com/news/college-admissions-scandal-bribery-cheating-today-felicity-huffman
-arrested-fbi-2019-03-12/.

4. Kate Taylor, "By Turns Tearful and Stoic, Felicity Huffman Gets 14-Day Prison Sentence," NYTimes.com, September 13, 2019, https://www.nytimes.com/2019 /09/13/us/felicity-huffman-sentencing.html.

5. Lisa Respers France, "Brands distance themselves from Lori Laughlin and daughter Olivia Jade," CNN.com, March 14, 2019, https://www.cnn.com/2019/03/14 /entertainment/olivia-jade-cheating-scandal/index.html.

6. Kerry Justich, "Celebrity kid called 'spoiled' and 'privileged brat' after saying she's going to college for 'game days' and 'partying,'" Yahoo.com, August 17, 2018, https://www.yahoo.com/lifestyle/celebrity-kid-called-spoiled-privileged-brat-saying -shes-going-college-game-days-partying-190101738.html.

7. "Percentage of the US population who have completed four years of college or more from 1940 to 2019, by gender," Statista.com, March 2020, https://www.statista .com/statistics/184272/educational-attainment-of-college-diploma-or-higher-by -gender/.

8. Joseph B. Fuller and Manjari Raman, "Dismissed by Degrees," Harvard Business School, October 2017, https://www.hbs.edu/managing-the-future-of-work/Documents /dismissed-by-degrees.pdf.

9. "Number of People with Master's and Doctoral Degrees Doubles Since 2000," Census.gov, February 21, 2019, https://www.census.gov/library/stories/2019/02 /number-of-people-with-masters-and-phd-degrees-double-since-2000.html#:~:text =Since%202000%2C%20the%20number%20of,from%208.6%20percent%20in%20 2000.

10. Connor Harris, "The Earning Curve: Variability and Overlap in Labor-Outcomes by Education Level," Manhattan Institute, February 26, 2020, https:// www.manhattan-institute.org/high-school-college-wage-gap?utm_source=press _release&utm_medium=email.

11. J. D. Vance, *Hillbilly Elegy: A Memoir of a Family and Culture in Crisis* (New York: HarperCollins, 2016).

12. Charles Murray, *Coming Apart* (New York: Crown Forum, 2012), 16–19.

13. Christopher Lasch, *The Revolt of the Elites and the Betrayal of Democracy* (New York: Norton, 1995), 6.

14. Joseph Epstein, "Is There a Doctor in the White House? Not if You Need an M.D.," WSJ.com, December 11, 2020, https://www.wsj.com/articles/is-there-a -doctor-in-the-white-house-not-if-you-need-an-m-d-11607727380.

15. Bryan Alexander, "Dr. Jill was blindsided by Wall Street Journal call to drop 'Dr.' title: 'It was really the tone of it,'" USAToday.com, December 17, 2020, https://www .usatoday.com/story/entertainment/tv/2020/12/17/jill-biden-speaks-out-wall -street-journal-column-drop-dr-title/3952529001/.

16. Paul A. Gigot, "The Biden Team Strikes Back," WSJ.com, December 13, 2020, https://www.wsj.com/articles/the-biden-team-strikes-back-11607900812.

17. Adam Harris, "America Is Divided by Education," *Atlantic*, November 7, 2018,

https://www.theatlantic.com/education/archive/2018/11/education-gap-explains
-american-politics/575113/.

18. Thomas Edsall, "Honestly, This Was a Weird Election," NYTimes.com, December 2, 2020, https://www.nytimes.com/2020/12/02/opinion/biden-trump
-moderates-progressives.html.

19. Helen Pluckrose and James Lindsay, *Cynical Theories* ([Durham, NC]: Pitchstone, 2020), 57.

20. Ibram X. Kendi, *How to Be an Antiracist* (New York: One World, 2019), 84.

21. Robin DiAngelo, *White Fragility* (Boston: Beacon Press, 2018), 17.

22. Ibram X. Kendi, "Pass an Anti-Racist Constitutional Amendment," Politico.com, 2019, https://www.politico.com/interactives/2019/how-to-fix-politics-in-america
/inequality/pass-an-anti-racist-constitutional-amendment/.

23. Ibram X. Kendi, *How to Be an Antiracist* (One World, 2019), 19.

24. Ibram X. Kendi, "A Battle Between the Two Souls of America," TheAtlantic
.com, November 11, 2020, https://www.theatlantic.com/ideas/archive/2020/11
/americas-two-souls/617062/.

25. Helen Pluckrose and James Lindsay, *Cynical Theories* ([Durham, NC]: Pitchstone, 2020), 210–11.

26. Richard Sosis and Candace Alcorta, "Signaling, Solidarity, and the Sacred: The Evolution of Religious Behavior," *Evolutionary Anthropology* 12 (2003): 264–74, http://sites.oxy.edu/clint/evolution/articles/SignalingSolidarityandtheSacredThe
EvolutionofReligiousBehavior.pdf.

27. Christopher Lasch, *The Revolt of the Elites and the Betrayal of Democracy* (New York: Norton, 1995), 21.

28. Mike McRae, "A Massive Hoax Involving 20 Fake Culture Studies Papers Just Exploded in Academia," ScienceAlert.com, October 4, 2018, https://www.sciencealert
.com/cultural-studies-sokal-squared-hoax-20-fake-papers.

29. Yascha Mounk, "What an Audacious Hoax Reveals About Academia," The Atlantic.com, October 5, 2018, https://www.theatlantic.com/ideas/archive/2018
/10/new-sokal-hoax/572212/.

30. Christine Emba, "The 'Sokal Squared' hoax sums up American politics," Washington Post.com, October 10, 2018, https://www.washingtonpost.com/opinions/what
-do-the-kavanaugh-confirmation-and-the-sokal-squared-hoax-have-in-common
/2018/10/10/f7efabf8-ccc6-11e8-a3e6-44daa3d35ede_story.html.

31. Heather Mac Donald, *The Diversity Delusion* (New York: St. Martin's, 2018), 2.

32. David Randall, "Social Justice Education in America," NAS.org, November 29, 2019, https://www.nas.org/reports/social-justice-education-in-america/full-report
#Preface&Acknowledgements.

33. O. Carter Snead, *What It Means to Be Human* (Cambridge, MA: Harvard University Press, 2020), 68–70.

34. Ibid., 84–85.

35. Helen Pluckrose and James Lindsay, *Cynical Theories* ([Durham, NC]: Pitchstone, 2020).

36. Roger Kimball, *The Long March* (New York: Encounter Books, 2000), 106–11.

37. Ibid., 112–18.

38. Shelby Steele, *White Guilt* (New York: HarperCollins, 2006).

39. Jon Street, "Less than 2 percent of Harvard faculty are conservative, survey finds," CampusReform.org, March 4, 2020, https://www.campusreform.org/?ID=14469.

40. Rachel Treisman and David Yaffe-Bellany, "Yale faculty skews liberal, survey shows," YaleDailyNews.com, September 14, 2017, https://yaledailynews.com/blog/2017/09/14/yale-faculty-skews-liberal-survey-shows/.

41. James Freeman, "Yale Prof Estimates Faculty Political Diversity at '0%,'" WSJ.com, December 9, 2019, https://yaledailynews.com/blog/2017/09/14/yale-faculty-skews-liberal-survey-shows/.

42. Jon Street, "STUDY: Profs donate to Dems over Republicans by 95:1 ratio," CampusReform.org, January 22, 2020, https://www.campusreform.org/?ID=14255.

43. Bradford Richardson, "Liberal professors outnumber conservatives nearly 12 to 1, study finds," WashingtonTimes.com, October 6, 2016, https://www.washingtontimes.com/news/2016/oct/6/liberal-professors-outnumber-conservatives-12-1/.

44. Jon A. Shields, "The Disappearing Conservative Professor," NationalAffairs.com, Fall 2018, https://www.nationalaffairs.com/publications/detail/the-disappearing-conservative-professor.

45. Nick Gillespie, "Would the ACLU Still Defend Nazis' Right to March in Skokie?," Reason.com, January 2021, https://reason.com/2020/12/20/would-the-aclu-still-defend-nazis-right-to-march-in-skokie/.

46. Scott Jaschik, "Who Defines What Is Racist?," InsideHigherEd.com, May 30, 2017, https://www.insidehighered.com/news/2017/05/30/escalating-debate-race-evergreen-state-students-demand-firing-professor.

47. Tom Knighton, "Leftists Storm Out of Lecture Over Claim Men, Women Have Different Bodies," PJMedia.com, March 16, 2018, https://pjmedia.com/news-and-politics/tom-knighton/2018/03/16/leftists-storm-lecture-claim-men-women-different-bodies-n56793.

48. Conor Friedersdorf, "The Perils of Writing a Provocative Email at Yale," The Atlantic.com, May 26, 2016, https://www.theatlantic.com/politics/archive/2016/05/the-peril-of-writing-a-provocative-email-at-yale/484418/.

49. Jon A. Shields, "The Disappearing Conservative Professor," NationalAffairs.com, Fall 2018, https://www.nationalaffairs.com/publications/detail/the-disappearing-conservative-professor.

50. Norimitsu Onishi, "Will American Ideas Tear France Apart? Some of Its Leaders Think So," NYTimes.com, February 9, 2021, https://www.nytimes.com/2021/02/09/world/europe/france-threat-american-universities.html?action=click&module=Top%20Stories&pgtype=Homepage.

51. Joseph B. Fuller and Manjari Raman, "Dismissed by Degrees," Harvard Business School, October 2017, https://www.hbs.edu/managing-the-future-of-work/Documents/dismissed-by-degrees.pdf.

CHAPTER 4: HOW SCIENCE™ DEFEATED ACTUAL SCIENCE

1. Adam Gabbatt, "US anti-lockdown rallies could cause surge in Covid-19 cases, experts warn," TheGuardian.com, April 20, 2020, https://www.theguardian.com /us-news/2020/apr/20/us-protests-lockdown-coronavirus-cases-surge-warning.

2. Michael Juliano, "Some LA parks are closing until further notice after a busy weekend on the trails," Timeout.com, March 22, 2020, https://www.timeout.com /los-angeles/news/some-l-a-parks-are-closing-until-further-notice-after-a-busy -weekend-on-the-trails-032220.

3. Bruce Ritchie and Alexandra Glorioso, "Florida won't close its beaches. Here's exactly what DeSantis said about that," Politico.com, March 19, 2020, https://www .politico.com/states/florida/story/2020/03/19/florida-wont-close-its-beaches -heres-exactly-what-desantis-said-about-that-1268185.

4. Heather Mac Donald, "The Myth of Systemic Police Racism," WSJ.com, June 2, 2020, https://www.wsj.com/articles/the-myth-of-systemic-police-racism-11591119883.

5. Larry Buchanan, Quoctrung Bui, and Jugal K. Patel, "Black Lives Matter May Be the Largest Movement in US History," NYTimes.com, July 3, 2020, https://www .nytimes.com/interactive/2020/07/03/us/george-floyd-protests-crowd-size.html.

6. Craig Mauger and James David Dickson, "With little social distancing, Whitmer marches with protesters," DetroitNews.com, June 4, 2020, https://www.detroitnews .com/story/news/local/michigan/2020/06/04/whitmer-appears-break-social -distance-rules-highland-park-march/3146244001/.

7. Jaclyn Cosgrove, Tania Ganguli, Julia Wick, Hailey Branson-Potts, Matt Hamilton, and Liam Dillon, "Mayor Garcetti takes a knee amid chants of 'Defund police!' at downtown LA protest," LATimes.com, June 2, 2020, https://www.latimes.com /california/story/2020-06-02/mayor-garcetti-takes-a-knee-amid-chants-of-defund -police-at-downtown-l-a-protest.

8. Vincent Barone, "NYC Black Lives Matter marches can continue despite large-event ban, de Blasio says," NYPost.com, July 9, 2020, https://nypost.com/2020/07/09 /nyc-allows-black-lives-matter-marches-despite-ban-on-large-events/.

9. Rachel Weiner, "Political and health leaders' embrace of Floyd protests fuels debate over coronavirus restrictions," WashingtonPost.com, June 11, 2020, https:// www.washingtonpost.com/health/political-and-health-leaders-embrace-of-floyd -protests-fuels-debate-over-coronavirus-restrictions/2020/06/11/9c60bca6-a761-11 ea-bb20-ebf0921f3bbd_story.html.

10. Julia Marcus and Gregg Gonsalves, "Public-Health Experts Are Not Hypocrites," TheAtlantic.com, June 11, 2020, https://www.theatlantic.com/ideas/archive /2020/06/public-health-experts-are-not-hypocrites/612853/.

11. Terrance Smith, "White coats and black lives: Health care workers say 'racism is a pandemic too,'" June 12, 2020, https://abcnews.go.com/Politics/white-coats-black -lives-health-care-workers-racism/story?id=71195580.

12. Michael Powell, "Are Protests Dangerous? What Experts Say May Depend on Who's Protesting What," NYTimes.com, July 6, 2020, https://www.nytimes.com /2020/07/06/us/Epidemiologists-coronavirus-protests-quarantine.html.

13. Joseph P. Williams, "Pandemic, Protests Cause Racism to Resonate as a Public Health Issue," USNews.com, July 8, 2020, https://www.usnews.com/news/healthiest-communities/articles/2020-07-08/racism-resonates-as-public-health-crisis-amid-pandemic-protests.

14. Isaac Scher, "NYC's contact tracers have been told not to ask people if they've attended a protest," BusinessInsider.com, June 15, 2020, https://www.businessinsider.com/nyc-contact-tracers-not-asking-people-attend-george-floyd-protest-2020-6.

15. "COVID-19 Hospitalization and Death by Age," CDC.gov, August 18, 2020, https://www.cdc.gov/coronavirus/2019-ncov/covid-data/investigations-discovery/hospitalization-death-by-age.html.

16. Yascha Mounk, "Why I'm Losing Trust in the Institutions," Persuasion.community, December 23, 2020, https://www.persuasion.community/p/why-im-losing-trust-in-the-institutions.

17. Abby Goodnough and Jan Hoffman, "The Elderly vs. Essential Workers: Who Should Get the Coronavirus Vaccine First?," NYTimes.com, December 5, 2020, https://www.nytimes.com/2020/12/05/health/covid-vaccine-first.html.

18. Yascha Mounk, "Why I'm Losing Trust in the Institutions," Persuasion.community, December 23, 2020, https://www.persuasion.community/p/why-im-losing-trust-in-the-institutions.

19. Stephen Pinker, *Enlightenment Now: The Case for Reason, Science, Humanism and Progress* (New York: Viking, 2018), 4

20. M. Collins, R. Knutti, J. Arblaster, J.-L. Dufresne, T. Fichefet, P. Friedlingstein, X. Gao, W. J. Gutowski, T. Johns, G. Krinner, M. Shongwe, C. Tebaldi, A. J. Weaver, and M. Wehner, "2013: Long-term Climate Change: Projections, Commitments and Irreversibility," in *Climate Change 2013: The Physical Science Basis. Contribution of Working Group I to the Fifth Assessment Report of the Intergovernmental Panel on Climate Change* (Cambridge and New York: Cambridge University Press, 2013), https://www.ipcc.ch/site/assets/uploads/2018/02/WG1AR5_Chapter12_FINAL.pdf.

21. Alan Buis, "Making Sense of 'Climate Sensitivity,'" Climate.NASA.gov, September 8, 2020, https://climate.nasa.gov/blog/3017/making-sense-of-climate-sensitivity/.

22. "Economics Nobel goes to inventor of models used in UN 1.5C report," Climate ChangeNews.com, October 8, 2018, https://www.climatechangenews.com/2018/10/08/economics-nobel-goes-inventor-models-used-un-1-5c-report/.

23. Paul Krugman, "The Depravity of Climate-Change Denial," NYTimes.com, November 26, 2018, https://www.nytimes.com/2018/11/26/opinion/climate-change-denial-republican.html.

24. Nicolas Loris, "Staying in Paris Agreement Would Have Cost Families $20K," Heritage.org, November 5, 2019, https://www.heritage.org/environment/commentary/staying-paris-agreement-would-have-cost-families-20k.

25. Michael Greshko, "Current Climate Pledges Aren't Enough to Stop Severe Warming," NationalGeographic.com, October 31, 2017, https://www.nationalgeographic.com/news/2017/10/paris-agreement-climate-change-usa-nicaragua-policy-environment/#close.

26. Kevin D. Dayaratna, PhD, and Nicolas D. Loris, "Assessing the Costs and Benefits of the Green New Deal's Energy Policies," Heritage.org, July 24, 2019, https://www.heritage.org/sites/default/files/2019-07/BG3427.pdf.

27. Helen Pluckrose and James Lindsay, *Cynical Theories* ([Durham, NC]: Pitchstone, 2020), 37.

28. Lawrence Krauss, "The Ideological Corruption of Science," WSJ.com, July 12, 2020, https://www.wsj.com/articles/the-ideological-corruption-of-science-1159457 2501?mod=article_inline.

29. Richard Haier, "No Voice at VOX: Sense and Nonsense about Discussing IQ and Race," Quillette.com, June 11, 2017, https://quillette.com/2017/06/11/no-voice-vox-sense-nonsense-discussing-iq-race/.

30. Lawrence H. Summers, "Remarks at NBER Conference on Diversifying the Science & Engineering Workforce," Office of the President of Harvard University, January 14, 2005, https://web.archive.org/web/20080130023006/http://www.president.harvard.edu/speeches/2005/nber.html.

31. Editorial Board, "Science Eats Its Own," WSJ.com, December 23, 2020, https://www.wsj.com/articles/science-eats-its-own-11608765409.

32. Ben Shapiro, "A Brown University Researcher Released a Study About Teens Imitating Their Peers by Turning Trans. The Left Went Insane. So Brown Caved," DailyWire.com, August 28, 2018, https://www.dailywire.com/news/brown-university-researcher-released-study-about-ben-shapiro.

33. Abigail Shrier, "Amazon Enforces 'Trans' Orthodox," WSJ.com, June 22, 2020, https://www.wsj.com/articles/amazon-enforces-trans-orthodoxy-11592865818.

34. Abigail Shrier, "Does the ACLU Want to Ban My Book?," WSJ.com, November 15, 2020, https://www.wsj.com/articles/does-the-aclu-want-to-ban-my-book-11605475898.

35. Kathleen Doheny, "Boy or Girl? Fetal DNA Tests Often Spot On," WebMD.com, August 9, 2011, https://www.webmd.com/baby/news/20110809/will-it-be-a-boy-or-girl-fetal-dna-tests-often-spot-on#1.

36. "AMA Adopts New Policies at 2018 Interim Meeting," AMA-Assn.org, November 13, 2018, https://www.ama-assn.org/press-center/press-releases/ama-adopts-new-policies-2018-interim-meeting.

37. "AMA Adopts New Policies During First Day of Voting at Interim Meeting," American Medical Association, November 19, 2019, https://www.ama-assn.org/press-center/press-releases/ama-adopts-new-policies-during-first-day-voting-interim-meeting.

38. Vadim M. Shteyler, M.D., Jessica A. Clarke, J.D., and Eli Y. Adashi, M.D., "Failed Assignments—Rethinking Sex Designations on Birth Certificates," NEJM .org, December 17, 2020, https://www.nejm.org/doi/full/10.1056/NEJMp2025974.

39. Lawrence Krauss, "The Ideological Corruption of Science," WSJ.com, July 12, 2020, https://www.wsj.com/articles/the-ideological-corruption-of-science-115945 72501?mod=article_inline.

40. "An Open Letter to the Communications of the ACM," December 29, 2020,

https://docs.google.com/document/d/1-KM6yc416Gh1wue92DHReoyZqheIaIM 23fkz0KwOpkw/edit.

41. "Yann LeCun Quits Twitter Amid Acrimonious Exchanges on AI Bias," Synced Review.com, June 30, 2020, https://syncedreview.com/2020/06/30/yann-lecun -quits-twitter-amid-acrimonious-exchanges-on-ai-bias/.

42. Bridget Balch, "Curing health care of racism: Nikole Hannah-Jones and Ibram X. Kendi, PhD, call on institutions to foster change," AAMC.org, November 17, 2020, https://www.aamc.org/news-insights/curing-health-care-racism-nikole-hannah -jones-and-ibram-x-kendi-phd-call-institutions-foster-change.

43. Heather Mac Donald, "How Identity Politics Is Harming the Sciences," City -Journal.org, Spring 2018, https://www.city-journal.org/html/how-identity-politics -harming-sciences-15826.html.

44. Philip Ball, "Prejudice persists," ChemistryWorld.com, June 9, 2020, https:// www.chemistryworld.com/opinion/viewing-science-as-a-meritocracy-allows -prejudice-to-persist/4011923.article.

45. Katrina Kramer, "*Angewandte* essay calling diversity in chemistry harmful de-cried as 'abhorrent,' 'egregious,'" ChemistryWorld.com, June 9, 2020, https://www .chemistryworld.com/news/angewandte-essay-calling-diversity-in-chemistry -harmful-decried-as-abhorrent-and-egregious/4011926.article.

46. Editors, "*Scientific American* Endorses Joe Biden," *Scientific American*, October 1, 2020, https://www.scientificamerican.com/article/scientific-american-endorses-joe -biden1/.

47. Editorial, "Why Nature supports Joe Biden for US president," Nature.com, October 14, 2020, https://www.nature.com/articles/d41586-020-02852-x?utm _source=twitter&utm_medium=social&utm_content=organic&utm_campaign =NGMT_USG_JC01_GL_Nature.

48. Editors, "Dying in a Leadership Vacuum," *New England Journal of Medicine*, Oc-tober 8, 2020, https://www.nejm.org/doi/full/10.1056/NEJMe2029812.

CHAPTER 5: YOUR AUTHORITARIAN BOSS

1. Alma Cohen, Moshe Hazan, Roberto Tallarita, and David Weiss, "The Politics of CEOs," National Bureau of Economic Research, May 2019, https://www.nber.org /system/files/working_papers/w25815/w25815.pdf.

2. Doug McMillon, "Advancing Our Work on Racial Equity," Walmart.com, June 12, 2020, https://corporate.walmart.com/newsroom/2020/06/12/advancing-our-work -on-racial-equity.

3. Rachel Lerman and Todd C. Frenkel, "Retailers and restaurants across the US close their doors amid protests," WashingtonPost.com, June 1, 2020, https://www .washingtonpost.com/technology/2020/06/01/retailers-restaurants-across-us-close -their-doors-amid-protests/.

4. Tim Cook, "Speaking up on racism," Apple.com, https://www.apple.com/speaking -up-on-racism/.

5. Mitchell Schnurman, "'Silence is not an option': What CEOs are saying about

racial violence in America," DallasNews.com, June 7, 2020, https://www.dallasnews .com/business/commentary/2020/06/07/silence-is-not-an-option-what-ceos-are -saying-about-racial-violence-in-america/.

6. "Addressing racial injustice," Microsoft.com, June 23, 2020, https://blogs.micro soft.com/blog/2020/06/23/addressing-racial-injustice/.

7. Joseph Guzman, "Netflix pledges $100 million to support Black communities in the US," Thehill.com, June 30, 2020, https://thehill.com/changing-america/respect /equality/505229-netflix-pledges-100-million-to-support-black-communities-in.

8. Mitchell Schnurman, "'Silence is not an option': What CEOs are saying about ra- cial violence in America," DallasNews.com, June 7, 2020, https://www.dallasnews .com/business/commentary/2020/06/07/silence-is-not-an-option-what-ceos-are -saying-about-racial-violence-in-america/.

9. https://twitter.com/gushers/status/1269110304086114304.

10. Katie Canales, "A 'handful' of Cisco employees were fired after posting offensive comments objecting to the company's support of the Black Lives Matter movement," BusinessInsider.com, July 17, 2020, https://www.businessinsider.com/cisco-employ ees-fired-racist-comments-black-lives-matter-2020-7.

11. Associated Press, "Sacramento Kings broadcaster Grant Napear fired after 'all lives matter' tweet," DetroitNews.com, June 3, 2020, https://www.detroitnews .com/story/sports/nba/pistons/2020/06/03/sacramento-kings-broadcaster-grant -napear-out-after-all-lives-matter-tweet/3132629001/.

12. Vandana Rambaran, "Dean fired after saying 'BLACK LIVES MATTER, but also, EVERYONE'S LIFE MATTERS' in email," FoxNews.com, July 2, 2020, https://www.foxnews.com/us/dean-fired-after-saying-black-lives-matter-but-also -everyones-life-matters-in-email.

13. Dunja Djudjic, "B&H Employee 'removed' after publicly opposing Black Lives Matter movement," DIYPhotography.net, June 11, 2020, https://www.diypho tography.net/bh-employee-removed-after-publicly-opposing-black-lives-matter -movement/.

14. Jemimi McEvoy, "Every CEO and Leader That Stepped Down Since Black Lives Matter Protests Began," Forbes.com, July 1, 2020, https://www.forbes.com/sites /jemimamcevoy/2020/07/01/every-ceo-and-leader-that-stepped-down-since-black -lives-matter-protests-began/?sh=595688765593.

15. Brad Polumbo, 'Is Black Lives Matter Marxist? No and Yes," FEE.org, July 7, 2020, https://fee.org/articles/is-black-lives-matter-marxist-no-and-yes/.

16. Alyssa Newcomb, "How to delete old tweets before they come back to haunt you," NBCNews.com, August 3, 2018, https://www.nbcnews.com/tech/tech-news/how -delete-old-tweets-they-come-back-haunt-you-n896546.

17. Christopher Caldwell, *The Age of Entitlement* (New York: Simon & Schuster, 2020), 169.

18. "#BrandsGetReal: What consumers want from brands in a divided society," SproutSocial.com, November 2018, https://sproutsocial.com/insights/data/social -media-connection/.

19. James R. Bailey and Hillary Phillips, "How Do Consumers Feel When Companies Get Political?," HBR.org, February 17, 2020, https://hbr.org/2020/02/how-do-consumers-feel-when-companies-get-political.

20. Alexander Osipovich and Akane Otani, "Nasdaq Seeks Board-Diversity Rule That Most Listed Firms Don't Meet," WSJ.com, December 1, 2020, https://www.wsj.com/articles/nasdaq-proposes-board-diversity-rule-for-listed-companies-11606829244.

21. Klaus Schwab, "A Better Economy Is Possible. But We Need to Reimagine Capitalism to Do It," Time.com, October 22, 2020, https://time.com/collection/great-reset/5900748/klaus-schwab-capitalism/.

22. Jesse Pound, "Biden says investors 'don't need me,' calls for end of 'era of shareholder capitalism,'" CNBC.com, July 9, 2020, https://www.cnbc.com/2020/07/09/biden-says-investors-dont-need-me-calls-for-end-of-era-of-shareholder-capitalism.html.

23. Biz Carson, "Expensify's CEO emailed users to encourage them to 'vote for Biden,'" Protocol.com, October 22, 2020, https://www.protocol.com/bulletins/expensifys-ceo-emailed-all-of-his-users-to-encourage-them-to-protect-democracy-vote-for-biden.

24. Robin DiAngelo, *White Fragility* (Boston: Beacon Press, 2018).

25. Benjamin Zeisloft, "UConn agrees to pay 'White Fragility' author $20k for 3.5 hour anti-racism lecture," CampusReform.org, August 12, 2019, https://www.campusreform.org/?ID=15430.

26. Edward H. Chang et al., "Does Diversity Training Work the Way It's Supposed To?," *Harvard Business Review*, July 9, 2019, https://hbr.org/2019/07/does-diversity-training-work-the-way-its-supposed-to.

27. Frank Dobbin and Alexandra Kalev, "Why Diversity Programs Fail," *Harvard Business Review*, July–August 2016, https://hbr.org/2016/07/why-diversity-programs-fail.

28. Pamela Newkirk, "Diversity Has Become a Booming Business. So Where Are the Results?," Time.com, October 19, 2019, https://time.com/5696943/diversity-business/.

29. Emily Heil, "The Goya boycott could impact the brand, experts say—just not the way you think," WashingtonPost.com, July 28, 2020, https://www.washingtonpost.com/news/voraciously/wp/2020/07/28/the-goya-boycott-could-impact-the-brand-experts-say-just-not-the-way-you-think/.

30. Meera Jagannathan, "Equinox could experience lasting damage from the anti-Trump boycott, despite other companies escaping unscathed," Marketwatch.com, August 14, 2019, https://www.marketwatch.com/story/equinox-could-experience-lasting-damage-from-the-anti-trump-boycott-while-other-companies-have-escaped-unscathed-2019-08-13.

31. Steven Overly and Laura Kayali, "The moment of reckoning for the Facebook advertiser boycott," Politico.com, July 29, 2020, https://www.politico.com/news/2020/07/29/facebook-advertiser-boycott-zuckerberg-385622.

32. "Do Boycotts Work?," Northwestern Institute for Policy Research, March 28, 2017, https://www.ipr.northwestern.edu/news/2017/king-corporate-boycotts.html.

33. Noorie Malik, "New Consumer Alert on Yelp Takes Firm Stance Against Racism," Yelp.com, October 8, 2020, https://blog.yelp.com/2020/10/new-consumer-alert-on-yelp-takes-firm-stance-against-racism.

34. Emery P. Dalesio and Jonathan Drew, "Exclusive: 'Bathroom bill' to cost North Carolina $3.75B," APNews.com, March 30, 2017, https://apnews.com/article/e6c7a15d2e16452c8dcbc2756fd67b44.

35. Peter O'Dowd, "Cities, Businesses Boycott Arizona Over New Law," NPR.org, May 4, 2010, https://www.npr.org/templates/story/story.php?storyId=126486651.

36. Lisa Richwine, "Disney CEO says it will be 'difficult' to film in Georgia if abortion law takes effect," Reuters.com, May 29, 2019, https://www.reuters.com/article/us-usa-abortion-walt-disney-exclusive/disney-ceo-says-it-will-be-difficult-to-film-in-georgia-if-abortion-law-takes-effect-idUSKCN1T003X.

37. Kevin Dugan, "Credit cards are clamping down on payments to hate groups," NYPost.com, August 16, 2017, https://nypost.com/2017/08/16/credit-cards-are-clamping-down-on-payments-to-hate-groups/.

38. Associated Press, "First National Bank of Omaha drops NRA credit card," CBSNews.com, February 22, 2018, https://www.cbsnews.com/news/first-national-bank-of-omaha-drops-nra-credit-card/.

39. Chase Purdy, "Even America's worst airline couldn't stomach the National Rifle Association," QZ.com, February 24, 2018, https://qz.com/1215137/the-nra-loses-the-support-of-united-americas-most-hated-legacy-airline/.

40. Zachary Warmbrodt, "GOP split as banks take on gun industry," Politico.com, April 22, 2018, https://www.politico.com/story/2018/04/22/banks-guns-industry-gop-split-544739.

41. John Aidan Byrne, "JPMorgan Chase accused of purging accounts of conservative activists," NYPost.com, May 25, 2019, https://nypost.com/2019/05/25/jpmorgan-chase-accused-of-purging-accounts-of-conservative-activists/.

42. Dana Loesch,"Mailchimp Deplatforming a Local Tea Party Is a Hallmark of Fascism," Federalist.com, December 16, 2020, https://thefederalist.com/2020/11/16/mailchimp-deplatforming-a-local-tea-party-is-a-hallmark-of-fascism/.

43. Caleb Parke, "Conservatives call for PayPal boycott after CEO says Southern Poverty Law Center helps ban users," FoxNews.com, February 28, 2019, https://www.foxnews.com/tech/conservatives-call-for-paypal-boycott-after-ceo-admits-splc-helps-ban-users.

44. "US businesses cut Republican party donations in wake of riot," DW.com, https://www.dw.com/en/us-businesses-cut-republican-party-donations-in-wake-of-riot/a-56189263.

45. Theo Francis, "Why You Probably Work for a Giant Company, in 20 Charts," WSJ.com, April 6, 2017, https://www.wsj.com/graphics/big-companies-get-bigger/.

46. Austan Goolsbee, "Big Companies Are Starting to Swallow the World," NY Times.com, September 30, 2020, https://www.nytimes.com/2020/09/30/business/big-companies-are-starting-to-swallow-the-world.html.

CHAPTER 6: THE RADICALIZATION OF ENTERTAINMENT

1. "Academy Establishes Representation and Inclusion Standards for Oscars Eligibility," Oscars.org, September 8, 2020, https://www.oscars.org/news/academy-establishes-representation-and-inclusion-standards-oscarsr-eligibility.

2. Reggie Ugwu, "The Hashtag That Changed the Oscars: An Oral History," NY Times.com, February 6, 2020, https://www.nytimes.com/2020/02/06/movies/oscarssowhite-history.html.

3. Anna North, "#MeToo at the 2018 Oscars: The good, the bad, and the in between," Vox.com, March 5, 2018, https://www.vox.com/2018/3/5/17079702/2018-oscars-me-too-times-up-frances-mcdormand-jimmy-kimmel.

4. Casey Newton, "How Kevin Hart tweeted himself out of a job hosting the Oscars," TheVerge.com, December 8, 2018, https://www.theverge.com/2018/12/8/18131221/kevin-hart-oscar-hosting-homophobia-twitter-tweets.

5. Stephen Daw, "A Complete Timeline of Kevin Hart's Oscar-Hosting Controversy, from Tweets to Apologies," Billboard.com, January 13, 2020, https://www.billboard.com/articles/events/oscars/8492982/kevin-hart-oscar-hosting-controversy-timeline.

6. Ben Shapiro, *Primetime Propaganda* (New York: HarperCollins, 2011), 71.

7. "The Motion Picture Production Code (as Published 31 March, 1930)," https://www.asu.edu/courses/fms200s/total-readings/MotionPictureProductionCode.pdf.

8. Ben Shapiro, *Primetime Propaganda* (New York: HarperCollins, 2011), 59.

9. Ibid., 62.

10. Shonda Rhimes, *Year of Yes: How to Dance It Out, Stand in the Sun, and Be Your Own Person* (New York: Simon & Schuster, 2015), 235–37.

11. Jim Rutenberg, "How to Write TV in the Age of Trump: Showrunners Reveal All," NYTimes.com, April 12, 2017, https://www.nytimes.com/2017/04/12/arts/television/political-tv-in-age-of-trump-shonda-rhimes-scandal-veep-madame-secretary-house-of-cards-hbo.html?_r=0].

12. Elaine Low, "Disney Plus Subscribers Surpass 73 Million as of October," Variety.com, November 12, 2020, https://variety.com/2020/tv/news/disney-plus-subscribers-surpass-73-million-subscribers-as-of-october-1234830555/.

13. "The Nielsen Total Audience Report: August 2020," Nielsen.com, August 13, 2020, https://www.nielsen.com/us/en/insights/report/2020/the-nielsen-total-audience-report-august-2020/.

14. John Koblin, "The Obamas and Netflix Just Revealed the Shows and Films They're Working On," NYTimes.com, April 30, 2019, https://www.nytimes.com/2019/04/30/business/media/obama-netflix-shows.html.

15. Todd Spangler, "Susan Rice Will Leave Netflix Board to Join Biden Administration," Variety.com, December 10, 2020, https://variety.com/2020/biz/news/susan-rice-exits-netflix-board-biden-administration-1234850756/.

16. Ari Levy, "The most liberal and conservative tech companies, ranked by employees' political donations," CNBC.com, July 2, 2020, https://www.cnbc.com/2020/07/02/most-liberal-tech-companies-ranked-by-employee-donations.html.

17. Megan Graham, "Netflix says it will rethink its investment in Georgia if 'heartbeat' abortion law goes into effect," CNBC.com, May 28, 2019, https://www.cnbc.com/2019/05/28/netflix-would-rethink-investment-in-georgia-if-abortion-law-stands.html.

18. Sherisse Pham, "Netflix finally finds a way into China," CNN.com, May 3, 2017, https://money.cnn.com/2017/04/26/technology/netflix-china-baidu-iqiyi/.

19. Lisa Richwine, "Disney CEO says it will be 'difficult' to film in Georgia if abortion law takes effect," Reuters.com, May 29, 2019, https://www.reuters.com/article/us-usa-abortion-walt-disney-exclusive/disney-ceo-says-it-will-be-difficult-to-film-in-georgia-if-abortion-law-takes-effect-idUSKCN1T003X.

20. Amy Qin and Edward Wong, "Why Calls to Boycott 'Mulan' Over Concerns About China Are Growing," NYTimes.com, September 8, 2020, https://www.nytimes.com/2020/09/08/world/asia/china-mulan-xinjiang.html.

21. Johanna Blakley et al., "Are You What You Watch?," LearCenter.org, May 2019, https://learcenter.org/wp-content/uploads/2019/05/are_you_what_you_watch.pdf.

22. "GLAAD works with Hollywood to shape transgender stories and help cast trans actors," GLAAD.org, May 12, 2020, https://www.glaad.org/blog/glaad-works-hollywood-shape-transgender-stories-and-help-cast-trans-actors.

23. Dave Nemetz, "*The Office* Edits Out Blackface Scene, *Community* Pulls Entire Episode," TVLine.com, June 26, 2020, https://tvline.com/2020/06/26/the-office-community-blackface-cut-removed-streaming/.

24. "Gone with the Wind removed from HBO Max," BBC.com, June 10, 2020, https://www.bbc.com/news/entertainment-arts-52990714.

25. Samuel Gelman, "Disney+ Updates Offensive Content Disclaimer for Aladdin, Peter Pan and More," CBR.com, October 15, 2020, https://www.cbr.com/disney-plus-update-disclaimer-aladdin-peter-pan/.

26. "*Cops* TV series canceled after 31 years in wake of protests," EW.com, June 9, 2020, https://ew.com/tv/cops-canceled/.

27. Sarah Whitten, "'Live P.D.' canceled by A&E following report that the reality show filmed police custody death," CNBC.com, June 11, 2020, https://www.cnbc.com/2020/06/11/live-pd-canceled-over-report-that-show-filmed-police-custody-death.html.

28. "Scarlett Johansson quits trans role after LGBT backlash," BBC.com, July 13, 2018, https://www.bbc.com/news/entertainment-arts-44829766.

29. "You would say that wouldn't you! Sarah Silverman says progressives should allow cancel-culture victims a 'path to redemption'—after she was fired from film role for blackface," DailyMail.co.uk, October 26, 2020, https://www.dailymail.co.uk/news/article-8880547/Sarah-Silverman-slams-non-forgiving-cancel-culture-progressives-warns-digging-mistakes.html.

30. Nick Vadala, "Dave Chappelle defends Kevin Hart in controversial new Netflix comedy special 'Sticks & Stones,'" Inquirer.com, August 28, 2019, https://www.inquirer.com/entertainment/tv/dave-chappelle-netflix-comedy-kevin-hart-louis-ck-michael-jackson-20190828.html.

31. Christian Toto, "Bill Burr: Cancel Culture Made Me a Better Stand-up Comedian," HollywoodInToto.com, https://www.hollywoodintoto.com/bill-burr-cancel -culture-stand-up-comedian/.

32. Ben Cost, "'Mr. Bean' actor Rowan Atkinson equates cancel culture to 'medieval mob,'" NYPost.com, January 5, 2021, https://nypost.com/2021/01/05/mr-bean -rowan-atkinson-says-cancel-culture-to-medieval-mob/.

33. Center Is Sexy, "Graphing Rotten Tomatoes' Political Bias," Medium.com, September 18, 2019, https://medium.com/@centerissexy/graphing-rotten-tomatoes -political-bias-957e43986461.

34. Owen Gleiberman, "Healthy Tomatoes? The Danger of Film Critics Speaking as One," Variety.com, August 20, 2017, https://variety.com/2017/film/columns /rottentomatoes-the-danger-of-film-critics-speaking-as-one-1202533533/.

35. Peter Bradshaw, "Variety's apology to Carey Mulligan shows the film critic's ivory tower is toppling," TheGuardian.com, January 28, 2021, https://www.theguardian .com/film/2021/jan/28/variety-apology-carey-mulligan-film-critics.

36. Megan Garber, "Hey, Look, the New Ghostbusters Didn't Kill *Ghostbusters*," TheAtlantic.com, July 15, 2016, https://www.theatlantic.com/entertainment/archive /2016/07/hey-look-ghostbusters-didnt-kill-feminism/491414/.

37. Matt Miller, "The Year *Star Wars* Fans Finally Ruined *Star Wars*," Esquire.com, December 13, 2018, https://www.esquire.com/entertainment/movies/a25560063 /how-fans-ruined-star-wars-the-last-jedi-2018/.

38. Hannah Giorgis, "The Fear in Chappelle's New Special," TheAtlantic.com, August 28, 2019, https://www.theatlantic.com/entertainment/archive/2019/08/dave -chappelle-doubles-down-sticks-and-stones/596947/.

39. Jordan Hoffman, "Dave Chappelle Releases a Passionate and Raw Comedy Set, Making George Floyd Protests Personal," VanityFair.com, June 12, 2020, https:// www.vanityfair.com/hollywood/2020/06/dave-chappelle-releases-a-passionate -and-raw-comedy-set-making-george-floyd-protests-personal.

40. Lorraine Ali, "Review: Dave Chappelle's new special isn't stand-up. It's an anguished story of violence," June 12, 2020, https://www.latimes.com/entertainment -arts/tv/story/2020-06-12/dave-chappelle-846-youtube-netflix-george-floyd.

41. David Sims, "*Hillbilly Elegy* Is One of the Worst Movies of the Year," TheAtlantic .com, November 23, 2020, https://www.theatlantic.com/culture/archive/2020/11 /hillbilly-elegy/617189/.

42. Todd Spangler, "Netflix Launches 'Black Lives Matter' Collection of Movies, TV Shows, and Documentaries," Variety.com, June 10, 2020, https://variety.com/2020 /digital/news/netflix-black-lives-matter-collection-1234630160/.

43. Kiersten Willis, "Netflix, Amazon and Hulu spotlight black stories with film collections," AJC.com, June 11, 2020, https://www.ajc.com/entertainment/netflix -amazon-and-hulu-spotlight-black-stories-with-film-collections/vMxIsfPV3ksp7x 2W7AtlQM/.

44. John Mossman, "Abdul-Rauf Suspended Over National Anthem," Associated Press, March 13, 1996, https://apnews.com/article/0a244b7bf3d7c3882229d7f0e84587d6.

45. Tim Bontemps, "Michael Jordan stands firm on 'Republicans buy sneakers, too' quote, says it was made in jest," ESPN.com, May 4, 2020, https://www.espn.com /nba/story/_/id/29130478/michael-jordan-stands-firm-republicans-buy-sneakers -too-quote-says-was-made-jest.

46. Clay Travis, *Republicans Wear Sneakers, Too* (New York: HarperCollins, 2018), 41–49.

47. Ibid., 55.

48. "Pro Football Is Still America's Favorite Sport," TheHarrisPoll.com, January 26, 2016, https://theharrispoll.com/new-york-n-y-this-is-a-conflicting-time-for-football -fans-on-the-one-hand-with-the-big-game-50-no-less-fast-approaching-its-a-time -of-excitement-especial/.

49. "Average daily time spent watching TV per capita in the United States in 2009 and 2019, by ethnicity," Statista.com, https://www.statista.com/statistics/411806 /average-daily-time-watching-tv-us-ethnicity/.

50. Kerwin Kofi Charles, Erik Hurst, and Nikolai Roussanov, "Conspicuous Consumption and Race," *Quarterly Journal of Economics* 124, no. 2 (2009): 425–67, https:// repository.upenn.edu/fnce_papers/413/.

51. "St. Louis police officers angered by Rams' 'hands up, don't shoot' pose," SI.com, November 30, 2014, https://www.si.com/nfl/2014/11/30/st-louis-rams-ferguson -protests.

52. "NFL won't discipline Rams players for 'hands up, don't shoot' gesture," SI.com, December 1, 2014, https://www.si.com/nfl/2014/12/01/nfl-discipline-st-louis -rams-players-hands-dont-shoot.

53. "NFL denies Cowboys' request to wear decal honoring fallen Dallas officers," Foxnews.com, August 12, 2016, https://www.foxnews.com/sports/nfl-denies-cow boys-request-to-wear-decal-honoring-fallen-dallas-officers.

54. David K. Li, "Colin Kaepernick reveals the specific police shooting that led him to kneel," NBCNews.com, August 20, 2019, https://www.nbcnews.com/news/us -news/colin-kaepernick-reveals-specific-police-shooting-led-him-kneel-n1044306.

55. Christopher Ingraham, "What Colin Kaepernick means for America's racial gap in patriotism," WashingtonPost.com, September 23, 2016, https://www.wash ingtonpost.com/news/wonk/wp/2016/09/23/what-colin-kaepernick-means-for -americas-racial-gap-in-patriotism/.

56. Jenna West, "Colin Kaepernick Returns to 'Madden' for First Time Since 2016," SI.com, September 8, 2020, https://www.si.com/nfl/2020/09/08/colin-kaepernick -returns-madden-nfl-ea-sports-2020.

57. Darren Rovell, "NFL television ratings down 9.7 percent during 2017 regular season," ESPN.com, January 4, 2018, https://www.espn.com/nfl/story/_/id /21960086/nfl-television-ratings-97-percent-2017-regular-season.

58. Ben Shapiro, "ESPN Admits They Mistreat Conservatives, and It's Killing Their Ratings," DailyWire.com, November 17, 2016, https://www.dailywire.com/news /espn-admits-they-mistreat-conservatives-and-its-ben-shapiro.

59. Ben Strauss, "As ESPN tries to stick to sports, President Jimmy Pitaro must de-

fine what that means," WashingtonPost.com, July 26, 2019, https://www.washington post.com/sports/2019/07/26/jimmy-pitaro-espn-president-politics/.

60. Nikole Tower, "In an ethnic breakdown of sports, NBA takes lead for most diverse," GlobalSportMatters.com, December 12, 2018, https://globalsportmatters .com/culture/2018/12/12/in-an-ethnic-breakdown-of-sports-nba-takes-lead-for -most-diverse/.

61. Tom Huddleston, "These are the highest paid players in the NBA right now," CNBC.com, October 22, 2019, https://www.foxnews.com/sports/nfl-denies-cow boys-request-to-wear-decal-honoring-fallen-dallas-officers.

62. The Undefeated, "Social Justice Messages Each Player Is Wearing on His Jersey," TheUndefeated.com, July 31, 2020, https://theundefeated.com/features/social -justice-messages-each-nba-player-is-wearing-on-his-jersey/.

63. Dan Wolken, "Opinion: LeBron James undermines values he's espoused in most disgraceful moment of career," USAToday.com, October 15, 2019, https://www.usa today.com/story/sports/columnist/dan-wolken/2019/10/14/lebron-james-daryl -morey-china-hong-kong-tweet/3982436002/.

64. Paul P. Murphy, "Baseball is making Black Lives Matter on Opening Day," CNN .com, July 24, 2020, https://www.cnn.com/2020/07/23/us/opening-day-baseball -mlb-black-lives-matter-trnd/index.html.

65. Associated Press, "Baltimore Ravens' Matthew Judon blasts NFL Commissioner Roger Goodell's 'Black Lives Matter' speech," USAToday.com, June 15, 2020, https://www.usatoday.com/story/sports/nfl/ravens/2020/06/15/roger-goodells -black-lives-matter-speech-blasted-matthew-judon/3196057001/.

66. Scott Polacek, "NFL Plans to Include Social Justice Messages in End Zone Borders for Week 1," BleacherReport.com, July 27, 2020, https://bleacherreport.com /articles/2901950-nfl-plans-to-include-social-justice-messages-in-end-zone-borders -for-week-1.

67. Rick Porter, "NFL Ratings Slip in 2020, Remain Dominant on Broadcast," Holly woodReporter.com, January 6, 2021, https://www.hollywoodreporter.com/live -feed/nfl-ratings-slip-in-2020-remain-dominant-on-broadcast#:~:text=The%20 league%20drops%20about%2010,draw%20on%20ad%2Dsupported%20television.

68. "NBA Ratings Decline Points to Broader Trouble in TV Watching," Bloomberg .com, October 13, 2020, https://www.bloomberg.com/news/articles/2020-10-13 /nba-ratings-decline-points-to-broader-trouble-in-tv-watching.

69. Chris Haney, "TV Ratings: MLB 2020 World Series Least-Watched of All-Time," Outsider.com, October 29, 2020, https://www.bloomberg.com/news/articles /2020-10-13/nba-ratings-decline-points-to-broader-trouble-in-tv-watching.

CHAPTER 7: THE FAKE NEWS

1. Richard Read, "Attorney for Minneapolis police officer says he'll argue George Floyd died of an overdose and a heart condition," LATimes.com, August 20, 2020, https://www.latimes.com/world-nation/story/2020-08-20/george-floyd-derek -chauvin-defense.

2. "988 people have been shot and killed by police in the past year," WashingtonPost .com, Updated January 26, 2021, https://www.washingtonpost.com/graphics/inves tigations/police-shootings-database/?itid=lk_inline_manual_5.

3. "Groups March into Beverly Hills, Loot Stores on Rodeo Drive," CBSLocal.com, May 30, 2020, https://losangeles.cbslocal.com/2020/05/30/rodeo-drive-protest -looting-george-floyd/.

4. Jonathan Lloyd, "Dozens of Businesses Damaged at Flashpoint of Violence in the Fairfax District," NBCLosAngeles.com, May 31, 2020, https://www.nbclosangeles .com/news/local/fairfax-district-melrose-damaged-looting-grove-fire-natioal -guard-lapd/2371497/.

5. Alejandra Reyes-Velarde, Brittny Mejia, Joseph Serna, Ruben Vives, Melissa Etehad, Matthew Ormseth, and Hailey Branson-Potts, "Looting hits Long Beach, Santa Monica as countywide curfew goes into effect," LATimes.com, May 31, 2020, https://www.latimes.com/california/story/2020-05-31/looting-vandalism-leaves -downtown-l-a-stunned.

6. "NYC Protests Turn Violent," NYTimes.com, May 31, 2020, https://www.ny times.com/2020/05/31/nyregion/nyc-protests-george-floyd.html.

7. Isaac Stanley-Becker, Colby Itkowitz, and Meryl Kornfield, "Protests mount and violence flares in cities across US, putting the nation on edge," WashingtonPost.com, May 30, 2020, https://www.washingtonpost.com/national/protests-gain-force-across -us/2020/05/30/fccf57ea-a2a8-11ea-81bb-c2f70f01034b_story.html.

8. Tim Hains, "MSNBC's Ali Velshi Downplays Riot in Front of Burning Building: 'Mostly a Protest,' 'Not Generally Speaking Unruly," RealClearPolitics.com, May 28, 2020, https://www.realclearpolitics.com/video/2020/05/28/msnbcs_ali_velshi _downplays_riot_in_front_of_burning_building_mostly_a_protest_not_generally _speaking_unruly.html.

9. Joe Concha, "CNN ridiculed for 'Fiery but Mostly Peaceful' caption with video of burning building in Kenosha," TheHill.com, August 27, 2020, https://thehill.com /homenews/media/513902-cnn-ridiculed-for-fiery-but-mostly-peaceful-caption -with-video-of-burning.

10. "Costliest US civil disorders," Axios.com, https://www.axios.com/riots-cost -property-damage-276c9bcc-a455-4067-b06a-66f9db4cea9c.html.

11. Ariel Zilber, "REVEALED: Widespread vandalism and looting during BLM protests will cost insurance $2 billion after violence erupted in 140 cities in the wake of George Floyd's death," DailyMail.co.uk, September 16, 2020, https://www.daily mail.co.uk/news/article-8740609/Rioting-140-cities-George-Floyds-death-cost -insurance-industry-2-BILLION.html.

12. Lois Beckett, "At least 25 Americans were killed during protests and political un- rest in 2020," TheGuardian.com, October 31, 2020, https://www.theguardian.com /world/2020/oct/31/americans-killed-protests-political-unrest-acled.

13. Ebony Bowden, "More than 700 officers injured in George Floyd protests across US," NYPost.com, June 8, 2020, https://nypost.com/2020/06/08/more-than-700 -officers-injured-in-george-floyd-protests-across-us/.

14. https://twitter.com/CBSNews/status/1267877443911778306.

15. Virginia Allen, "New York Times Mum on '1619 Project' Creator Calling '1619 Riots' Moniker an 'Honor,'" DailySignal.com, June 22, 2020, https://www.daily signal.com/2020/06/22/new-york-times-mum-on-1619-project-creator-calling -1619-riots-moniker-an-honor/.

16. https://twitter.com/theMRC/status/1267818603807567872.

17. "Chris Cuomo demands to know where it says protests must be 'peaceful.' Then he gets a lesson on the Constitution," TheBlaze.com, June 3, 2020, https://www.the blaze.com/news/chris-cuomo-protests-peaceful-constitution.

18. Andrew Kerr, "Here Are 31 Times the Media Justified or Explained Away Riot-ing and Looting After George Floyd's Death," DailySignal.com, September 4, 2020, https://www.dailysignal.com/2020/09/04/here-are-31-times-the-media-justified -or-explained-away-rioting-and-looting-after-george-floyds-death/.

19. Tonya Mosley, "Understand Protests as 'Acts of Rebellion' Instead of Riots, Marc Lamont Hill Says," WBUR.org, June 2, 2020, https://www.wbur.org/hereandnow /2020/06/02/protests-acts-of-rebellion.

20. Heather Mac Donald, "Taking Stock of a Most Violent Year," WSJ.com, Janu-ary 24, 2021, https://www.wsj.com/articles/taking-stock-of-a-most-violent-year -11611525947.

21. Brian Flood, "CNN's Don Lemon says anti-police violence of 2020 built on 'facts' so 'you can't compare' to Capitol riot," FoxNews.com, January 13, 2021, https:// www.foxnews.com/media/cnns-don-lemon-2020-built-facts-riot.

22. Lindsey Ellefson, "Don Lemon on His Journalistic Approach: My 'Lens' Is 'Not Necessarily a Bias,' but 'Experience,'" TheWrap.com, July 7, 2020, https://www .thewrap.com/don-lemon-on-his-journalistic-approach-my-lens-is-not-necessarily -a-bias-but-experience/.

23. Paul Bedard, "90% of media political donations to Biden, Sanders, AOC, Dem-ocrats: Report," WashingtonExaminer.com, October 28, 2020, https://www .washingtonexaminer.com/washington-secrets/90-of-media-political-donations-to -biden-sanders-aoc-democrats-report.

24. Jack Shafer and Tucker Doherty, "The Media Bubble Is Worse Than You Think," Politico.com, May/June 2017, https://www.politico.com/magazine/story /2017/04/25/media-bubble-real-journalism-jobs-east-coast-215048.

25. Keith Griffith, "American trust in the mainstream media hits an all-time low with just 18% of Republicans saying they believe journalists after the 2020 election," Daily Mail.co.uk, January 21, 2021, https://www.dailymail.co.uk/news/article-9173711 /American-trust-media-hits-time-low.html.

26. "James Callendar," Monticello.org, https://www.monticello.org/site/research -and-collections/james-callender.

27. Amy Solomon Whitehead, "The Unattainable Ideal: Walter Lippmann and the Limits of the Press and and Public Opinion," LSU master's thesis, LSU.edu, 2015, https://digitalcommons.lsu.edu/cgi/viewcontent.cgi?article=3281&context=grad school_theses.

28. Walter Lippmann, *Liberty and the News* (New York: Harcourt, Brace & Howe, 1920), 88–89.

29. Ravi Somaiya and Ashley Southall, "Arrested in Ferguson Last Year, 2 Reporters Are Charged," NYTimes.com, August 11, 2015, https://www.nytimes.com/2015/08/11/us/arrested-in-ferguson-2014-washington-post-reporter-wesley-lowery-is-charged.html?_r=0.

30. Wesley Lowery, *They Can't Kill Us All* (New York: Hachette Book Group, 2016), 37.

31. Maxwell Tani, "Washington Post Threatened Another Star Reporter Over His Tweets," DailyBeast.com, February 3, 2020, https://www.thedailybeast.com/washington-post-threatened-another-star-reporter-wesley-lowery-over-his-tweets.

32. Ben Smith, "Inside the Revolts Erupting in America's Big Newsrooms," NY Times.com, June 7, 2020, https://www.nytimes.com/2020/06/07/business/media/new-york-times-washington-post-protests.html.

33. Oliver Darcy, "New York Times staffers revolt over publication of Tom Cotton op-ed," CNN.com, June 4, 2020, https://www.cnn.com/2020/06/03/media/new-york-times-tom-cotton-op-ed/index.html.

34. Marc Tracy, "James Bennet Resigns as New York Times Opinion Editor," NY Times.com, June 7, 2020, https://www.nytimes.com/2020/06/07/business/media/james-bennet-resigns-nytimes-op-ed.html.

35. Michael M. Grynbaum, "The Atlantic Cuts Ties with Conservative Writer Kevin Williamson," NYTimes.com, April 5, 2018, https://www.nytimes.com/2018/04/05/business/media/kevin-williamson-atlantic.html.

36. Kyle Smith, "Politico Staff in Uproar over Ben Shapiro Appearance," National Review.com, January 14, 2021, https://www.nationalreview.com/corner/politico-staff-in-uproar-over-ben-shapiro-appearance/.

37. https://twitter.com/ErikWemple/status/1349900614470393864.

38. Maxwell Tani, "100+ Politico Staffers Send Letter to Publisher Railing Against Publishing Ben Shapiro," TheDailyBeast.com, January 25, 2021, https://www.thedailybeast.com/more-than-100-politico-staffers-send-letter-to-ceo-railing-against-publishing-ben-shapiro.

39. https://twitter.com/ErikWemple/status/1349804843439894532.

40. Karen Attiah, "The media had a role to play in the rise of Trump. It's time to hold ourselves accountable," WashingtonPost.com, January 20, 2021, https://www.washingtonpost.com/opinions/2021/01/20/media-had-role-play-rise-trump-its-time-hold-ourselves-accountable/.

41. Marc Tracy, "Top Editor of Philadelphia Inquirer Resigns After 'Buildings Matter' Headline," NYTimes.com, June 6, 2020, https://www.nytimes.com/2020/06/06/business/media/editor-philadephia-inquirer-resigns.html.

42. Bari Weiss, "Resignation Letter," BariWeiss.com, July 14, 2020, https://www.bariweiss.com/resignation-letter.

43. Victoria Bynum, James M. McPherson, James Oakes, Sean Wilentz, and Gordon S. Wood, "RE: The 1619 Project," *New York Times Magazine*, December 29, 2019,

https://www.nytimes.com/2019/12/20/magazine/we-respond-to-the-historians-who-critiqued-the-1619-project.html.

44. K. C. Johnson, "History Without Truth," City-Journal.org, December 31, 2019, https://www.city-journal.org/1619-project-history-without-truth.

45. Leslie M. Harris, "I Helped Fact-Check the 1619 Project. The Times Ignored Me," Politico.com, March 6, 2020, https://www.politico.com/news/magazine/2020/03/06/1619-project-new-york-times-mistake-122248.

46. Brian Stelter and Oliver Darcy, "1619 Project faces renewed criticism—this time from *The New York Times*," CNN.com, October 12, 2020, https://www.cnn.com/2020/10/12/media/new-york-times-1619-project-criticism/index.html.

47. "Oprah Winfrey, Nikole Hannah-Jones to Adapt '1619 Project' for Film, TV," HollywoodReporter.com, July 8, 2020, https://www.hollywoodreporter.com/video/oprah-winfrey-nikole-hannah-jones-adapt-1619-project-watch-1302506.

48. Jacques Steinberg, "An All-Out Attack on 'Conservative Misinformation,'" NY Times.com, October 31, 2008, https://www.nytimes.com/2008/11/01/washington/01media.html.

49. Tucker Carlson and Vince Coglianese, "Inside Media Matters: Sources, memos reveal erratic behavior, close coordination with White House and news organizations," DailyCaller.com, February 12, 2012, https://dailycaller.com/2012/02/12/inside-media-matters-sources-memos-reveal-erratic-behavior-close-coordination-with-white-house-and-news-organizations/.

50. Nicholas Kristof, "A Letter to My Conservative Friends," NYTimes.com, January 27, 2021, https://www.nytimes.com/2021/01/27/opinion/trump-supporters-conspiracy-theories.html.

51. Margaret Sullivan, "Fox News is a hazard to our democracy. It's time to take the fight to the Murdochs. Here's how," WashingtonPost.com, January 24, 2021, https://www.washingtonpost.com/lifestyle/media/fox-news-is-a-hazard-to-our-democracy-its-time-to-take-the-fight-to-the-murdochs-heres-how/2021/01/22/1821f186-5cbe-11eb-b8bd-ee36b1cd18bf_story.html.

52. Max Boot, "Trump couldn't have incited sedition without the help of Fox News," WashingtonPost.com, January 18, 2021, https://www.washingtonpost.com/opinions/2021/01/18/trump-couldnt-have-incited-sedition-without-help-fox-news/.

53. Oliver Darcy, "Analysis: TV providers should not escape scrutiny for distributing disinformation," CNN.com, January 8, 2021, https://www.cnn.com/2021/01/08/media/tv-providers-disinfo-reliable-sources/index.html.

54. https://twitter.com/tomselliott/status/1351140855478947844.

55. Kara Swisher, "Zuckerberg's Free Speech Bubble," NYTimes.com, June 3, 2020, https://www.nytimes.com/2020/06/03/opinion/facebook-trump-free-speech.html?action=click&module=RelatedLinks&pgtype=Article.

56. Kevin Roose, "The Making of a YouTube Radical," NYTimes.com, June 8, 2019, https://www.nytimes.com/interactive/2019/06/08/technology/youtube-radical.html.

57. Jim VandeHei, "Our new reality: Three Americas," Axios.com, January 10, 2021,

https://www.axios.com/capitol-siege-misinformation-trump-d9c9738b-0852-408d
-a24f-81c95938b41b.html?stream=top.

58. Armin Rosen, "Journalists Mobilize Against Free Speech," TabletMag.com, January 24, 2021, https://www.tabletmag.com/sections/news/articles/jounalists-against
-free-speech.

59. Caitlin Flanagan, "The Media Botched the Covington Catholic Story," The Atlantic.com, January 23, 2019, https://www.theatlantic.com/ideas/archive/2019
/01/media-must-learn-covington-catholic-story/581035/.

60. "Statement of Nick Sandmann, Covington Catholic High School junior, regarding incident at the Lincoln Memorial," CNN.com, January 23, 2019, https://www.cnn
.com/2019/01/20/us/covington-kentucky-student-statement/index.html.

61. Caitlin Flanagan, "The Media Botched the Covington Catholic Story," The Atlantic.com, January 23, 2019, https://www.theatlantic.com/ideas/archive/2019
/01/media-must-learn-covington-catholic-story/581035/.

62. https://grabien.com/story.php?id=321993.

63. https://twitter.com/Acosta/status/1351649797820862465.

64. Isaac Schorr, "Jen Psaki Is Living Her Best Life," NationalReview.com, January 25, 2021, https://www.nationalreview.com/2021/01/jen-psaki-is-living-her-best
-life/.

65. Margaret Sullivan, "The media can be glad for the Biden White House's return to normalcy. But let's not be lulled," WashingtonPost.com, January 21, 2021, https://
www.washingtonpost.com/lifestyle/media/the-media-can-be-glad-for-the-biden
-white-houses-return-to-normalcy-but-lets-not-be-lulled/2021/01/20/ea444ac6
-5b81-11eb-a976-bad6431e03e2_story.html.

CHAPTER 8: UNFRIENDING AMERICANS

1. Emma-Jo Morris and Gabrielle Fonrouge, "Smoking-gun email reveals how Hunter Biden introduced Ukrainian businessman to VP dad," NYPost.com, October 14, 2020, https://nypost.com/2020/10/14/email-reveals-how-hunter-biden-intro
duced-ukrainian-biz-man-to-dad/.

2. Ben Schreckinger, "Biden Inc.," Politico.com, August 2, 2019, https://www
.politico.com/magazine/story/2019/08/02/joe-biden-investigation-hunter-brother
-hedge-fund-money-2020-campaign-227407.

3. Tim Marcin, "Hunter Biden Admits His Last Name Has Opened Basically Every Door for Him," Vice.com, October 15, 2019, https://www.vice.com/en/article/a35y9k
/hunter-biden-admits-his-last-name-has-opened-basically-every-door-for-him.

4. Mark Moore, "Joe Biden's testy response to NBC question about Hunter's dealings in Ukraine," NYPost.com, February 3, 2020, https://nypost.com/2020/02/03/joe
-bides-testy-response-to-nbc-question-about-hunters-dealings-in-ukraine/.

5. "Read Trump's phone conversation with Volodymr Zelensky," CNN.com, September 26, 2019, https://www.cnn.com/2019/09/25/politics/donald-trump-ukraine
-transcript-call/index.html.

6. Ebony Bowden and Steven Nelson, "Hunter's ex-partner Tony Bobulinski: Joe

Biden's a liar and here's the proof," NYPost.com, October 22, 2020, https://nypost
.com/2020/10/22/hunter-ex-partner-tony-bobulinski-calls-joe-biden-a-liar/.

7. Natasha Bertrand, "Hunter Biden story is Russian disinfo, dozens of former in-
tel officials say," Politico.com, October 19, 2020, https://www.politico.com/news
/2020/10/19/hunter-biden-story-russian-disinfo-430276.

8. Evan Perez and Pamela Brown, "Federal criminal investigation into Hunter Biden
focuses on his business dealings in China," CNN.com, December 10, 2020, https://
www.cnn.com/2020/12/09/politics/hunter-biden-tax-investigtation/index.html.

9. Paul Bedard, "Media's hiding of Hunter Biden scandal robbed Trump of clear
win: Poll," MSN.com, November 13, 2020, https://www.msn.com/en-us/news
/politics/media-s-hiding-of-hunter-biden-scandal-robbed-trump-of-clear-win-poll
/ar-BB1aZGcF.

10. Benjamin Hart, "Twitter Backs Down After Squelching New York Post's Hunter
Biden Story," NYMag.com, October 16, 2020, https://nymag.com/intelligencer
/2020/10/twitter-facebook-block-ny-post-hunter-biden-article.html.

11. Audrey Conklin, "Facebook official who said platform is reducing distribution of
Hunter Biden has worked for top Dems," FoxNews.com, October 14, 2020, https://
www.foxnews.com/politics/facebook-spokesperson-top-democrats-new-york-post.

12. https://twitter.com/andymstone/status/1316395902479872000.

13. https://twitter.com/andymstone/status/1316423671314026496.

14. Alex Hern, "Facebook leak reveals policies on restricting New York Post's Biden
story," TheGuardian.com, October 30, 2020, https://www.theguardian.com/tech
nology/2020/oct/30/facebook-leak-reveals-policies-restricting-new-york-post
-biden-story.

15. 47 U.S. Code §230.

16. "Section 230 of the Communications Decency Act," EFF.org, https://www.eff
.org/issues/cda230.

17. "CDA 230: Legislative History," EFF.org, https://www.eff.org/issues/cda230
/legislative-history.

18. 47 U.S. Code §230.

19. Mark Zuckerberg, "Bring the World Closer Together," Facebook.com, June 22,
2017, https://techcrunch.com/2017/06/22/bring-the-world-closer-together/.

20. Justin Fox, "Why Twitter's Mission Statement Matters," HBR.org, November 13,
2014, https://hbr.org/2014/11/why-twitters-mission-statement-matters.

21. Angie Drobnic Holan, "2016 Lie of the Year: Fake news," Politifact.com, December 13, 2016, https://www.politifact.com/article/2016/dec/13/2016-lie-year-fake
-news/.

22. David Remnick, "Obama Reckons with a Trump Presidency," NewYorker.com,
November 18, 2016, https://www.newyorker.com/magazine/2016/11/28/obama
-reckons-with-a-trump-presidency.

23. Scott Shackford, "Senator Feinstein's Threat to 'Do Something' to Social Media
Companies Is a Bigger Danger to Democracy Than Russia," Reason.com, November 3,
2017, https://reason.com/2017/11/03/sen-feinsteins-threat-to-do-something-to/.

24. Kurt Wagner, "Mark Zuckerberg says it's 'crazy' to think fake news stories got Trump elected," Vox.com, November 11, 2016, https://www.vox.com/2016/11/11/13596792/facebook-fake-news-mark-zuckerberg-donald-trump.

25. Mark Zuckerberg, "Building Global Community," Facebook.com, February 16, 2017, https://www.facebook.com/notes/mark-zuckerberg/building-global-community/10103508221158471/?pnref=story.

26. "Transcript of Mark Zuckerberg's Senate hearing," WashingtonPost.com, April 10, 2018, https://www.washingtonpost.com/news/the-switch/wp/2018/04/10/transcript-of-mark-zuckerbergs-senate-hearing/.

27. Tony Romm, "Zuckerberg: Standing for Voice and Expression," WashingtonPost.com, October 17, 2019, https://www.washingtonpost.com/technology/2019/10/17/zuckerberg-standing-voice-free-expression/.

28. Alison Durkee, "Jack Dorsey Sees a 'Major Gap and Flaw' in Mark Zuckerberg's Free Speech Argument," VanityFair.com, October 25, 2019, https://www.vanityfair.com/news/2019/10/jack-dorsey-mark-zuckerberg-free-speech-political-ads-facebook.

29. Sara Rimer, "Jack Dorsey, Twitter and Square Cofounder, Donates $10 Million to BU Center for Antiracist Research," BU.edu, August 20, 2020, https://www.bu.edu/articles/2020/jack-dorsey-bu-center-for-antiracist-research-gift/.

30. Kara Swisher, "Zuckerberg's Free Speech Bubble," NYTimes.com, June 3, 2020, https://www.nytimes.com/2020/06/03/opinion/facebook-trump-free-speech.html.

31. Alison Durkee, "'So You Won't Take Down Lies?' AOC Blasts Mark Zuckerberg in Testy House Hearing," VanityFair.com, October 24, 2019, https://www.vanityfair.com/news/2019/10/mark-zuckerberg-facebook-house-testimony-aoc.

32. Cecilia Kang, "Biden Prepares Attack on Facebook's Speech Policies," NYTimes.com, June 11, 2020, https://www.nytimes.com/2020/06/11/technology/biden-facebook-misinformation.html.

33. "Report of the Select Committee on Intelligence on Russian Active Measures Campaigns and Interference in the 2016 Election, Volume 2: Russia's Use of Social Media with Additional Views," Intelligence.senate.gov, https://www.intelligence.senate.gov/sites/default/files/documents/Report_Volume2.pdf.

34. Nicholas Thompson and Issie Lapowsky, "How Russian Trolls Used Meme Warfare to Divide America," Wired.com, December 17, 2018, https://www.wired.com/story/russia-ira-propaganda-senate-report/.

35. Molly Ball, "The Secret History of the Shadow Campaign That Saved the 2020 Election," Time.com, February 4, 2021, https://time.com/5936036/secret-2020-election-campaign/.

36. Eliza Shearer and Elizabeth Grieco, "Americans Are Wary of the Role Social Media Sites Play in Delivering the News," Journalism.org, October 2, 2019, https://www.journalism.org/2019/10/02/americans-are-wary-of-the-role-social-media-sites-play-in-delivering-the-news/.

37. Kevin Roose, "The Making of a YouTube Radical," NYTimes.com, June 8, 2019, https://www.nytimes.com/interactive/2019/06/08/technology/youtube-radical.html.

38. Lesley Stahl, "How Does YouTube Handle the Site's Misinformation, Conspiracy Theories, and Hate?," CBSNews.com, December 1, 2019, https://www.cbsnews.com/news/is-youtube-doing-enough-to-fight-hate-speech-and-conspiracy-theories-60-minutes-2019-12-01/.

39. Josh Constine, "Facebook will change algorithm to demote 'borderline content' that almost violates policies," TechCrunch.com, November 15, 2018, https://techcrunch.com/2018/11/15/facebook-borderline-content/?guccounter=1.

40. Kevin Roose, Mike Isaac, and Sheera Frankel, "Facebook Struggles to Balance Civility and Growth," NYTimes.com, November 24, 2020, https://www.nytimes.com/2020/11/24/technology/facebook-election-misinformation.html.

41. Ben Shapiro, "Facebook Unveils Plan to Defeat 'Fake News': Rely on leftist Fact-Checkers," DailyWire.com, December 15, 2016, https://www.dailywire.com/news/facebook-unveils-plan-defeat-fake-news-rely-ben-shapiro.

42. Bethania Palma, "Did AOC Exaggerate the Danger She Was in During Capitol Riot?," Snopes.com, February 3, 2021, https://www.snopes.com/fact-check/aoc-capitol-attack/.

43. Stephen J. Ceci, "The Psychology of Fact-Checking," ScientificAmerican.com, October 25, 2020, https://www.scientificamerican.com/article/the-psychology-of-fact-checking1/.

44. Elizabeth Dwoskin, Nitasha Tiku, and Heather Kelly, "Facebook to start policing anti-Black hate speech more aggressively than anti-White comments, documents show," WashingtonPost.com, December 3, 2020, https://www.washingtonpost.com/technology/2020/12/03/facebook-hate-speech/.

45. Emine Saner, "YouTube's Susan Wojcicki: 'Where's the line of free speech—are you removing voices that should be heard?,'" TheGuardian.com, August 10, 2019, https://www.theguardian.com/technology/2019/aug/10/youtube-susan-wojcicki-ceo-where-line-removing-voices-heard.

46. https://www.facebook.com/communitystandards/hate_speech/.

47. Tony Romm and Elizabeth Dwoskin, "Trump banned from Facebook indefinitely, CEO Mark Zuckerberg says," WashingtonPost.com, January 7, 2021, https://www.washingtonpost.com/technology/2021/01/07/trump-twitter-ban/.

48. "Permanent suspension of @realDonaldTrump," Twitter.com, January 8, 2021, https://blog.twitter.com/en_us/topics/company/2020/suspension.html.

49. "Yann LeCun Quits Twitter Amid Acrimonious Exchanges on AI Bias," Synced Review.com, June 30, 2020, https://syncedreview.com/2020/06/30/yann-lecun-quits-twitter-amid-acrimonious-exchanges-on-ai-bias/.

50. Dan Levin, "A Racial Slur, a Viral Video, and a Reckoning," NYTimes.com, December 26, 2020, https://www.nytimes.com/2020/12/26/us/mimi-groves-jimmy-galligan-racial-slurs.html.

51. Jon Ronson, "How One Stupid Tweet Blew Up Justine Sacco's Life," NYTimes
.com, February 12, 2015, https://www.nytimes.com/2015/02/15/magazine/how
-one-stupid-tweet-ruined-justine-saccos-life.html.

52. Ari Levy, "Trump fans are flocking to the social media app Parler—its CEO is
begging liberals to join them," CNBC.com, June 27, 2020, https://www.cnbc.com
/2020/06/27/parler-ceo-wants-liberal-to-join-the-pro-trump-crowd-on-the-app.html.

53. Brian Fung, "Parler has now been booted by Amazon, Apple and Google," CNN
.com, January 11, 2021, https://www.cnn.com/2021/01/09/tech/parler-suspended
-apple-app-store/index.html.

54. https://twitter.com/jason_kint/status/1358467793323257857.

55. Brian X. Chen and Kevin Roose, "Are Private Messaging Apps the Next Misinformation Hot Spot?," NYTimes.com, February 3, 2021, https://www.nytimes
.com/2021/02/03/technology/personaltech/telegram-signal-misinformation
.html?smtyp=cur&smid=tw-nytimes.

56. Eliza Shearer and Elizabeth Grieco, "Americans Are Wary of the Role Social
Media Sites Play in Delivering the News," Journalism.org, October 2, 2019, https://
www.journalism.org/2019/10/02/americans-are-wary-of-the-role-social-media
-sites-play-in-delivering-the-news/.

57. H. Tankovska, "Facebook: Number of monthly active users worldwide 2008–
2020", https://www.statista.com/statistics/264810/number-of-monthly-active-face
book-users-worldwide/#:~:text=With%20roughly%202.8%20billion%20monthly
,network%20ever%20to%20do%20so.

58. Jeff Desjardins, "How Google retains more than 90% of market share," Business
Insider.com, April 23, 2018, https://www.businessinsider.com/how-google-retains
-more-than-90-of-market-share-2018-4.

59. Greg Stirling, "Almost 70% of digital ad spending going to Google, Facebook, Amazon, says analyst firm," MarketingLand.com, June 17, 2019, https://marketingland
.com/almost-70-of-digital-ad-spending-going-to-google-facebook-amazon-says
-analyst-firm-262565#:~:text=However%2C%20eMarketer%20revised%20down
ward%20its,nearly%2050%25%20to%2038%25.&text=Google%2C%20Facebook%20
and%20Amazon%20are,dollars%20spent%20according%20to%20eMarketer.

THE CHOICE BEFORE US

1. Emma Nolan, "What Did Gina Carano Say? 'The Mandalorian' Star Fired after
Instagram Holocaust Post," Newsweek.com, February 11, 2021, https://www.news
week.com/what-gina-carano-said-about-holocaust-mandalorian-fired-1568539.

2. "'The Mandalorian' Star Gina Carano Fired Amid Social Media Controversy,"
THR.com, February 10, 2021, https://www.hollywoodreporter.com/news/the
-mandalorian-star-gina-carano-fired-amid-social-media-controversy.

3. Emma Nolan, "What Did Gina Carano Say? 'The Mandalorian' Star Fired after
Instagram Holocaust Post," Newsweek.com, February 11, 2021, https://www.news
week.com/what-gina-carano-said-about-holocaust-mandalorian-fired-1568539.

4. "'The Mandalorian' Star Gina Carano Fired Amid Social Media Controversy,"

THR.com, February 10, 2021, https://www.hollywoodreporter.com/news/the -mandalorian-star-gina-carano-fired-amid-social-media-controversy.

5. https://twitter.com/benshapiro/status/1359833571075227648.

6. Andreas Wiseman, "Carano Hits Back, Announces New Movie Project with Ben Shapiro's Daily Wire: 'They Can't Cancel Us If We Don't Let Them,'" Deadline .com, February 12, 2021, https://deadline.com/2021/02/gina-carano-mandalorian -ben-shapiro-hits-back-cancel-culture-1234692971/.

7. Marc Tracy, "Two Journalists Exit New York Times After Criticism of Past Be- havior," NYTimes.com, February 5, 2021, https://www.nytimes.com/2021/02/05 /business/media/donald-mcneil-andy-mills-leave-nyt.html.

8. Dylan Byers, "New York Times editor walks back statement on racial slurs," NBCNews.com, February 11, 2021, https://www.nbcnews.com/news/all/new-york -times-editor-walks-back-statement-racial-slurs-n1257482.

9. Joe Pompeo, "'It's Chaos': Behind the Scenes of Donald McNeil's *New York Times* Exit," VanityFair.com, February 11, 2021, https://www.vanityfair.com/news /2021/02/behind-the-scenes-of-donald-mcneils-new-york-times-exit.

10. Pedro Domingos, "Beating Back Cancel Culture: A Case Study from the Field of Artificial Intelligence," January 27, 2021, https://quillette.com/2021/01/27/beating -back-cancel-culture-a-case-study-from-the-field-of-artificial-intelligence/.

INDEX

universities and colleges (*continued*)
wokeism's carriage into culture,
government, and science, 85–86,
94–95
USA Today, 166
US Business Roundtable, 130
U.S. Capitol, January 6, 2021, storming
of, 1–3
authoritarian responses to, 2, 11–14
democratic institutions and, 9–11, 14
media's coverage of compared to BLM
coverage, 166–68
Parler's deplatforming and, 12–13,
136, 209–10
social media and banning of Trump,
205
U.S. Constitution
checks and balances to restrain
government and, 5–6
Revolutionary Impulse and, 53, 54
Utopian Impulse and, 51
see also freedom of speech and the
press
utopian brutality, 5
Utopian Impulse
authoritarian leftism and, 47
Critical Race Theory and, 57–59
ideal of the state as solution to societal
ills, 48–52
identity politics and, 66
intersectional coalition and, 63–64
tension with Revolutionary Impulse, 70
waning of interest in, in 1980s, 52–53

vaccines, social justice and COVID 19,
104–6
Vance, J. D., 76–77
VandeHei, Jim, 21, 184
Vanity Fair, 220
Variety, 151
Velshi, Ali, 165

Vimeo, 194
Visa, 135

Wall Street Journal, 92, 137
Walmart, 120
Warzel, Charlie, 174
Washington Post, 164–65, 176–77, 203–4
Waters, Maxine, 198
Weingarten, Randi, 136
Weinstein, Bret, 93
Weinstein, Harvey, 142
Weiss, Bari, 178
Wemple, Erik, 176
white supremacy. *See* Critical Race
Theory (CRT)
"whiteness," museum exhibition
condemning, 66–67
Whitmer, Gretchen, 100–101
Wilentz, Sean, 179
Williamson, Kevin, 175
Wilson, Darren, 172
Wilson, Woodrow, 48–49
Wischnowski, Stan, 177
Wojcicki, Susan, 204
Wood, Gordon S., 179
Woods, Mario, 157
Wortham, Jenna, 174
Wright, Jeremiah, 60
Wyden, Ron, 13

Yale Daily News, 90–92
Yancy, George, 93–94
Year of Yes (Rhimes), 145
Yelp, and "woke snitching," 133
Yglesias, Matthew, 16, 41–42
YouTube, 184, 194, 201–2, 204–5, 210,
211

Zelensky, Volodymyr, 190
Zucker, Jeff, 25
Zuckerberg, Mark, 183–84, 196–98, 205

ABOUT THE AUTHOR

Ben Shapiro is founding editor in chief and editor emeritus of the Daily Wire and host of *The Ben Shapiro Show*, the top conservative podcast in the nation. A three-time *New York Times* bestselling author, Shapiro is a graduate of Harvard Law School and an Orthodox Jew. He is widely considered one of the most influential conservative voices in America.